KU-034-591

New Perspectives in International Development

International Development

This book forms part of the series *International Development* published by Bloomsbury Academic in association with The Open University. The two books in the series are:

International Development in a Changing World
(edited by Theo Papaioannou and Melissa Butcher)
ISBN 978-1-78093-234-7 (hardback)
ISBN 978-1-78093-237-8 (paperback)
ISBN 978-1-78093-235-4 (Epub eBook)
ISBN 978-1-78093-236-1 (PDF eBook)

New Perspectives in International Development
(edited by Melissa Butcher and Theo Papaioannou)
ISBN 978-1-78093-243-9 (hardback)
ISBN 978-1-78093-251-4 (paperback)
ISBN 978-1-78093-248-4 (Epub eBook)
ISBN 978-1-78093-249-1 (PDF eBook)

This publication forms part of the Open University module
TD223 *International development: making sense of a changing world*. Details of this and other Open University modules can be obtained from the Student Registration and Enquiry Service, The Open University, PO Box 197, Milton Keynes MK7 6BJ, United Kingdom (tel. +44 (0)845 300 60 90, email general-enquiries@open.ac.uk).

www.open.ac.uk

New Perspectives in International Development

Edited by Melissa Butcher
and Theo Papaioannou

The Open University

BLOOMSBURY ACADEMIC

Published by

Bloomsbury Academic
an imprint of Bloomsbury Publishing Plc
50 Bedford Square
London WC1B 3DP
United Kingdom

and

175 Fifth Avenue
New York
NY10010
USA
www.bloomsburyacademic.com

In association with

The Open University
Walton Hall, Milton Keynes
MK7 6AA
United Kingdom

First published 2013

Copyright © 2013 The Open University

All rights reserved. No part of this publication may be reproduced, stored in a retrieval system, transmitted or utilised in any form or by any means, electronic, mechanical, photocopying, recording or otherwise, without written permission from the publisher or a licence from the Copyright Licensing Agency Ltd. Details of such licences (for reprographic reproduction) may be obtained from the Copyright Licensing Agency Ltd, Saffron House, 6–10 Kirby Street, London EC1N 8TS (website www.cla.co.uk).

Edited and designed by The Open University.

Typeset by The Open University.

Printed and bound in the United Kingdom by Page Bros, Norwich.

CIP records for this book are available from the British Library and the Library of Congress.

ISBN 978-1-78093-243-9 (hardback)
ISBN 978-1-78093-251-4 (paperback)
ISBN 978-1-78093-248-4 (Epub eBook)
ISBN 978-1-78093-249-1 (PDF eBook)

1.1

Contents

Introduction

Melissa Butcher and Theo Papaioannou

Welcome to *New Perspectives in International Development*, the second volume of the companion text book to the Open University module *International development: making sense of a changing world*. This book will focus on some of the latest thinking in international development that is moving the debate into areas such as the connection between fear, security, conflict and sustainable development. Looming energy crises and concerns surrounding the impact of environmental and climate change have led to an increasing focus in Development Studies on the role of technology and resources. Finally, the book takes up the theme of wellbeing, a growing body of research that is attempting to find new ways to assess development policies and practices, including making development personal.

The book maintains the theme of development as a process of change, examined through the lens of historical transformation, contested sites of power, the capacity for human agency to affect change, and the different scales, from the local to the transnational, at which change can occur. The interaction between these threads and the particular case studies highlights the complex processes involved in international development that cannot be understood in isolation.

This interaction extends to academic research and the chapters in this book represent an interdisciplinary understanding of new perspectives in international development. Writers bring their own theoretical and empirical tools from social sciences including geography, politics, international relations, economics and environmental science. As noted in the companion volume to this book (*International Development in a Changing World*), every subject has its own 'language' with a 'vocabulary' of terms that are used to engage with, describe, analyze and interpret the subject. Development is no different and this second volume adds to this vocabulary, enabling you to learn and practice new terminology through its application to relevant case studies. If you have a social science background you will already be familiar with some of the terms used here. If you come from a natural science or technological background, you may need to be a bit more patient, although there's no need to feel daunted. In order to help you with the vocabulary of *New Perspectives in International Development*, we have produced a glossary located at the end of this book; key terms are highlighted in the text in bold.

The theoretical concepts you will come across, such as 'risk society' (see Chapter 5), 'positive and negative freedom' (see Chapter 4), or 'modernization' (see Chapter 6), provide general and normative explanations about how social transformations and deliberative human actions are thought to occur, informing policy and practice. However, as all theory is context dependent, and therefore cannot be understood in abstraction from the concrete relations of history, power and agency, and scale, chapters move from the theoretical to include case studies. Theory is placed in the context of the deliberate actions of people to improve their livelihoods, communities and societies. For this reason, as you read through the chapters in this book you will come across many activities that give you an opportunity to apply the theories you read about to real-world examples. These activities are of three kinds:

- Activities that allow you to check particular skills. For example, checking that you can interpret numerical data about human development that is presented in table form; or identifying the main points made in an argument.

- Activities that ask you to check your understanding of a topic or concept, or to relate that understanding to your own experience and prior knowledge. Often such activities will ask you to make notes which can become the basis of personal and critical reflection. International development is, after all, inherently personal, as discussed in Chapter 10.

- Activities that ask you to critically engage in a hypothetical discussion about a development idea, or debate an issue for which there is no clear 'right' answer, only arguments one way or the other. In such activities you are an active part of the story or argument, and can take ownership of it.

As in *International Development in a Changing World*, these different kinds of activity also start from the basic assumption that you only really learn something when you have to teach it, even if that is teaching yourself. However, we follow these activities with a 'Discussion' text of our own which can give you ideas to build on or compare your own thoughts with.

New Perspectives in International Development begins by asking the question 'what is it that we are afraid of?' The answer to this question will obviously vary depending on context but, as Joseph Hanlon points out, fears and vulnerabilities are interconnected. The rise of China may cause concern for policy makers in the USA who fear a loss of influence, workers in Detroit may fear losing their livelihoods, while others may worry about the impact on the environment of China's demand for more resources. Rural migrants in China's burgeoning cities may fear starvation and homelessness with the decline of the welfare state in that country. The interconnected processes of development generate and exacerbate many of these fears.

Introducing emotional content into the analysis makes a clear connection between the personal and the institutional in international development. It is also evident in the manipulation of conflict, both civil and inter-state wars as examined by Joseph Hanlon and William Brown. Their chapters discuss how security concerns have entered development policies and actions, exploring the 'security–development nexus' with a focus on different forms of insecurity: from national to individual, and from global to local. Both authors raise the question of whether we need security to have development and how insecurity, conflict and vulnerability hamper development goals.

Brown raises the controversial debate of whether in fact some conflicts can be 'good' for development, the driving force for the formation of liberal democratic states and social organization that enhances, for future generations at least, greater opportunities. The normative judgement of what is 'good' policy is also raised by Hanlon in his analysis of the blurring of boundaries between development aid and foreign policy, and whether in fact humanitarian aid in conflict zones can do more harm than good. Claudia Aradau's chapter takes up this theme by using a theoretical analysis of positive and negative freedom to assess whether the interventions in human trafficking are necessarily positive for the women involved. Being trafficked for some, it could be argued, is part of a livelihood strategy.

There are obvious questions of power and choice raised by this discussion, for example patriarchy and the lack of opportunities available to women in developing countries to engage in work other than the sex trade that increases their vulnerability. But one solution to having less power, and greater insecurity as a result, is to build solidarity with others. This idea is taken up by Mark Smith in his work on Haiti and Trinidad. Haiti struggles with the damage done by a colonial past, natural disasters, internal political and social conflict, and inequality. However, its neighbour, Trinidad, has followed a different trajectory, not only because of its different history and context but, as Smith argues, the formation of non-governmental organizations (NGOs) that have acted to combat corruption and work towards a more collaborative approach to development. Such forms of solidarity are a means for the most vulnerable people to protect themselves or at least prepare for the future.

While solidarity may be one way of addressing vulnerabilities, innovative technology has also been highlighted as an integral, necessary, component of development aimed at improving living standards and decreasing insecurity. We can think of agricultural technology that has meant a steady supply of food to feed a growing population, or water and sanitation infrastructure that has meant we are less likely to die of disease. Yet new technologies also generate fears and risks, raising the question of whether they will save us or create more problems in the long run, for us or for other people. Debates on the impact of genetically modified food, for example, illustrate these arguments.

Peter Robbins situates these questions within a discussion on the hegemony of 'modernization', a set of theories translated into policies and institutions that have marked the direction and philosophy underpinning much of international development in the 20th and into the 21st century. With modernisation came the idea that new technologies were required for development to occur. Yet as we know today, much of the technologies of the 20th century that enabled a carbon-based economy also created environmental damage and climate change, and the resources necessary to maintain economic growth, such as oil, are not renewable (see Roger Blackmore's chapter). This has particular implications for emerging economies and rising powers. As Kelly Gallagher argues, while China is investing heavily in alternative energy sources, to date the take-up rate of more energy efficient and cleaner technologies in the country is limited. The idea that a 'late industrializing' country like China could leapfrog to a more sustainable model of development does not appear to be borne out.

Raphael Kaplinsky outlines how this tension between development and the need to manage its environmental impacts, has created a set of internal contradictions that are likely to undermine globalization itself. Global economic growth is unsustainable in environmental terms and the flexibilization of the economic system has meant increasing levels of inequality and insecurity for many, not just the poorest. Linking back to previous chapters, this world of insecurity and fear is likely to generate opposition to aspects of globalization (something we have seen in the 'Occupy' movement) and presents us with the very real prospect of resource wars in the future (including over water as much as oil).

So a final question in this volume is how can equitable development be sustained in a world of scarce resources, where demand for energy is pressing and where issues such as climate change threaten past, present and future gains? The answer may lie in rethinking what we mean by development, how we classify it and measure it. As noted in this and the companion volume (*International Development in a Changing World*), development has often been conceptualized as a process of economic growth. However, as Sarah White argues, there may be other ways of perceiving development, focused on a critique that comes from making development personal. This can involve thinking about more holistic conceptualizations of development, such as 'wellbeing'.

There has been a growing momentum to focus on wellbeing as the goal of international development, with the personal at its centre. Rather than just measuring economic indicators, wellbeing implies participatory processes where what we think and feel also matters. It is inflected by our identities and culture, including the power relationships inherent in these terms, and is being applied not only to 'developing' countries but is spoken about by leaders in countries such as France and Britain as a means to understand societies there. Taking these ideas, this final chapter provides you with the opportunity to reflect upon your own capacity to make development personal, to be a part of change, or more importantly to be part of determining the direction of change.

The perspectives in this volume raise some challenging questions, such as whether conflict can be useful in driving development, whether strategies of humanitarian intervention may create more harm than good, or whether it is in fact possible to balance economic development and environmental change. However, we have also set out analytical tools that can be applied both practically and theoretically in different contexts. Using these concepts you will be able to reach your own perspectives on the processes that make up international development.

Fear and development

Joseph Hanlon

Introduction

What are you afraid of? Do you fear that your children will go hungry, or that you will be unable to find a job, or that your crop will fail? Are you concerned about personal violence in the streets or at home – robbery, rape, gang attacks? Are you worried about flood or cyclones? Or do you fear civil war or global violence – terrorist attacks or an attack on your town by a rebel group or an invasion of your country by a neighbour?

Your answers to these sorts of questions will be determined by who you are, what social position you occupy, your location in the world, perhaps your culture or religion, and, of course, your age, gender and social class. These fears are expressions of vulnerability and insecurity, and, wherever you live, all are possible. But the risks vary. If you live in a city you are unlikely to fear crop failure, but you may fear being caught up in a terrorist attack, which is something the author of this chapter has experienced. Our fears are signs of our vulnerability, which in turn reflects both the risk of a harmful event and presence (or lack) of support structures to help us if such an event occurs. For example, a farmer is less frightened of a bad crop season due to climate change if there are support structures, such as government agencies or charitable groups who can help in bad times.

Why do we start this book with the concept and experience of **fear**? Security is often seen as the opposite of fear; a goal that needs to be attained in everyday life. In order to achieve security or even to get nearer to it, throughout history people have tried to reduce fear and eliminate or deal with the threats causing it, including implementing development programmes to enhance security. Security is, therefore, also a practice or a process through which people, governments and institutions attempt to reduce or eradicate fear, and make it manageable.

Peoples' experiences around the world are shaped by fears of conflict, unemployment, famine, poverty, disease, and so on. Many of our efforts at 'development' are aimed at reducing fears – by improving healthcare and producing more food – and also by developing new policies and creating support structures in case our fears come true. But sometimes the harmful effects of the development process, for example creating conflict or displacement, can be what we are afraid of. Therefore, the relation between fear and development is not a simple one. Which fears are reduced by development and which fears can be sparked by developmental processes? By the end of the chapter, you should have a better understanding of how fear both promotes and retards development and how it shapes the complex relationship between conflict and security. Specifically, this chapter aims to:

- analyze the links between fear, security and development
- assess complexities around conflict and development

- investigate historical responses to insecurity
- understand the causes of **civil war**.

1.1 Understanding fear, security and development

It is the deaths due to war and organized violence or those caused by earthquakes and other disasters that capture the attention of the media, because they encapsulate our own worst fears. Civilian deaths in Sierra Leone's civil war in the 1990s, victims in the Twin Towers of New York in 2001 or in the Gaza strip in 2009, all highlight the social toll of conflict, and that it can be dramatic, random and outside our control. We can be victims of political violence waged by leaders far away. Such conflict stresses our vulnerability and can create heightened feelings of insecurity. However, more people die 'silent', preventable deaths caused by hunger or illness than die in wars. And in the poorer parts of cities like Shanghai and Detroit, other fears are present – of an inability to put food on the table, of crime and social violence, of cultural and material loss. But which fears are important and relevant for international development?

Fear is also a double-edged emotion – it can spur people into action but it can also be paralyzing, making us passive. In short it can promote and retard development. For instance, if we look at inequality both within and between societies, we can see that these inequalities can lead to poor health or social conflict (see Hanlin and Brown, 2013); some will act to try to reduce inequality, while others will say 'I am so poor and powerless there is nothing I can do.'

Such fears are not just contemporary phenomena. In fact our deepest fears date back millennia. The Four Horsemen of the Apocalypse in the Book of Revelation of the Christian Bible are usually taken to symbolise disease, war, famine and death (Figure 1.1). Cultures may represent fears differently, but these four have been dominant both culturally and historically. Consequently, much of our social organization – family, community, state, and most recently international organizations – has been created to keep the metaphors of the four horsemen at bay. And throughout the world, that struggle continues. Of course, the nature of specific fears changes, for example from bows and arrows to nuclear weapons, and from losing farm land to losing industrial jobs.

Figure 1.1   The Four Horsemen of the Apocalypse; engraving by Albrecht Durer

The links between disease, war, famine and death have also been long understood. War brings famine and pestilence, but the opposite is also true. People who believe they are starving may use force to obtain the assets of another society or challenge their own social order because their rulers are taking an unfair share of the wealth. For example, Algerians blamed the French for pushing them off their land to make room for French settlers, thus causing poverty and hunger. While the national liberation movement won the 1954–62 independence war, up to one million people died. Many similar wars have been fought to throw off colonial rulers and declare independence, for example the USA in the 18th century, Venezuela and five other South American countries in the 19th century, and various African and Asian countries in the 20th century. As in Algeria, national statehood sometimes only came about after bitter civil wars.

These links alert us to the complex connections between security and development. Indeed, it could be argued that 'development' is the battle against the fear of disease, war, famine, and death. Higher yielding crops are developed to try to stave off food shortages and hunger; better houses are designed to withstand earthquakes; new organizational systems are created to manage more complex cities. As was stressed by Hanlin and Brown (2013), *development is about change*, and, as not all change is positive, it can be conflictual – some people benefit, some people are not affected, and some lose out. Conflicts may come about because of change that induces greater benefits for one group, or displaces another. This can lead to overt resistance to change. If unplanned development creates a large number of losers, intentional development is often needed to support the poorest and those who may not benefit. This led, as noted in Hanlin and Brown (2013), to structuralist and interventionist development models, in an attempt to increase the percentage of those who gain and protect those who lose.

An example of the contested nature of change can be seen in the development of India (see Mohan, 2013). Industrialization raised living standards for some, but it also caused job losses for millions of handcraft workers (in both the UK and India). To combat this change, the Indian independence leader, Mahatma Gandhi, promoted the wearing of *khadi*, that is, hand spun and woven cotton cloth. However, the argument made against Gandhi's approach was that, while industrialization created unemployment for handloom weavers, it provided poor people with much cheaper, mass produced, clothing. Gandhi's struggle for Indian independence also had an international dimension because he made an important critique of colonial control of resources and labour. For example, in India, under colonial rule, cotton production was controlled by the British in ways that favoured the export of raw materials to the mills and factories of Northwest England (primarily Manchester and Lancashire), where it was manufactured into textiles to be exported back to India (among other countries). Indian cotton producers became dependent on fluctuating international market prices, while unequal trade arrangements, including tariffs imposed by the British, hampered the ability of the indigenous Indian textile industry to develop through exporting its own cloth. Therefore, while employment and wealth was created for communities in Britain, poverty was often exacerbated for those in India whose livelihoods were associated with cotton and textile production.

An example perhaps of a better balance between security and development can be found in Sweden where its rapid industrialization in the mid-20th century was driven by state-supported small firms and labour market flexibility. Companies were able to hire and fire workers with ease, and thus to take more risks in expanding production. This was acceptable because it was backed up by generous unemployment benefits provided by the state for those workers in periods when they were not able to work. Unlike in the Indian example, above, in this case we can see a positive circle where development promoted security, which, in turn, promoted development.

Therefore, there is a certain tension between fear and development: fear of disease, war, famine, and death pushes us toward development, yet fear of the side effects of development may cause us to resist changes that disrupt established social organization and hierarchies. We look to development to reduce our fears and create security, but we need security to accept the possible harmful effects of development.

Activity 1.1

Read US President Franklin D. Roosevelt's definition of freedom from want and freedom from fear, see below. If you had to rank the four freedoms he outlines, which one should come first in your view?

> We look forward to a world founded upon four essential human freedoms.
>
> The first is freedom of speech and expression – everywhere in the world.
>
> The second is freedom of every person to worship God in his own way – everywhere in the world.
>
> The third is freedom from want – which, translated into world terms, means economic understandings which will secure to every nation a healthy peacetime life for its inhabitants – everywhere in the world.
>
> The fourth is freedom from fear – which, translated into world terms, means a worldwide reduction of armaments to such a point and in such a thorough fashion that no nation will be in a position to commit an act of physical aggression against any neighbour – anywhere in the world.
>
> *(Roosevelt, 1941)*

Spend about 5 minutes on this activity.

Roosevelt understood the importance of fear. In his inaugural address on 4 March 1933, at the depths of the Great Depression, he said 'the only thing we have to fear is fear itself – nameless, unreasoning, unjustified terror which paralyzes needed efforts.' He returned to this in his famous 'four freedoms' speech in 1941. His third freedom is 'freedom from want' – effectively, development to end want and poverty. And his fourth freedom is 'freedom from fear' – effectively, creating security against physical aggression. Fear and want are real, and Roosevelt in 1941 was already setting out development goals to reduce insecurity and poverty.

Leaders often use fear as a mobilizing tool, for example creating divisions along lines of perceived difference – race, ethnicity, religion, gender – or around economic or social change that is presented as detrimental. For example, the **Cold War** (1947–91) was in part promoted by political and military leaders building their power bases by creating the fear that communism or capitalism would destroy the other side. This led to massive military expenditure in the name of 'security'.

How much 'security' we need or we can have is never a simple or clear question. It is a personal, social and political judgement, and different countries and communities reach different balances. But many scholars and policy makers understand the relation between security and development as a positive spiral in which development feeds our feelings of security and results in a reduction of fear.

Roosevelt separated freedom from want and freedom from fear, but the two have always been intertwined, and the introduction noted that fears can involve hunger or physical security. Thus a security continuum runs from hunger through war, as security is increasingly seen to include human needs, as you will see in this chapter and later on in Chapter 3.

Globalization and environmental change have brought the two more firmly together: national or local governments still have primary responsibility and attempt to find developmental responses to insecurities, but the problems are common to many countries and across frontiers, and the solutions are increasingly seen as international.

Activity 1.2

List a few of your fears.

Are they related to 'development' in some way?

Can you give an example of exaggerated or unjustified fears? Were they promoted by leaders or the media?

Spend no more than 10 minutes on this activity.

Discussion

Our worst fears are often of things we cannot control – that we will lose our job, that we will be struck down by a pandemic disease like flu, or that someone, perhaps a mugger or a terrorist, will attack us. Fears like these are often exaggerated by politicians or the media, and we have to be careful to judge how great the risk really is. A woman who gives birth may be afraid of dying, and that is a real fear – women do die in childbirth. But for a woman in Europe the risk is relatively low; for a woman in Malawi the risk is more than 100 times as great (Hanlon, 2013). Part of development is improved healthcare and a sharp reduction in maternal mortality, and therefore is a direct response to a woman's fear of dying in childbirth.

We may fear hunger or at least food shortages and high prices for basic staple foods, but where do we locate that fear? For a peasant, it will be partly the fear that bad rains may destroy the crop. But in an increasingly globalized world, food shortages can also be due to a lost crop in another country or even global market shortages. Even terrorist attacks can have different roots. Bombs in Madrid and London were planted by both domestic nationalist groups and those linked to Al Qaeda.

As you have seen in the introduction, one way to define 'security' is as the absence of fear. This implies that there is a set of systems that allow us to go about our daily business with some assurance that there will be adequate food, that our children can go to school, and so on. It also means – and this has often been the most immediate implication of the concept of security – that there are a series of backup and preventive systems in place that provide the institutional mechanisms for protecting the vulnerable. Obviously this could range from armies to protect us and flood prevention measures for communities on rivers and coastal regions, to unemployment benefits and health services to cover income shortfalls, disability and sickness. Before moving on to the next section summarize your understanding of this complex relationship between development and fear in the following activity.

Activity 1.3

When does development stop fear?

When does development create fear?

When does fear stop development?

When does fear create development?

Consider these four questions. Can you think of a real-life scenario for each one?

Spend about 15 minutes on this activity.

Discussion

When does development stop fear? The development of health services can reduce the fear of pandemics, disease, and death in childbirth.

When does development create fear? Industrialization can exacerbate inequalities and create fear of unemployment, for example the experience of the Indian cotton workers during the time of Gandhi and the British Empire.

When does fear stop development? People who must be moved may stop the building of a road or dam because they fear their land and livelihoods will not be replaced. Or fear of another group could bring civil war, which stops development.

When does fear create development? Fear of death in childbirth has been a prime motivator in improving healthcare. Fear of hunger and oppression triggered independence wars that led to statehood and possibilities for development.

Section 1.2 will show how we have dealt with these difficult relations between our myriad fears, development and the goal of security. As you have seen, the problems of security and development go far back in history. Yet, it was only in the 20th century that international institutions were put in place to ameliorate the four horsemen of disease, war, famine and death.

1.2 Pursuing security in the 20th century

Much of the 20th century saw the four horsemen on the rampage, but also saw more serious academic and political discussion of how the horsemen might be corralled. World War II (1939–45) was the deadliest conflict in human history, with 50 to 70 million fatalities. It was truly global, with 100 million military personnel mobilized for wartime action and many more civilians in supportive occupations. It was particularly brutal and directed more than earlier wars at civilians, for example by the bombing of major non-military targets such as cities on both sides of the conflict. It also saw an unprecedented genocide, with the German regime engaged in organized murder on a scale so far unseen in human history. Ultimately, the war resulted in the development of nuclear weapons with enormous destructive power, as witnessed in Hiroshima and Nagasaki in 1945.

The end of the war saw movements from two directions to make sure it never happened again and also to prevent a nuclear war. The first was the creation of international institutions designed to prevent such conflicts. The United Nations (UN) (Figure 1.2) was established in 1945 in the hope that it might be possible to prevent wars of this kind where earlier attempts, such as the League of Nations, had failed. It should be noted that there have been no major military conflicts on that scale, between large industrial powers, since the formation of the UN. In the late 1940s it was believed that economic instability was one cause of the rise of Fascism in central Europe, the Great Depression of the 1930s and bitter economic and political conflicts between nations. So, the International Monetary Fund (IMF) and the International Bank for Reconstruction and Development (IBRD) were established in 1944 in Bretton Woods, New Hampshire, USA (see Hanlin and Brown, 2013). The IBRD was initially to fund rebuilding of Europe after the war. This was later expanded to developing countries and it is now better known as the World Bank. Membership in all three organizations is composed of governments.

But in parallel to this state-based response to social problems such as unemployment and the fiscal crises of states, there was also an understanding that the war had grown out of human suffering and in turn had done immense harm. That led to a closer look at the rights of individuals as well as the responsibilities of nation states, and was codified in the Universal Declaration of Human Rights adopted by the UN in 1948. As well as political rights such as freedom of mobility, association and expression and a prohibition against discrimination, the declaration includes social and economic rights, including rights to free primary education and social security, a right to work, and a right to an 'adequate' standard of living. Thus, implicit in these institutions and the rhetorical devices used to support them, there was an individual right to something which later would be called 'development'.

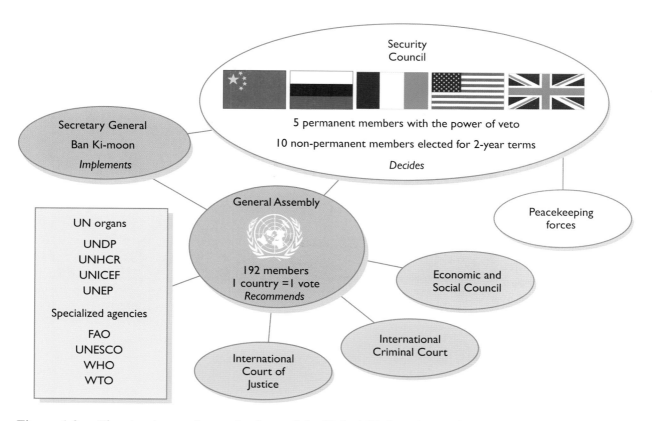

Figure 1.2 The structure and organizations of the United Nations (Ban Ki-moon was appointed in 2007, before this the Secretary General was Kofi Annan 1997–2006) (Adapted from: http://blogs.ubc.ca/astu400e2010/2010/09/16/un-structure-simplified/)

These measures in the international arena took place at the same time that welfare states in countries such as the UK were established, bringing security and development into a closer relationship. Both were needed to mitigate against the fear and insecurity that could generate another conflict. In the UK, the 1942 report by William Beveridge talked of five 'giant evils' in society: want, disease, ignorance, squalor and idleness (Figure 1.3). His report served as the basis for the post-World War II Welfare State with national insurance and a National Health Service. While some of the specific measures would be applied in different ways across Europe, in retrospect the combined effects and the institutions that emerged are often described as the Keynesian Welfare State. Similar forms of social democracy or corporatism in other European countries formed the basis for the rapid economic growth of the 1950s and 1960s, the most successful economies being those that generated exports of capital goods (i.e. the export of machines, technical capacity and systems to produce goods and services).

Figure 1.3 The 'Five Giants'

1.3   Civil wars and insecurity

These global institutions seem to have contributed to avoiding another inter-state war on the scale of World War II. Although there have been some smaller border wars, such as between India and Pakistan, and Israel and its neighbours, the only major inter-state war in the second half of the 20th century was the Iran–Iraq war (1980–8) in which more than one million people were killed. This does not mean that older forms of violent conflict will never return, for historical practices have an amazing capacity to sneak in the back door in the present. And while we have avoided larger inter-state wars, the 20th century has still been marked by civil wars within states, at times though fuelled by international tensions.

The second half of the 20th century was characterized by the global political hostility of the Cold War (1947–91), between the capitalist 'West' led by the USA and the socialist 'East', led by the Soviet Union. As well as economic competition and an arms race, there was a political battle to try to gain allies among the world's countries, and especially those colonies becoming independent. However, despite periods of heightened tensions, the 'Cold War' gained its name because it did not lead to direct war between the two sides. But East and West did go to war by proxy in specific strategically important regions such as the Korean Peninsula, 1950–53, Southeast Asia (and in particular the Vietnam War), 1955–79, and conflicts in and around Afghanistan. Other flashpoints included conflicts in Central and South America, including Cuba; Africa, including Mozambique; the Middle East and so on, often taking the form of covert wars and involving third-party military support for actors supporting East or West. Proxy conflicts in the Cold War were manifest in a whole range of regional, international and civil wars, with some countries shifting sides as circumstances changed. Interventions in single countries continued after the end of the Cold War, with the USA and its allies invading Iraq in 1990–91 and 2003–2010 and Afghanistan from 2001.

In the late 20th century, civil wars – those fought mainly inside a single country and largely by people of that country – became much more common than inter-state wars, and remain a serious challenge to development. Here the fear–development matrix shifts – fear of violence and related lack of security are no longer about another country, but about a different group within the same country. However, we should bear in mind that civil wars still often have an interstate component, as in the example of the Cold War above, such as external support for one or both sides in the conflict, and also in terms of the impacts of war (such as refugees flowing into neighbouring countries). In the Libyan Civil War, from 2011, both of these have been evident. Given the increased importance of this type of conflict on development and security, the following sections will look more closely at its origins and the ways in which civil wars differ from interstate wars.

The growing emphasis on the nation state in the late 19th and early 20th centuries fixed boundaries and sometimes through amalgamations, such as Yugoslavia and colonial demarcations in Africa, brought together groups of different wealth, culture, language and religion. This created tensions and conflicts within countries over resources, rights and power, which sometimes led to war.

Additional inequalities in power alongside divisions of culture, language and religion add fuel to civil strife. The Cold War era saw a rise in the number of 'civil wars', as is shown in Figure 1.4, which drop dramatically after 1992 (after the fall of the Berlin Wall in 1989). The more recent rise in the number of conflicts, to 37 in 2008, makes clear that there are now new causes of these conflicts.

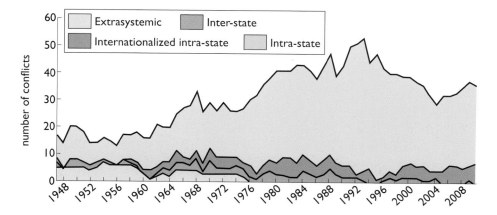

Figure 1.4 Number of armed conflicts by type, 1946–2009. Extrasystemic armed conflict occurs between a state and a non-state group outside its own territory; these conflicts are by definition territorial. Inter-state armed conflict occurs between two or more states. Internationalized intra-state armed conflict occurs between the government of a state and internal opposition groups, with intervention from other states in the form of troops. Intra-state armed conflict occurs between the government of state and internal opposition groups (Source: Harbom and Wallensteen, 2010)

Civil wars rarely have a single cause, and every conflict is different, but what seems fundamental is that a group of people see an issue that is so serious they are willing to risk their own lives and be prepared to kill even neighbours and relatives. Referring back to the earlier discussion above on fears and development as a process of transformation, civil wars are often marked by one group fighting for change, to address inequalities, and another to protect the status quo, although obviously there are more complex scenarios than outlined here. Also bear in mind that explanation is not justification; nothing can justify the genocide in Rwanda in which an estimated 800 000 people were massacred in 1994, or the war in Cambodia in the late 1970s in which the Khmer Rouge killed more than two million people, one-third of the population. But other civil wars have brought transformations which proved to be propitious for development, such as the US War of Independence (1775–83), the Russian Revolution of 1917, or the Mexican revolution of 1910–20.

Ideas of political rights, sovereignty and self-determination led colonies of European powers across the Americas, Africa and Asia to demand autonomy and independence in the 20th century. Sometimes this was granted voluntarily, and sometimes it required hard-fought liberation wars. One root of these wars was usually 'development', in that people in the colony argued that exploitation by the colonial power was restricting their development. Colonial powers managed colonies largely to extract agricultural, mineral and labour resources, not only without any benefit to local people, but often leading to their impoverishment. To prevent opposition, there were usually restrictions on the press and on association. Portuguese colonial authorities required Mozambicans to do forced labour until the 1960s; they allowed few black children to have more than four years of primary school; and prohibited black Mozambicans from running businesses. Japan's 1910–45 rule of its colony Korea was similar, with forced labour and restrictions on Koreans being educated and running businesses. In Zimbabwe, British colonial authorities in 1930 gave the best half of all farmland to 11 000 white settlers, and violently pushed one million black Zimbabweans onto the remaining poorer half of the land. In Kenya in the 1950s, tens of thousands of people opposed to colonial rule were put into concentration camps. In the Congo, vast tracts were handed over to foreign companies for plantations and mines, often using forced labour.

When states were granted, or won, their independence they often suffered from internal splits, caused by economic and social divisions, as well as colonial boundaries which did not correspond to traditional ones. This led to some bitter secession wars. In the US Civil War (1861–65), 11 US states were defeated in their attempt to secede to maintain what they perceived as a beneficial form of economic organization that utilized slavery. But more than 620 000 soldiers died: 10% of all US 'white' and 'free coloured' men between 15 and 40 years old, as well as many civilians (Government Printing Office, 1864). A more recent example is Bangladesh's separation from Pakistan in 1971. However, the Biafra region failed to secede from Nigeria in a war in 1967–70 in which up to one million people died, many of whom were civilians who starved after the Nigerian government blockaded the breakaway state.

Civil wars often have a heightened brutality and ferocity, in part because the fighting can be between families, neighbours and co-workers and because civilians do much of the killing and dying. In a conventional interstate war, the enemy belongs to the other country and thus has a different identity. In a civil war the enemy is just like you, so it becomes increasingly important to dehumanize and demonize in order to turn the former neighbour into an evil 'other' who no longer deserves respect. The result is the use of tactics such as rape and mutilation as the war takes on a personal character, and social accountability collapses, especially within poorly trained militias and guerrilla forces. In addition, civil wars tend to be conducted at closer quarters to the opposition, using small calibre weapons such as hand guns, or knives, rather than at a distance with aircraft; the killer and victim actually see each other. This breakdown of social structures, in particular the trust necessary for social capital that underpins communities, has an immediate impact on development, both social and economic.

The development economist Mary B. Anderson noted that in civil wars people commit atrocities against former acquaintances, friends or colleagues, or do nothing to stop someone being attacked, and feel very strong guilt at committing such acts of violence. They can only assuage the guilt and justify the action by believing that the former friend is now – perhaps always was – evil and likely to attack them (Anderson, 1999, pp. 11, 16). The other factor, as Anderson points out, is that 'civilian-based civil wars are fought in everyday living spaces. The outdoor café, the inter-village bus and the marketplace become battlegrounds, targeted because they are places in which civilians live and work.' The targeting and terrorizing of civilians to undermine opponent combatants has become a frequent feature of armed conflict.

This also means that opponents can actually be unidentified within our midst – the spy or potential terrorist can be anywhere. Again, this creates a level of fear and distrust which is seen to justify a degree of repression and loss of civil liberties that would not be allowed in 'normal' times. Non-combat related criminal acts and inter-personal violence then become easier because they can be done under the cloak of the civil war. If the war continues long enough, violence and distrust can become the norm.

The necessity to justify brutal acts against former friends and neighbours who were once trusted creates a spiral of violence and hatred that can last for generations, and makes peace-building and development very difficult when the war is over. For example, the US Civil War of 1861–65 continues to this day to have an impact on US politics. Finland remains divided after a brief but brutal civil war in 1918 in which over 36 000 people died; probably more were executed than killed in battle (Roselius, 2009). At least 500 000 people died in the Spanish civil war 1936–39 which left a nation traumatized. It was 60 years later that elderly survivors began to identify mass graves of those who had been executed during and after the war, and a programme was begun to exhume the bodies. Most recently such brutality was witnessed in Europe during the conflicts in the former Yugoslavia. These examples highlight how such things are not exclusively located in developing societies outside of the West or global North.

Leaders and followers

So if the effects of civil war stay with us for generations, how can we react to their causes? Can something be done before fear becomes so pervasive that trust cannot be restored? A central debate in the study of civil wars has been characterized by Yanacopulos and Hanlon (2006) as 'big bad men' versus 'people under pressure'. Collier et al. (2004, 2005) have succinctly put it as the 'Greed versus Grievance' debate. The first view is that wars are largely driven by leaders, often acting out of greed for money or power, and who may keep a war going unnecessarily or be complicit in its continuation because of their profits, for example from diamonds or other rare and valuable minerals or access to other assets such as potential power and water supplies.

It may be true that civil wars rarely go forward without strong leaders, but leaders can only succeed if they have followers, and people do not choose to go to war lightly. Civil wars start when at least one group sees no other alternative, and their solution, therefore, often lies in providing one. Cramer (2006) tried to drive this point home when he entitled his book *Civil War is Not a Stupid Thing*. The grievance is usually about resources, power relations or defending and asserting an identity, with a group starting a war because they feel they are disadvantaged and can do nothing else to redress the situation.

Grievances

Most important for us in this context, grievances are very often, directly or indirectly, about lack of development, improper sharing of resources, or unfairly sharing the costs. We do not ignore the issue of leaders, good or bad, but here we wish to concentrate on grievances and related development issues. There have been two important insights to explain this, 'structural violence' and 'group inequality'.

Johan Galtung, one of the seminal thinkers of peace studies, in 1969 declared that 'if people are starving when this is objectively avoidable, then violence is committed' (Galtung, 1969, p. 171). He made an important distinction between an actual and an ideal state of affairs. The larger the gap between the actual and the ideal, he argued, the more structural violence can be said to have taken place. As an important rider to this argument, he suggested that this did not include events that could not be anticipated such as a new epidemic like Swine Flu. However, if a person contracted a disease that could have been avoided by a more effective and fair distribution of the assets of a society then it counted as structural violence. The same logic could be applied to the distribution of food, school resources or shelter. If people starved, remained poorly educated or suffered in any other way and these could have been addressed had social relations and processes been organized differently, then violence had still occurred. In many ways, Galtung was one of the first to explicitly link security to development and in a fairly complex way.

Galtung called these forms of inequality 'structural violence', to distinguish it from direct or military violence which is carried out by an institution or specific actor. He also distinguished structural violence from the forms of psychological violence or torture that can take place between actors or in small groups in situations as diverse as interrogation interviews, legal trials and family relationships. In developing these ideas more recently, Cornwall (2002) argued that there is 'structural violence at the international level, which consists in the deliberate maintenance of a global system based on fundamental and self-reinforcing inequity'. Structural violence can be directly linked to fear, when people see others living in relative luxury and when they are unsure if they can feed their families. Such comparisons can lead to actual physical violence when people fear that some other group is responsible.

Activity 1.4

This activity asks you a series of difficult questions that relate to the ideas of grievance and structural inequalities. There is no right or wrong answer to these questions. Use them to check your comprehension of points made in the previous materials.

If I have extra food and you are starving, and I refuse to give you food, do you have a right to take it? Can you use violence against me?

If the state possesses food and resources but I am starving, do I have a right to rebel and seize those assets? Do I have a responsibility to distribute those food resources fairly and to whom?

The human rights declaration says there is a 'right' to an 'adequate' standard of living. Can people in poor countries use violence to claim that right?

Are 'illegal' migrants to the USA and Europe simply claiming the right to an adequate standard of living?

Spend no more than 30 minutes on this activity.

Structural violence can therefore be seen as occurring when inequality becomes harmful (see Hanlon, 2013). Inequalities, whether physical or structural, emerge in the context of societies. In the 1990s and since, Frances Stewart (2010) argued that relative inequality between self-defined groups is a major cause of civil wars, and offered a classification of the types of inter-group inequalities:

- *economic* (less access to jobs, food or other assets as a result of ownership and control)
- *political* (less access to power and control plus fewer political opportunity structures)
- *social* (discrimination in state services such as education, housing or welfare)
- *cultural* (failures in the recognition of standing based on religion, language and custom).

Groups themselves can be ethnic-, religious-, language- or clan-based, or they can be geographic (one region feels discriminated against) or class-based. However, her key point is that it is not the group identification that causes the war, but the inequalities at stake. For example, it could be argued that the civil war in Northern Ireland in the UK (1968–98) was not primarily about religion, but discrimination. Catholics considered that they were discriminated against with respect to jobs, education, housing and voting rights compared to Protestants. This implies that it was necessary to resolve those inequalities before the violence could be stopped. Thus developmental processes such as house building and job creation were central to reducing group inequalities and, with the Good Friday Agreement (1998), helped to end the 'Troubles'.

That leads back to the question at the start of this chapter – what are you afraid of? Fear reflects vulnerability or insecurity. But the object of fear is also important. In Northern Ireland, fear could be about not being able to obtain a house or job. The object of fear was seen to be not just a physical shortage of houses, but another group who was perceived as having preferred access to housing and other social and economic benefits. Economic and social inequality was reinterpreted as religious inequality. Linked to political discrimination, this led to a civil rights and separatist campaign, repressive policing and eventually to violence. As the violence escalated, insecurity and fear of violence increased on both sides.

This spiral of violence is common in most conflicts and civil wars. The initial violence, perhaps in response to structural violence and group inequality, may have seemed sensible and justified as the only way to redress an untenable situation. War, however, often takes on a dynamic of its own. Violence which is intended to provoke a concession by the other side also creates fear and insecurity on that side and may bring retaliation. Soon the issue can become lost, and the war is driven by mutual insecurity and fear of violence.

Box 1.1 A case study

This case study encapsulates some of the issues discussed in this section about the causes of civil war.

After 27 years in prison for leading an armed struggle against the government, Nelson Mandela was released in 1990. He served as President of South Africa from 1994 to 1999. Mandela won the Nobel Peace Prize in 1993 but was only taken off the US official list of terrorists in 2008. Mandela's release and Nobel Prize marked a change in all of southern Africa, which had suffered several civil wars.

In the late 20th century the region consisted of an independent but pariah state of South Africa (ruled by the white minority of former settlers under a system known as 'apartheid'), Namibia, which was controlled by South Africa, three small independent countries closely linked to South Africa (Lesotho, Botswana and Swaziland), three British colonies (which became Malawi, Zambia and Zimbabwe) and two Portuguese colonies (Angola and Mozambique). Malawi and Zambia decolonized peacefully and became independent; white settlers in Zimbabwe (then called Rhodesia) declared their own independence with white rule and allied with the Apartheid Regime in South Africa. Portugal refused to grant independence to its colonies. By the late 1960s there were liberation wars in Angola, Namibia, Zimbabwe and Mozambique and an armed struggle (although not a full-scale war) in South Africa. The Cold War was in full force, so the Eastern bloc supported the five liberation movements while the West tended to support the status quo.

The government in Portugal was overthrown in 1974 by soldiers no longer willing to fight the colonial wars, and Mozambique and Angola became independent. But the USA and South Africa moved quickly to support an opposition movement in Angola, while Cuba and the Soviet Union backed the government, in the first of the region's **proxy wars**.

Guerrillas won in Zimbabwe, which become independent in 1980. But when Ronald Reagan took office as President of the USA in 1980, he intensified the Cold War; the governments of Mozambique, Zimbabwe and Angola and the South African and Namibian liberation movements were labelled as communist, and white minority-ruled South Africa was backed as a bastion against communism. South Africa began to destabilize its neighbours with economic sanctions and military raids. In Mozambique it set up and supported an opposition movement which waged a brutal war. This became a region with two proxy wars, in which instead of fighting a global hot war, the East and West fought small hot wars inside African countries. In the 17 years 1975–92, two million people died in the proxy wars in Angola and Mozambique.

Mozambique was an example of the bizarre complexities of the Cold War. An African saying is that 'when the elephants fight, the grass suffers.' While East and West fought in Mozambique, many European countries, including Italy and the Nordic states, tried to bind the wounds. Donors began to label it 'permanent emergency' or 'chronic emergency', implying they knew that the 'emergency' was caused by a Cold War proxy war which they were unable or unwilling to stop. They could not persuade the elephants to stop fighting in Mozambique, and aid reached US$1 billion per year by the end of the 1980s. Aid was sometimes highly politicized. Food aid was withheld at least twice to force political concessions, and the USA forced Mozambique to accept the involvement of NGOs which were said to have reported on the war to US security services (Hanlon, 1991).

With the fall of the Berlin Wall in 1989 and the end of the Cold War, fighting in southern Africa largely stopped. In 1990 Mandela was released leading to majority rule in South Africa, and Namibia became independent. The war in Mozambique stopped in 1992, and in 1994 the existing government was overwhelmingly elected to power over a party led by the former apartheid-backed guerrillas. Liberation movements which had been opposed by the USA and the West won elections in South Africa, Namibia, Angola, Zimbabwe and Mozambique. Only in Angola had the civil war taken on an internal dynamic, and it continued until 2002; elsewhere, there was finally peace.

As well as the high death rates, damage caused by three decades of war was huge. A major priority across the region was reconstruction and development, and a rebalancing of economies to raise the living standard of the majority of the population that had been kept poor and uneducated under colonialism and apartheid. The end of the Cold War meant that all of the liberation movements abandoned any pretence of socialism. But the 1990s saw confrontations with the donors, who seemed not to trust the former socialists. Donors imposed neoliberal models which encouraged foreign investment but failed to reduce poverty. Zimbabwe took a more outspoken and interventionist approach and received less aid. Mozambique, where destruction had been particularly devastating, needed the money and had to accept the conditions, but riots in the capital, Maputo, in 2008 and 2010 led to a more interventionist approach.

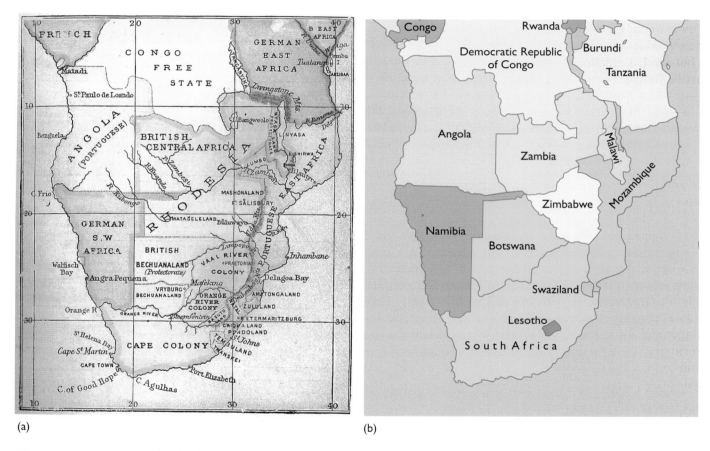

(a)

(b)

Figure 1.5 (a) Map of colonial Southern Africa; (b) map of post-colonial Southern Africa (Source: www.latrobe. edu.au/screeningthepast/25/rose-of-rhodesia/appendix-f.html)

Activity 1.5

Look at the maps in Figure 1.5 and read through the text in Box 1.1. Draw up a list of the many factors which led to the civil wars in southern Africa that lasted for three decades.

Spend about 15 minutes on this activity.

Discussion

Civil wars by definition are between groups within a country, and in southern Africa key factors were racism and the attempt by a white or European-origin minority to maintain dominance over an African majority. But most civil wars have outside factors too, and in southern Africa these included colonialism and the Cold War. This case study also raises two other important questions. One is about terrorism. Nelson Mandela was jailed for using violence against the white apartheid regime in South Africa and he won the Nobel Peace Prize – but the US labelled him a terrorist. Were they right? Can violence be justified against a brutal regime?

1.4 Changing perceptions of security

As you have seen in the earlier discussion on civil war, perceptions are important for how we experience fear. How we perceive the source of fear, of inequality and violence is also instrumental for the causes of civil war. For instance, power differences and inequalities in the Cold War era were even reflected in language – the capitalist West was the 'First World' and the socialist East was the 'Second World', which led to the developing countries being grouped as the 'Third World', where the First and Second Worlds were fighting for dominance, through aid and military intervention. Meanwhile poor and developing countries looked for assistance and tried to deal with fear of hunger and joblessness within their individual states and communities. Third World leaders struggled to decide if they should take aid and policy advice from East or West, and sometimes successfully played the two sides off against each other.

The end of the Cold War led to three important changes. First, the capitalist world's international financial institutions, the World Bank and the IMF, became more powerful and imposed on developing countries a policy of strict free-market policies that minimized the role of government in the economy.

Second was the coming together of the economic powers of the Second and Third World – including Brazil, India and China – as a group with interests different from those of smaller and poorer countries. This also led to new language. Demarcation of a 'rich north' and 'poor south' no longer made sense when there were higher income countries south of the equator, such as Australia. That led activists in the poorer and less powerful countries to coin the term 'global South' as a political rather than a geographic description. The third change brought about at the end of the Cold War was also concerned with perceptions. The UN Development Programme's 1994 *Human*

Development Report defined a new concept of 'human security' and declared that 'there have always been two major components of human security: freedom from fear and freedom from want', explicitly using terms from the 1941 speech by US President Franklin Roosevelt noted above. In an earlier speech in 1933, Roosevelt had spoken of the fear of unemployment and the inability of farmers and industry to sell their production, which is drawn into his category of 'want' in the 1941 speech. In 1941, with World War II already under way, 'fear' was of other nations. With the new concept of 'human security', Pakistani economist and founder of the *Human Development Report*, Mahbub ul Haq, drew these two together. So the concept of human security brought together security and development in a response to disease, war, famine and death.

The *Human Development Report* argued that a change in perceptions was needed to define security:

> For too long, the concept of security has been shaped by the potential for conflict between states. For too long, security has been equated with the threats to a country's borders. For too long, nations have sought arms to protect their security.
>
> For most people today, a feeling of insecurity arises more from worries about daily life than from the dread of a cataclysmic world event. Job security, income security, health security, environmental security and security from crime – these are the emerging concerns of human security all over the world.
>
> *(United Nations, 1994, p. 3)*

The new concept of human security was a 'developmental' concept that included human needs and human agency:

> In the final analysis, human security is a child who did not die, a disease that did not spread, a job that was not cut, an ethnic tension that did not explode in violence, a dissident who was not silenced. Human security is not a concern with weapons – it is a concern with human life and dignity.
>
> *(United Nations, 1994, p. 22)*

The report goes on to define seven 'main categories' that constitute human security (Figure 1.6).

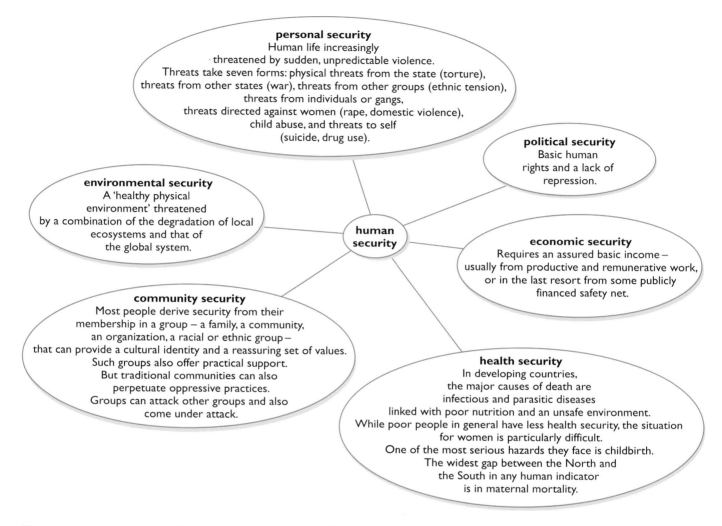

personal security
Human life increasingly
threatened by sudden, unpredictable violence.
Threats take seven forms: physical threats from the state (torture),
threats from other states (war), threats from other groups (ethnic tension),
threats from individuals or gangs,
threats directed against women (rape, domestic violence),
child abuse, and threats to self
(suicide, drug use).

political security
Basic human
rights and a lack of
repression.

environmental security
A 'healthy physical
environment' threatened
by a combination of the degradation of local
ecosystems and that of
the global system.

human security

economic security
Requires an assured basic income –
usually from productive and remunerative work,
or in the last resort from some publicly
financed safety net.

community security
Most people derive security from their
membership in a group – a family, a community,
an organization, a racial or ethnic group –
that can provide a cultural identity and a reassuring set of values.
Such groups also offer practical support.
But traditional communities can also
perpetuate oppressive practices.
Groups can attack other groups and also
come under attack.

health security
In developing countries,
the major causes of death are
infectious and parasitic diseases
linked with poor nutrition and an unsafe environment.
While poor people in general have less health security, the situation
for women is particularly difficult.
One of the most serious hazards they face is childbirth.
The widest gap between the North and
the South in any human indicator
is in maternal mortality.

Figure 1.6 Categories of human security (Source: United Nations, 1994)

Activity 1.6

Compare Figure 1.6 to the list of fears discussed in Section 1.1. Do they fit into these definitions of security?

What do you think about the order of these categories? To which would you give priority?

Spend no more than 10 minutes on this activity.

Although the terms of the UN report have not been used exactly, the fears discussed in this chapter cover most categories. You will also explore many of these fear and categories of human security later in this book.

How did the language of human security change the perception of, and responses, to fear? A 2001 Organization for Economic Co-operation and Development (OECD) study *'Security issues and development cooperation'* said that 'the security of states and the security of people should be seen as mutually reinforcing, suggesting that unmet social, political and economic needs may provoke popular unrest and opposition to governments, ultimately making them more vulnerable to internal and external threats' (OECD, 2001, p. 42). This reading of the relation between development and fear has given rise to another aspect of the debate, namely concerning the form that states need to take in order to achieve security.

At the end of the 20th century and the beginning of the 21st, two terms, 'failed states' and 'fragile states', gained increased currency; however, there was no clear definition for either. Rather, a debate ensued over which states counted as failed or fragile. The US journal *Foreign Policy* and the Fund for Peace, an independent research centre, have been publishing a ranking of 'failed states' since 2005, based on a dozen subjective indicators, such as 'illegitimate governments', 'human rights', 'brain drain' and 'inequality'. Its worst 10 countries in 2010 were Somalia (worst), Chad, Sudan, Zimbabwe, Democratic Republic of the Congo (DRC), Afghanistan, Iraq, Central African Republic, Guinea and Pakistan (Foreign Policy, 2010). But in 2006, the London School of Economics (LSE) Crisis States Research Centre rejected what it called 'a tendency to label a "poorly performing" state as "failed"'. It said a state was 'failed' only if it 'can no longer perform its basic security, and development functions and … has no effective control over its territory and borders' (LSE, 2006). Given inconsistent definitions of what a failed state is, the numbers of failed states also vary substantially.

Similar problems exist with 'fragile states'. In 2009, the UK Department for International Development (DfID) said its 'working definition of "fragile states" covers states where the government cannot or will not deliver core functions to its people.' DfID continues:

'The term fragile states includes a variety of situations:

- Collapsed states – such as Somalia
- States in conflict or recovering from conflict – such as Afghanistan, Sudan, Nepal, Democratic Republic of Congo (DRC) and Angola
- States where governments are strong but are not committed to poverty reduction – Burma and Zimbabwe
- Gradually improving states (with occasional setbacks) – such as Ethiopia and Yemen
- States where development has stopped or is in decline – such as Côte d'Ivoire.'

(DFID, 2009)

A number of points should be noted. First is the totally contradictory use of terms: DfID calls Zimbabwe 'strong' but 'fragile' based on a political judgement about commitment to 'poverty reduction', while Foreign Policy calls it 'failed'. Second is the emphasis on 'state-building' rather than broader social and economic development to resolve the grievances behind war. Third is an emphasis on looking for 'different ways to deliver aid', which could be regarded as a euphemism for bypassing a government the DfID does not like. Fourth is the importance of linking with the military.

These inconsistent definitions of failed and fragile states raise the question of perception once more. When the DfID talks about a 'government [that] cannot or will not deliver core functions to its people', is that something which can be measured, or is that a political judgement, to label governments in order to pave the way for future intervention? Chapter 2 argues that these labels had an important role in adding a new dimension to the relation between security and development: namely, that states in the global South represent a threat to the global North, particularly in terms of conflict. Chapter 3 will explore this further by focusing in particular on the role of intervention. As the earlier extract on southern Africa showed, during the Cold War the big powers assumed a right to intervene in developing countries. In the 1990s, the power was largely shifted to the international financial institutions, notably the World Bank and IMF, which made neoliberal economic policies a condition of aid. But with the turn of the century, there was a shift back to political and military intervention in poor countries, particularly those labelled 'failed' and 'fragile'. This is justified on the basis that poor development in some countries, such as Afghanistan, increases insecurity in others, such as the UK, because of the threat of terrorism generated in discourses of inequality between global South and North.

Mark Duffield (2001, 2007) has repeatedly criticized the merging of security and development by the aid industry. With changes in the structure of capitalism, peripheral areas are still important for minerals and raw materials, but are no longer important for markets and labour. This leaves many people in the global South (and in poor parts of the North) 'surplus to requirements'. In this thinking, aid increasingly becomes a tool for managing and pacifying unneeded people; it becomes part of a new global governance that some would describe as imperialism or neocolonialism, because it is often former colonies that are being managed. Duffield comments that the danger is no longer inter-state war, but 'the threat of an excluded South fomenting international instability through conflict, criminal activity and terrorism' – as well as migration to the rich North (Duffield, 2001, p. 2).

In *Development, Security and Unending War* (2007), Duffield argues:

> the benevolence with which development cloaks itself – its constant invocation of rights, freedoms and the people – conceals a stubborn will to manage and contain disorder rather than resolve it. Development seeks to control and ameliorate the unintended consequences of progress such as destitution, environmental collapse or humanitarian disasters.
>
> *(Duffield, 2007, viii)*

And he goes on to claim that 'Afghanistan is being pacified militarily so that aid agencies can operate and secure civilian loyalties.'

Duffield's arguments expand on the idea which began this chapter: that development and security are not simply connected in one country or in one part of the world (say, the East or West bloc during the Cold War). Development and security are at odds now in the global South and the global North as the argument is made that development in the South serves the security purposes of the North. Chapter 2 gives special attention to the problems that warfare raises for development, particularly given some of the changes in the international system and structures of global capitalism that Duffield also notes.

Perhaps one starting point would be an understanding that conflict is normal in any society, and the role of government and other social institutions is to resolve it. In addition, we should recognize that development itself is often conflictual, with some groups benefiting more than others, as noted earlier, and societies then needing to mediate and balance between these different groups. Most conflicts are resolved peacefully, and war is the exception, not the rule. However, some conflicts become violent when these social mechanisms break down – often when one group wishes to maintain an advantage over another. At that point, some processes will encourage violence. Wars need leaders, but leaders need followers, so a leader often emerges when there is a growing consensus in favour of violence. External influences may exacerbate the violence by supporting one side, as happened during the Cold War and which continues in many other wars today with neighbouring countries often taking one side. Chapter 3 will note that intervention can only be effective if we understand the nature of the specific war – that means knowing the underlying grievances and structural inequalities to ensure that interventions tackle the causes rather than widen the inequalities, but also knowing the leaders and external backers of combatants.

Summary and looking forward

This chapter opened by looking at fears, and then argued for a two-way relationship with development. Fear, particularly of disease, war, famine and death, can promote development as attempts are made to reduce the causes of fear. But development is about change, which in turn can provoke conflicts, and fear of being harmed by development, say by losing your job or land, might cause opposition. Therefore, fears can also stop or hinder development and need to be tackled first. Development has become increasingly focused on setting in place structures and processes that deal with the causes of conflict, such as inequality, providing an antidote to fear and creating a positive development spiral.

War has been a prevalent cause of fear in the 20th century, resulting in the deaths of more than 100 million people. This has led to the formation of global institutions, such as the UN, to improve security and prevent wars in the future. However, while inter-state wars declined, the number of civil wars increased, which required new ways of thinking about the relationship between development and security. Two important concepts were developed to understand the causes of these violent conflicts: structural violence by Galtung and group inequality by Stewart. Development policies also began to take on a new shape as it became clearer that disease, war, famine and death act together. Perspectives on human security led to development programmes that target countries regarded as impacting on the security of others, such as in the struggle to prevent terrorism. This has led to a re-conceptualization of security to refer to all four elements. War, human security, intervention and vulnerability will be discussed in more detail in the next four chapters of this book.

References

Anderson, M.B. (1999) *Do No Harm: How Aid Can Support Peace – Or War*, Boulder, Colorado, Lynne Reinner Publishers.

Beveridge, W. (1942) *Social Insurance and Allied Services*, London, HMSO.

Collier, P., Hoeffler, A. and Smbanis, N. (2005) 'The Collier–Hoeffler model of civil war onset and the case study project research design' in Collier, P. and Sambanis, N. (eds) *Understanding Civil War: Vol. 2 Evidence and Analysis*, Washington DC, The International Bank for Reconstruction and Development/World Bank.

Collier, P., Hoeffler, A. and Soderbom, M. (2004) 'On the duration of civil war', *Journal of Peace Research*, vol. 41, no. 3, pp. 253–73.

Cornwall, R. (2002) 'Conclusion – Where to from Here?' in Lind, J. and Sturman, K. (eds) *Scarcity and Surfeit: the Ecology of Africa's conflicts*, Pretoria, Institute for Security Studies.

Cramer, C. (2006) *Civil War Is Not a Stupid Thing: Accounting for Violence in Developing Countries*, London, Hurst and Co.

Department for International Development (DfID) (2009) 'Government: building states that are capable, responsive and accountable to their citizens – fragile states' [online] http://webarchive.nationalarchives.gov.uk/+/http://www.dfid.gov.uk/fightingpoverty/fragile_states.asp, (National Archives snapshot taken on 22 April 2009, Accessed 12 June 2011).

Duffield, M.R. (2001) *Global Governance and the New Wars: the Merging of Development and Security*, London, Zed Publications.

Duffield, M.R. (2007) *Development, Security and Unending War: Governing the World of Peoples*, Cambridge, Polity Press.

Foreign Policy (2010) 2010 Failed States Index, issue 180, pp. 74–79, available online at: http://www.foreignpolicy.com/articles/2010/06/21/2010_failed_states_index_interactive_map_and_rankings (Accessed 24 October 2011).

Galtung, J. (1969) 'Violence, peace and peace research', *Journal of Peace Research*, vol. 6, no. 3, pp. 167–91.

Government Printing Office (1864) *Population of the United States in 1860; Compiled from the Original Returns of the Eighth Census*, Washington DC, Government Printing Office.

Hanlin, R. and Brown, W. (2013) 'Contesting development in theory and practice' in Papaioannou, T. and Butcher, M. (eds) *International Development in a Changing World*, London, Bloomsbury Academic/Milton Keynes, The Open University.

Hanlon, J. (1991) *Mozambique: Who Calls the Shots?* London, Villiers Publications.

Hanlon, J. (2013) 'Inequality – does it matter?' in Papaioannou, T. and Butcher, M. (eds) *International Development in a Changing World*, London, Bloomsbury Academic/Milton Keynes, The Open University.

Harbom, L. and Wallensteen, P. (2010) 'Armed conflict, 1946–2009', *Journal of Peace Research*, vol. 47, issue 4, pp. 501–9.

London School of Economics (LSE) (2006) 'Crisis, fragile and failed States: definitions used by the CSRC', *Crises States Workshop*, London, March 2006.

Mohan, G. (2013) 'Rising powers' in Papaioannou, T. and Butcher, M. (eds) *International Development in a Changing World*, London, Bloomsbury Academic/ Milton Keynes, The Open University.

Organization for Economic Co-operation and Development (OECD) (2001), 'Security issues and development cooperation: a conceptual framework for enhancing policy coherence', *DAC Journal*, vol. 2, no. 3, pp. 33–68.

Robin, C. (2004), *Fear: The History of a Political Idea*, Oxford, Oxford University Press.

Roosevelt, F.D. (1941) *State of the Union Address to the Congress*, 6 January 1941.

Roselius, A. (2009) 'I bödlarnas fotspår: massavrättningar och terror i finska inbördeskriget' [Translation: The executioner's footsteps: mass execution and terror in the Finnish Civil War], Inbunden, Leopard Förlag.

Stewart, F.J. (2010) 'Horizontal inequalities as a cause of conflict: a review of CRISE's findings', *World Development Report Background Paper*, WDR/World Bank.

United Nations (1994) *1994 Human Development Report: New Dimensions of Human Security*, New York, United Nations, [online] http://hdr.undp.org/en/reports/global/ hdr1994/chapters/ (Accessed 24 October 2011).

Yanacopulos, H. and Hanlon, J. (2006) *Civil War, Civil Peace*, Milton Keynes, The Open University.

Further reading

Buzan, B. and Hansen, L. (2009) *The Evolution of International Security Studies,* Cambridge, Cambridge University Press.

Collier, P. (2007) *The Bottom Billion: Why the Poorest Countries are Failing and What Can be Done About it*, Oxford, Oxford University Press.

Cramer, C. (2006) *Civil War is Not a Stupid Thing*, London, Hurst.

Moisi, D. (2010) *The Geopolitics of Emotion: How Cultures of Fear, Humiliation, and Hope are Reshaping the World*, New York, Anchor Books.

Schneier, B. (2003) *Beyond Fear: Thinking Sensibly about Security in an Uncertain World*, New York, Copernicus Books.

Wilkinson, R. and Pickett, K. (2010) *Spirit Level*, London, Penguin.

Yanacopulos, H. and Hanlon, J. (2010) *Civil War, Civil Peace (Research in International Studies),* London, James Currey.

War, states and development

2

William Brown

Introduction

We cannot eradicate world poverty if we ignore countries affected by
conflict or bad governance ... Instability, violence and insecurity still blight
the lives of millions of men, women and children ... The best way to stem
the rise of violence and create a platform for sustained growth is to build a
state that is capable of delivering basic services effectively and fairly ...

(DfID, 2009, pp. 69–70)

Security is a precondition of development. Conflict not only destroys
infrastructure, including social infrastructure; it also encourages criminality,
deters investment and makes normal economic activity impossible.

(Council for the EU, 2003, p. 2)

From its beginnings, the World Bank has seen violent conflict as a profound
development challenge. ... Violent conflict has severe developmental
consequences: societies experiencing civil war and large-scale violent crime
generally achieve lower development outcomes than those able to prevent or
avoid it ...

(World Bank, 2010, p. 5 and p. 11)

These quotes show how leading aid donors (the World Bank, the UK and the
EU) view the limited prospects for development and poverty reduction in
conditions of violent conflict or warfare. Most major aid donor states, the UN
and numerous NGO and academic commentaries on development express
similar views. Indeed, since the end of the Cold War (1991), there has been an
increasingly prominent view that the problem of violent conflict in the South
was a major concern for development, as well as for the security of people
and states in the South, and for the security of those in the North. This
chapter provides a critical look at this viewpoint, focusing in particular on the
relationship between war and development.

The chapter aims to:

- investigate why the problem of warfare became a key concern of those
  interested in promoting development
- explore different ideas about the relationships between warfare and
  development
- consider how creating political order within states is seen as one way to
  resolve the developmental problems raised by civil war.

To do this, Section 2.1 looks at the historically changing character of war, and
the key problems warfare is seen to pose to the international community post
World War II, including the different ways in which wars in the South are

seen as a problem for the North. Section 2.2 looks at contrasting views about the relationship between warfare and development, including the ideas of donors expressed above that violence is a barrier to development, as well as some ideas that challenge this view. Finally, Section 2.3 explores the idea of political order within states, seen by many as a means by which to resolve the developmental problem of violence. The exploration of these areas draws on contemporary development and international relations literature, but will also introduce some ideas from the history of political thought and historical sociology.

2.1   Historical evolution of warfare

To understand the relationship between war and development in the contemporary world, it helps to have some awareness of the historical context of warfare, and in particular the changing character of warfare over time. This will help you understand why a particular form of war – **internal or civil war** – has become such a concern for states in the North and poses a number of difficult problems for development and for the international community as a whole as introduced in Chapter 1.

2.1.1   War – a recurrent problem in international relations?

For many scholars of international relations, war is seen as one of the basic and recurrent problems of international politics. The classical realist theorist Hans Morgenthau claimed that '[a]ll history shows that nations active in international politics are continuously preparing for, actively involved in, or recovering from organized violence in the form of war' (Morgenthau, 1948, p. 40). From his perspective, it was the nature of the international system that makes the world always prone to warfare because war is the ultimate means by which states settle their differences. Warfare between states is one of the most important processes of interaction in the international system, one that has played a fundamental role in shaping the world we live in.

The reason why the international system is 'war-prone' is classically explained through the notion of a **security dilemma**, a central idea in the realist school of thought in international relations. As many scholars in international relations point out, in formal political terms the international system is seen as an anarchy, in the sense of there being no 'world government' or 'world police force' able to impose a resolution where states are in conflict with each other (see Brown and Hanlin, 2013 for an overview). Realist scholars emphasize that this means states have to rely on their own resources, ultimately their own military resources, in order to protect themselves against potential or actual threats from other states – it is a 'self-help' system (Kiely, 2013).

As originally formulated by John Herz in 1950, the idea of a security dilemma suggests that one state's accumulation of greater military power, even if done with defensive intent, will be interpreted by others as potentially offensive, creating a threat to their security, and they will respond in kind. The result is a constant tendency in the international system towards a 'vicious cycle of security and power accumulation' (Herz, 1950, p. 157). In this view war, when it does break out, sees the deployment of military force by contending states in pursuit of specific goals – for example, gaining territory or resources.

However, while such a dynamic remains a constant possibility in the international system, a closer look at the historical patterns of warfare shows us a rather more complex picture, and a process of change and evolution that might be missed if one concentrates only on the perennial problem of the security dilemma.

2.1.2   The changing character of warfare

From a background in historical sociology, Michael Mann (1987) has suggested that there have been three 'phases' in the development of modern warfare (see Figure 2.1).

(a)

(b)

(c)

Figure 2.1   Three phases of warfare: (a) limited war (like the Seven Years War); (b) total war (World War II); and (c) nuclear war (threat of massive arsenals of weapons like this intercontinental ballistic missile) (Source: Getty Images)

First, Mann outlines what might be seen as the classical view of warfare, very much in line with the security dilemma outlined above. Mann terms this **limited war**, which he dates from the Peace of Westphalia (1648, which ended 30 years of religious warfare in Europe) to World War I (1914–18). Limited war is close to the concept of war famously defined by the 19th century Prussian militarist von Clausewitz 2008 ([1873]) as 'merely the continuation of policy by other means'. That is, war is seen as an instrument of political action, used by the leaders of states to attain identified goals, whether that be taking territory (as with the Iraqi invasion of Kuwait), reducing an enemy's military power, or some other specific strategic, political, economic or cultural goal. For Mann, war in this phase was limited in goals – what war aimed to achieve – and in the means used – the size of armies or weapons technology used. It was also limited in terms of the extent to which society as a whole was involved in warfare. Limited wars often drew on a small proportion of the population to do the fighting, while declaring war, formulating strategy and concluding peace deals were mainly decided by aristocratic and political elites. Wars of this kind were also typically of short duration. Many of these wars involved territorial expansion in the context of colonialism, such as the Boer War (1899–1902). As you will see in Subsection 2.2.2, even in this phase, for some historians, warfare had a very major developmental impact on the European states involved.

Mann suggests the second phase of warfare is **total war**, exemplified by the period of the two World Wars (1914–18 and 1939–45). Total war was unlimited in its goals – the aim was the complete destruction of the opponent. It utilized increasingly destructive and mobile forms of technology through the 'industrialization' of warfare, and the constant revolutionizing of the means of war through the application of industrial science and technology. In these wars, the whole manufacturing sector of respective states often became devoted to weapons production or forms of military support, such as medical supplies, aeronautics and communication. As a result, total war also drew in ever greater numbers of people, eventually seeking the total mobilization of societies through mass conscription and the diversion of economic output to achieve war ends, as was the case, in particular, in World War II. Such periods are also likely to lead to rapid technological development, as many areas receive investment resources from the state and private sector unlikely to be witnessed in peacetime.

The third phase of modern warfare came with the development of **nuclear warfare** from 1945 onwards. Nuclear weapons were first developed and used (in Hiroshima and Nagasaki in Japan in 1945) by the USA. The Soviet Union gained a nuclear capability in 1949, followed by the UK, France and China in the 1950s and 1960s. More recently a number of other states have declared or are thought to have nuclear capability including Israel, India and Pakistan. However, the key confrontation of the Cold War nuclear age was between the USA and the Soviet Union, both of whom held massive arsenals able to destroy each other several times over. In terms of ends and means, a full nuclear exchange could never be rational unless one imagines, as Mann notes, that the desired goals of war are combined murder and suicide. Yet, possession of nuclear weapons was rationalized in terms of deterrence – the strategy that one state's possession of such weapons would deter another from using them, for fear of retaliation and destruction. The possession of nuclear weapons played a major role in establishing a new pattern of warfare post World War II. Between the main contending parties in the Cold War, a kind of nuclear stalemate held, sometimes very precariously, and no inter-state war broke out between the members of NATO (North Atlantic Treaty Organization) and the Warsaw Pact. However, while a 'nuclear peace' ruled in Europe and the North more generally, the Cold War saw both sides heavily involved in conflicts in the South backing governments or rebels, depending on their political allegiances, as noted in Chapter 1.

Activity 2.1

Mann's forms of war have been introduced as three 'historical phases', implying each followed the other in succession. Can you think of any wars that do not fit Mann's pattern quite so neatly?

Spend about 5 minutes on this activity.

Discussion

You may have thought of revolutionary wars in Europe in the 18th and 19th century, or perhaps even of colonial wars as displaying some of the characteristics of total war. Or you may have thought of the Iraq war in 1990–91, which had elements of a limited war. In fact, Mann doesn't claim a completely neat chronological sequence of forms of warfare and notes that elements of total war were apparent much earlier – in the French revolutionary and Napoleonic wars (1792–1815) and in the American Civil War (1861–65), all of which relied on massive mobilizations of people in extended wars of attrition. In addition, the first Gulf War (Iran–Iraq: 1980–88) had clear similarities with total war at least for the two countries involved; while the second (1990–91) had elements of limited war in the sense of the limited goal of the expulsion of Iraq from Kuwait and the limited (albeit still very destructive) means used by both sides. Beyond that, the development of new technology has led some writers to speak of a newer phase of 'networked warfare' based on a so-called 'revolution in military affairs' with the use of advanced information technology and remotely controlled 'arms length' deployments, such as the use of drones by US forces in Afganistan.

You might also have noted some wars that do not fit this characterization of warfare as something that occurs between states. Chapter 1 introduced the concept of civil war. Internal or civil wars plausibly form a fourth category to add to Mann's list. In the period since World War II, the predominant form of actual fighting (as opposed to the 'cold' nuclear stand-off) has been violent conflict primarily within states rather than between them, and primarily in the global South. This trend has been noted by several writers (Holsti, 1995; Kaldor, 1999) who argue that warfare *between* states has been partially eclipsed by warfare *within* states. Furthermore, matching neither the conventional technology of Mann's first two phases of war nor the nuclear armaments of his third stage, such wars have been labelled, 'wars of the third kind' (Rice, 1988; Holsti, 1995), involving some form of guerrilla warfare by at least one side and being primarily directed at some kind of change to the state. Holsti has argued that, between 1945 and 1995, nearly two-thirds of all armed combat was in the form of internal wars – civil wars, wars of national liberation, wars of secession, and armed uprisings to oust governments: '… war today' he wrote 'is rooted in the lack, or disintegration of, community within states' (Holsti, 1995, p. 320).

This is not to say that internal wars are not 'international' as well. Such wars frequently spill over into other states, become internationalized through the actions of external supporters and opponents, those seeking to intervene to end violence, arms suppliers, ties between dissident groups and so on. For example, the wars in Sierra Leone (1991–2000) and Liberia (1989–96, 1998–2003), as well as the Democratic Republic of Congo (from 1996 onwards) were notable for the extensive international financial and trading links, particularly in valuable raw materials like diamonds, as well as for the cross-border actions of combatants and neighbouring states. They are also not 'limited' in Mann's sense, in that internal wars are increasingly 'repeat' events, rather than one-offs. In the first decade of the 21st century, 90 per cent of civil wars occurred in countries that had experienced a civil war in the previous 30 years (World Bank, 2011, p. 2).

Partially reflecting this, with the end of the Cold War, a new set of discourses around security and development came to the fore. On the one hand, the end of the Cold War seemed to offer the chance to resolve some long-running conflicts that had been sustained in part by the involvement of one or both superpowers. For example, there was an end to war in Mozambique, Angola and Namibia in southern Africa, and Nicaragua and El Salvador in Central America, all hotspots of Cold War rivalry. However, the end of the Cold War also saw wars emerge in the former Soviet bloc, where the disintegration of communist rule opened up disputes, such as over political boundaries in the former Yugoslavia and in some of the former states of the Soviet Union.

One consequence of these shifting patterns of warfare was the creation of a new set of political problems for the international community. Although it may seem odd that there are international rules and codes of practice around warfare – particularly given the emphasis this chapter has placed on a formal international anarchy – nevertheless, warfare between states has for many centuries been regulated to some extent through voluntary 'rules of the game'. Initially, these were accepted norms of practice shared among governing elites, in the main the aristocracy and monarchies of European states. However, with the development of modern states, the rules of war became more institutionalized in a series of conventions and treaties (Box 2.1).

Box 2.1 Regulating warfare internationally

There is an enormous body of international law pertaining to the conduct of war. Some of these rules of war arise from customary practice among states built up over centuries. However, a substantial body of law arises from treaties and conventions. Some examples of these include:

- regulation of the treatment of prisoners of war, the injured and civilians in the Geneva Conventions, which originally date back to 1864 but which were codified in four Conventions in 1949
- regulation of the declaration and ending of warfare, including restrictions on the declaration of war in the Kellogg–Briand Pact of 1928 and in the UN Charter, 1945
- regulation of the kinds of weapons that can be used, such as the Hague Conventions of 1899 and 1907; the Geneva Protocol on the use of gas and biological weapons; and the Ottawa Treaty of 1997 on the use of land mines, as well as treaties limiting the possession and testing of nuclear and chemical weapons
- legal processes governing those accused of war crimes and crimes against humanity, such as the International Criminal Court (ICC) established by the Rome Statute of 1998.

The norms that have been created to help minimize inter-state war, outlined briefly in Box 2.1, may not be as much use for preventing or resolving internal war. For example, the collective international commitment, through the UN, to uphold the territorial integrity of existing states by recognition of state sovereignty, may help to deter conventional inter-state conflicts but it does little to prevent challenges to states from within. Indeed, the rules of sovereignty go a long way to making it difficult for the international community to intervene effectively in cases of internal warfare, as you will see further in Chapter 3.

2.1.3 War as a 'threat' to the North

So why did internal war, in the South in particular, become such a concern for the international community, and the powerful Western states in particular? As noted in Chapter 1, after World War II up until the 1990s, most internal wars had some kind of Cold War dimension at work within them, even if there were often regional or domestic causes as well. So in the post-Cold War world there was a strong feeling that Western states would now 'pull out' with little strategic interest at stake. However, there are perhaps two general reasons why warfare – and development – in the South continued to feature so strongly in the policy concerns of the North:

- warfare in the South was thought to create a series of security threats to the North
- warfare in the South was thought to undermine donors' efforts in the North to successfully fund development in the South (for example, through international aid programmes).

These two concerns arise in rather different policy arenas in states in the North – the first in discussions over national security and the second directly in development cooperation policy itself. As you will see, security and development are in fact entwined in both cases. In the former area of policy, development also features because 'successful' development in the South is seen as a way of reducing national security threats in the North. In the latter, security also plays a role as underdevelopment in the South is seen to lead to potential violent conflict, thus creating a vicious circle of insecurity.

Activity 2.2

To check your understanding, look again at your responses to the questions in Activity 1.3 of Chapter 1. Note down how the policy concerns of the North about violent conflict in the South might be seen to fit within those questions.

Spend about 5 minutes on this activity.

Discussion

As suggested in Chapter 1, development features both as something that is a solution to security fears arising out of war *and* as something that can be undermined by war. As you saw, the result was a much closer relationship between security and development policies in the North. Section 2.2, giving a more historical outline of policy concerns in the North, illustrates this evolutionary process. In the years after the Cold War, many scholars, as well as politicians like Bill Clinton (US President 1993–2001) and Tony Blair (UK Prime Minister 1997–2005), identified a contrast between the continuation of 'stable', 'liberal' and 'peaceful' areas of the world – primarily Europe, Australasia, Japan and the USA – with areas of instability and internal warfare, both in areas surrounding Europe's borders (the Middle East and West Asia) and elsewhere in the developing world, particularly Africa. Robert Cooper, one-time advisor to Blair, summed up the view: 'there is a zone of safety in Europe and outside it a zone of danger and chaos' (Cooper, 2004, p. 55). Such language appears to echo the argument in Chapter 1 that fear is a tool manipulated by political leaders. Yet, with the continuation of peaceful relations and deep and extensive cooperation among Western states – even after the reduction of the Cold War nuclear confrontation – some writers began to argue that there was an inherent pacifism in relations between liberal democracies (an idea put forward by Doyle, 1983, and known as the 'democratic peace' thesis). And while war between liberal and non-liberal states remained both possible and actual (as with the US-led invasion of Iraq in 2003), it was threats emanating from the 'disorderly' areas of the world that concerned many Western politicians. Cooper again summarized some of the fears: 'If non-state actors, notably drug, crime or terrorist syndicates take to using [chaotic states as] bases for attacks on the more orderly parts of the world, then the organized parts will eventually have to respond' (Cooper, 2004, p. 18).

For states in the North, then, the collapse of states in the South due to internal warfare was a problem because they created spaces that allowed a variety of 'threatening' non-state actors (for example, terrorists, illegal migrants, drug and human traffickers, see Chapter 4) to emerge. The key term 'failing states' emerged in northern policy and in academic studies of security and development (see Chapter 1 for a discussion of this contentious term). These general fears around failing states took a much sharper and more specific form following the attacks on the USA by al-Qaeda on 11 September 2001

(Figure 2.2). Here, a terrorist network used the territory of Afghanistan, mired in internal warfare and largely left to its own devices after 1993 by the great powers, as the base from which to launch attacks on the USA. This new threat posed again the issue of total war (in the sense of aiming at the total destruction of the opponent) and nuclear war (in the fear terrorists might gain access to nuclear material).

Figure 2.2   The attack on the World Trade Centre, New York, 2001

Activity 2.3

Read the following three brief extracts from the *2010 USA National Security Strategy*. How are conflict and development viewed in relation to security concerns about terrorism?

> Within this environment, the attacks of September 11, 2001, were a transformative event for the United States, demonstrating just how much trends far beyond our shores could directly endanger the personal safety of the American people ... Failing states breed conflict and endanger regional and global security. Global criminal networks foment insecurity abroad and bring people and goods across our own borders that threaten our people ... Democracies that respect the rights of their people remain successful states and America's most steadfast allies. Yet the advance of democracy and human rights has stalled in many parts of the world.
>
> *(US Government, 2010, p. 8)*

> Wherever al-Qaeda or its terrorist affiliates attempt to establish a safe haven – as they have in Yemen, Somalia, the Maghreb, and the Sahel – we will meet them with growing pressure. ...We will also help states avoid becoming terrorist safe havens by helping them build their capacity for responsible governance and security through development and security sector assistance.
>
> *(US Government, 2010, p. 21)*

> The United States has an interest in working with our allies to help the world's poorest countries grow into productive and prosperous economies governed by capable, democratic, and accountable state institutions. ... And we will provide our support in multiple ways – by strengthening the ability of governments and communities to manage development challenges and investing in strong institutions that foster the democratic accountability that helps sustain development. This will expand the circle of nations – particularly in Africa – who are capable of reaping the benefits of the global economy, while contributing to global security and prosperity.
>
> *(US Government, 2010, p.33–4)*

Spend no more than 10 minutes on this activity.

Discussion

In these extracts it is clear that in 2010 the USA viewed 'failing states' as a source of multiple security concerns – criminal networks as well as terrorists – and most importantly as providing 'safe havens' for al-Qaeda. Development, in this view, is not just an end in itself ('an interest in helping the poorest') but also as a means to achieve greater security ('contributing to global security'). Notably, the way of achieving both, according to the strategy document, is to help build 'capable, democratic and accountable institutions'.

In summary, the changing character of warfare has created new problems for the international community. For many states in the North, the security–development nexus arises from two directions. First, conflict in the South is thought to pose a series of security threats to the North as well as to people and states in the South. 'Development' is seen as an answer to that threat. Second, and conversely, establishing peace is seen as an answer to development problems in the South. Development and security appear mutually reinforcing. However, in both analytical and policy debates about warfare and development, there are in fact divergent views on how far warfare and development should actually be seen as opposed to each other.

2.2 War and development: obstacle or driver?

Two rather contrasting views about the relationship between war and development are presented in this section. The first, mostly in tune with the quotes at the beginning of the chapter and the policy stances discussed in Section 2.1, sees warfare as a barrier to development in the South. The second is a line of argument that suggests wars can be seen as transformatory processes, contributing to social change that may stimulate or even be necessary for development. In thinking about your own view of this debate, you need to bear in mind that the choice may not be as stark as it is presented here. Different views of the relationship between war and development turn, in part, on different understandings of what development is.

2.2.1 Civil war: 'development in reverse'

As noted in the introduction, the dominant view of many people, including many donor agencies, is that civil war is a barrier to development (Figure 2.3). The kind of planned interventions by development agencies, in the form of macroeconomic policy, or development projects, school building, poverty reduction strategies and so on, are all made more difficult, if not impossible, in conditions of civil war.

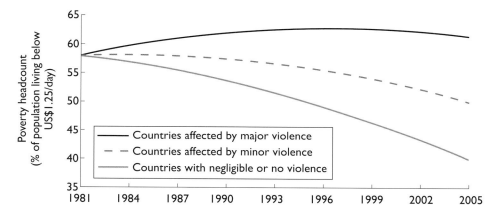

Figure 2.3 How violence disrupts development: in 2011 the World Bank claimed that countries experiencing major violence, including civil war, were lagging behind in poverty reduction (Source: World Bank 2011)

UK economics professor Paul Collier goes somewhat further, arguing in his highly influential, though controversial book, *The Bottom Billion*, that not only is war a barrier to development but that 'Civil war is development in reverse' (Collier, 2007, p. 27). For Collier, the reason lies in the effect of war on the social indicators of development. If 'development' is defined in terms of meeting a series of targets – indicators of social improvement (Brown and Hanlin, 2013) – then it is easy to see Collier's point.

Adapting methods of economic analysis to studying civil war, Collier estimated that civil war reduced growth by around 2.3 per cent per year making a country 15 per cent poorer after a seven-year war than would have otherwise been the case (Collier, 2007, p. 27–8). War, he went on, creates refugees and increased incidence of disease, both of which continue after wars have come to an end and typically affect neighbouring countries as well. War also creates the conditions for, or even is organized around, increased crime, with an estimated 95 per cent of illegal hard drugs produced from conflict zones (Collier 2007, p. 31). Civil wars tend to involve, and therefore negatively affect, the most economically active members of the population, further exacerbating the impact on societies involved. Overall, Collier estimated, the average cost of a civil war to a country and its neighbours was around US$64 billion. This is, he claimed 'a ballpark figure' but one which 'errs on the side of caution' (Collier, 2007, p. 32).

However, Collier's analysis of civil war also made a broader point related to why civil wars take place. His work formed an important contribution to the debate about whether civil wars were caused by 'greed or grievance'. This chapter is not primarily concerned with analyzing the causes of civil wars (this was covered in more depth in Chapter 1). However, this debate does have some relevance to the assessment of the developmental impact of civil war. If civil wars can serve some 'progressive' role, by challenging oppressive governments, achieving independence from colonial powers and instituting more democratic systems of rule or more equitable economic policies, they might be seen to serve a positive role in a country's development (Cramer, 2006a). Such a view of civil war sees it as primarily motivated by 'grievance' against repressive or corrupt governments. If, however, as Collier argued, civil wars are motivated by 'greed' – that combatants are primarily seeking to enrich themselves through either seizing control of the state, corruptly purloining its assets, or gaining control over valuable raw materials or valuable farm lands to finance military action or reward its supporters – then the 'anti-developmental' view of civil war is strengthened further (Collier and Hoeffler, 2002; Collier, 2007; Reno, 1998).

It is certainly true that some civil wars develop into 'war economies' based in particular around extraction of valuable resources. This was a notable feature of the civil wars in Sierra Leone (1991–2000) and in Angola (1975–2002), where access to diamond fields and oil became not just a necessity for rebel movements seeking to fund their war but a *raison d'etre* for the war itself (Figure 2.4). In a similar vein, control of cocaine and opium production was a major feature of the Colombian FARC rebels' activities and the Afghan Taliban, respectively. If Collier's analysis is right, it strengthens the view that civil war is, developmentally, very regressive.

However, this line of argument has faced a strong challenge both on empirical grounds and, as discussed in Subsection 2.2.2, from a more historical viewpoint. Empirically, several writers have challenged the evidence that civil wars were usually linked to motivations of 'greed' by using different case studies (Cramer, 2006b). Moreover, it was suggested that the 'greed' argument was guilty of confusing the question of why civil wars start with the question of why they continue. Few would suggest that the RUF rebels in Sierra Leone or Jonas Savimbi's UNITA movement in Angola were initially motivated by access to the riches of the diamond and oil fields – political questions were more important at the start. However, in both cases, access to sources of revenue became crucial to rebel movements' ability to continue fighting, giving both wars a new dynamic based on extracting and selling raw materials (Cramer, 2006a).

(a)   (b)

Figure 2.4   (a) Diamond mining was a key factor in Sierra Leone's civil war and (b) opium poppy production was key to the Taliban insurgency in Afghanistan (Source: Getty Images/AP Press Association)

Activity 2.4

Pause here and spend a few minutes noting down the conditions under which you think civil war might be justifiable, if ever, from a developmental point of view. You will come back to this question at the end of Subsection 2.2.2 so make a note of your ideas now.

Spend no more than 10 minutes on this activity.

2.2.2   War as a driver of social transformation

When you think of development as intentional action directed at achieving defined targets, whether they be levels of economic growth, poverty reduction or social indicators like decreased mortality, disease and suffering, it is not hard to see why you might come to the view that civil war is inherently 'bad' for development. After all, civil war is associated with the destruction of business and domestic property, government buildings and welfare centres, and on some occasions, schools and hospitals. In one example, the rebel Contras in Nicaragua deliberately targeted teachers and midwives in order to destabilize rural support for the Sandinista government during the early 1980s. In another case, teachers and monks have become targets as symbols of government authority, alongside the police and army, for the Muslim insurgency in the south of Thailand. For aid agencies and governments attempting to implement projects and policies aimed at achieving these targets it is hard to see how civil war could ever be seen as 'developmental'. However, a different view of development sees it as 'unplanned' processes of large-scale social change and transformation (see Brown and Hanlin, 2013).

From this view, it is possible to interpret warfare as having a significant developmental role.

In contrast to Collier's economics-based approach, this alternative view of civil war adopts a more historical perspective, focusing on the impact of warfare on long-term social development. One version of this view begins with the observation that the emergence of modern states in Europe was a profound developmental moment in modern history, laying the foundations from which the material and social transformations associated with the rise of capitalism could occur. Crucially, this change was in part driven by warfare. Both Michael Mann and Charles Tilly have set out versions of the argument that warfare between European states was the key driver of state formation in Europe (Mann, 1986; Tilly, 1995). Tilly begins with the idea of the security dilemma, an inherently competitive dynamic operating among Europe's many political units and states from the 10th century onwards (see Section 2.1). By the 15th century, Tilly notes, in Europe there were some 500 political units with ill-defined territories and overlapping jurisdictions, yet by 1900 there were just 25 states with clearly defined borders within which states claimed an exclusive right to rule (Figure 2.5 raises some questions about this claim, for while territories are more defined and jurisdictions were less likely to overlap in 1900, we should remember that state consolidation is a complex process that can even go into reverse).

While Tilly compares 1400 and 1900, these maps from 1786 and 2008, suggest that it is not clear at all that the numbers of political units has been reduced as drastically as Tilly claims. Tilly refers to a Europe of 25 states in 1900 whereas the 2008 map gives us a Europe of 36 states. In some cases such as Germany and Italy, state consolidation is fairly obvious, but a closer look highlights that some consolidated states have fragmented, such as the Austro–Hungarian Empire (in purple in 1786) under the rule of the Habsburg monarchy, which only ended in World War I. This suggests that state consolidation and fragmentation is a more fluid and dynamic process than Tilley suggests.

For Tilly, states that emerged from this competitive process were those that were able to mobilize resources for military ends. Before the 20th century, judged by contemporary standards, states' financial resources were very small, but the bulk of these resources – between 70 and 90 per cent of state expenditure in the case of Britain between the 12th and 19th centuries (Mann, 1986) – were devoted to military ends. The need to wage war demanded states increased the extraction of resources from their societies and this in turn served to develop state capabilities. Why might this be so?

Figure 2.5 The consolidation of states in central Europe: (a) 1786 and (b) the EU in 2008 (Source: Philips' Atlas of Modern History, 1964/Google Images)

The key reason was that the ability to wage war relied on extracting resources, whether those were men to fight, food, the production of weapons and ships, or revenue from raising taxes. One result was an expansion of a state's administrative and bureaucratic capacity, for instance to identify tax payers and process tax demands and payments. In addition, in many cases, the subject populations were likely to resist. As a result, the state's coercive apparatus, to enforce such levies, also increased. Processes of centralization of state apparatuses increased as did the state's monopoly on force as those landowners and feudal lords possessing arms were gradually subjugated. Held (1992, p. 95) notes: 'The development of some of the key organizations of the modern state emerged at the intersection of warfare and the attempt to pay for it.' War promoted 'territorial consolidation, centralization, differentiation of the instruments of government and monopolization of the means of coercion' (Tilly, 1995, p. 42).

> **Box 2.2 The modern state**
>
> The form or type of state emerging through the processes discussed, including war, is usually referred to as the 'modern state'. What does the term mean?
>
> The key features of the modern state, which emerged through these often violent processes in early modern Europe have been summarized by Held (1992) as follows:
>
> - Territoriality: the coincidence of clearly defined territories with unified systems of rule
> - Control of the means of violence: the monopolization of the means of violence by the state and pacification of domestic societies through defeat of rival centres of power within states and the introduction of standing armies and police forces
> - An impersonal structure of power: that is, the emergence of public offices of state distinct from the personal rule of monarchs and feudal lords
> - The centralization and unification of administration, systems of taxation and fiscal organization
> - New modes of law making and enforcement

Of course, the transformative impacts of warfare are probably only one of the factors that contributed to the developmental take-off in Europe from the late 18th century onwards. Other historians put much greater emphasis on the changing class relations within Europe as feudal agricultural economies transformed into capitalist and industrial ones (for example, Teschke, 2003). In addition, the rise of capitalism itself stimulated warmaking as states competed for overseas territories and markets, carving up the world into empires and spheres of influence.

Finally, Mann notes that another key impact of warfare on the internal character of European societies was in how they were ruled. As the cost and scale of warfare increased (particularly with the development of total war), the populations of European states were increasingly drawn into preparations for war making. In exchange for the state making these demands on the population, the population had a greater say in the decisions of states. In addition, governments became more concerned with the health and efficiency of the people, developing maternity services, basic welfare provision and unemployment protection. It was noted by the Bishop of London in 1917 that more babies died in Britain every hour than soldiers in the trenches (one in six babies died before the age of one). Although a number of other factors like these were also at work, war making therefore contributed significantly to the democratization of states, as happened with the expansion of the right to vote in the wake of World War I in Britain and elsewhere.

Activity 2.5

Pause here and check your understanding.

1   Identify why this historically based line of argument might have relevance for development debates today. You can use some suggestions from the following quote from the World Bank, which explains how the bank sees this historical legacy of warfare in development (World Bank, 2010, p. 9):

> War and violence have often played transformative roles in state-building, for all the suffering they have caused. Equally, injustice, exclusion and elite corruption have been standard features in many political dispensations in the past, including in most of today's developed countries. Today, however, the international community aspires to do better. International agreements now govern the use of force and define standards of human rights and governance behaviour, even if they are not always observed. Aggression and repression are no longer seen as acceptable tools of statecraft.

2   Identify how this idea of war and social transformation differs from the view of conflict and development in Chapter 1.

Spend about 15 minutes on this activity.

Discussion

1   The key idea is that if development today entails constructing forms of statehood more or less along the lines of the European model (see Box 2.2) – and such large-scale social change is central to development – then this European experience might have lessons for the South today. In this view, warfare in the South might be viewed more positively, as stimulating the kind of social change that transformed Europe in previous centuries. Cramer notes that all liberal states in the North have experienced significant episodes of warfare in their own development, be those civil wars in England (1642–51); wars of independence (1775–82) or civil war (1861–65) in the USA; or the impact of World War II on countries like South Korea, Japan, France and Germany (Cramer, 2006b).

The World Bank has a somewhat ambiguous position on this issue. In the quote above, the Bank acknowledges that development in Europe and elsewhere has come about through violent conflict. However, given the horrors of civil conflict noted in Chapter 1, it might be argued that some consideration should be given as to what alternatives could be pursued: is development necessarily violent or are there less violent means to the same end? If not, is it right to argue that development is 'worth the price' of war?

Perhaps not surprisingly, the World Bank steps back from this conclusion, suggesting that the international community 'aspires to do better'. While an honest acknowledgement of the conflict-driven nature of much past development, it does raise the question of whether 'doing better' is in fact possible.

2   In Chapter 1, you were presented with an idea of conflict as a normal, inherent part of the dynamics of development. Here, the historical impact of war is seen as something that is somewhat rarer, a non-routine occurrence that shifts the existing balance of societies and forges a new path. War can lead a relatively successful and prosperous society to the brink of collapse, as in the case of the Lebanon in the 1970s. In other cases, such as the large-scale destruction of Germany and Japan in the 1940s, war prepared the way for foreign occupation and aid programmes that generated new development pathways – as have also been witnessed by the Lebanon at the start of the 21st century.

Activity 2.6

Return to your answer to Activity 2.4. Has this historical discussion changed your view of when warfare is justifiable or necessary in developmental terms?

Spend no more than 10 minutes on this activity.

Discussion

You will have your own thoughts on this question, though it is perhaps easier for some to suggest the inevitability of warfare, particularly for Western commentators and academics who reside at a very safe distance from such 'necessary' violence, than those who have to suffer its grim reality up close.

Many aid donors and governments in the North see the solution to the problem of violent conflict in a particular state form: 'capable', 'effective', and 'fair' states (in the DfID's words). It is argued that this state form will both help to avoid civil war and promote development. How can this be done? Section 2.3 addresses this question by drawing on some political theory.

2.3   Political order within states: power and agency

The discussion of war and development repeatedly returns to the question of states. States appear in our discussion as a source of war, because they may be oppressive, prompting rebellions of one kind or another, because control of the state is seen as a route to accessing wealth, or because states go to war with one another. States also appear as a solution to the development–security problem, with donors claiming the construction of 'capable states' is a key prerequisite for achieving security and thus laying the foundation for development. But what is a capable state? There are a number of dimensions to this question, though an essential element is the ability to regulate organized violence within its borders by creating a legitimate form of government. This section first outlines why political theorists have emphasized the importance of the control of violence. It then looks at how the creation of legitimate political order plays a crucial role in preventing civil war and promoting development.

2.3.1 States, violence and political order

As you have seen in Chapter 1, violence is a broader category than warfare, encompassing both physical and structural dimensions, so here there is a shift to a slightly broader canvas than examined so far in this chapter. However, civil war might be seen as the most serious form of violence within a state. Ultimately, the ability of the state to uphold the rules or laws of a given society depends on the use of violence, through the police or armed forces. The existence of armed groups, as in a civil war situation, challenges this ability in a fundamental way. As you have seen in this chapter, if a state is unable to perform these functions, then much else that is necessary for development becomes less possible. Let's go through this argument in a bit more detail, focusing at first on questions on the role of power and agency in political order.

The state, in many views of politics, has a role in mediating conflicts of interest. It deals with and finds resolutions to issues where there are disagreements over collective rules and decisions in society, whether in terms of economic policy, taxation, or cultural and religious issues. The state in this guise has a **regulative role** in creating 'rules of the political game' and a **distributional role** in deciding 'who gets what, when and how' in the famous phrase used by political scientist Harold Laswell (1990 [1935]). Political scientists differ as to how to characterize these roles, some arguing the state is an impartial umpire mediating between competing groups, while others emphasize inherent biases within states that favour some groups over others. **Political power**, in this sense, is the ability to get your favoured outcomes in whatever area of politics is under consideration.

However, limiting political power exercised through the use of force is equally important, as Simon Bromley has suggested: '... collectively binding rules about the use of force play a basic and defining role in political life, or at least in the workings of any political order' (Bromley, 2010, p. 232–4). The reason, he argues, is that violence (he uses the term 'force' to mean the same thing) removes the ability of another person to act: 'The question of force is basic because the social use of force is quite different from other exercises of power' because it denies 'the agent's ability to act, thereby treating the agent as (literally) a merely physical object' (ibid). Rather than conflicts of interest being resolved through non-violent means – by persuasion, say, or by agreeing compromises and offering incentives to the other person – using violence actually stops your opponent having political agency at all. In summary, he claims 'Force constrains, or destroys, agency in the way that no other source of social power seeks to do ... in all other cases, the exercise of social power always presupposes a capacity for agency, however limited, on the part of its subordinate targets' (ibid, p. 23–4).

Activity 2.7

What would a society look like if everyone had the ability to resort to violence to settle disputes without any constraint? Would development be possible in such a circumstance?

Spend no more than 10 minutes on this activity.

Discussion

Your answer will depend in part on your view of the ability of human beings to resolve differences peacefully. However, there is a strong argument to say that levels of insecurity and fear in such a situation would be very high.

It was just this kind of question that motivated one of the most famous works of political theory, Thomas Hobbes' *Leviathan*.

2.3.2 Hobbes: 'In such condition there is no place for industry ...'

Thomas Hobbes is one of the most well-known and influential political theorists, writing at a time of violent upheaval in Europe. Not only did Hobbes live through the English civil wars (1642–51) but also the turmoil of the Thirty Years War in Europe which came to an end in 1648. This was a formative moment in the emergence of European states and, not surprisingly, questions of violence and political order dominated Hobbes' thinking. However, Hobbes' work remains relevant today for contemporary questions about civil war, development and the role of the state in creating political order.

Hobbes' work is an example of an approach known as **social contract** theory, which aims to analyze politics as a contract between rulers and the ruled, between states and citizens, according to which the latter renounce some (or most) of their freedoms in exchange for security. In *Leviathan*, Hobbes' most famous work, he seeks to explain political obligation and outline the reason why people would limit their freedoms by agreeing to allow a state to rule over them. Contemporary examples of authoritarian states are China or Singapore, where economic development may mean greater wealth but where the state still has a large degree of control over everyday private life and political freedoms or rights are strictly limited.

Hobbes begins by painting a picture of what life would be like in a situation suggested by Activity 2.7, where there is no state and no control over peoples' use of violence. 'Without a power to keep them in awe,' he suggests, there would be 'warre ... of every man against every man'. In a clear precursor to the idea that began this chapter – that without security, development is impossible – Hobbes argues that where 'men live without other security, than what their own strength, and their own invention shall furnish them with all' then all other aspects of civilized life – arts, culture, travel, trade, building – become impossible. In a famous passage he claims:

> In such condition, there is no place for Industry; because the fruit thereof is uncertain: and consequently no Culture of the Earth; no Navigation, nor use of the commodities that may be imported by Sea; no commodious Building; no Instruments of moving, and removing such things as require much force; no Knowledge of the face of the Earth; no account of Time; no Arts; no Letters; no Society; and which is worst of all, continuall feare, and danger of violent death; And the life of man, solitary, poore, nasty, brutish, and short.

> *(Hobbes 1996[1651])*

The account of civil war given in Chapter 1 has clear echoes of Hobbes' fear of life as 'poor, nasty, brutish, and short'. Brutal wars such as those in the Democratic Republic of the Congo, Sierra Leone and Iraq all suggest some support for Hobbes' view that where there is no organized constraint on the population, life will be very grim indeed (Figure 2.6).

Figure 2.6 Hobbes predicted that where there is no effective authority, as in Iraq in 2006–7, violence often escalates

The problem of political order for Hobbes is how people can get 'themselves out from that miserable condition of Warre'. For Hobbes, the answer lies in creating a 'Common Power' (a state) that will be able to enforce order.

Activity 2.8

Hobbes' answer is contained in the following passage. Read through it and try to identify what is the 'social contract' Hobbes is proposing:

> The only way to erect such a Common Power, as may be able to defend them from the invasion of Forraigners, and the injuries of one another, and thereby to secure them in such sort, as that by their owne Industrie, and by the fruites of the Earth, they may nourish themselves and live contentedly; is, to conferre all their power and strength upon one Man, or upon one Assembly of men,

that may reduce all their Wills, by plurality of voices, unto one Will … and therein to submit their Wills, every one to his Will, and their Judgements, to his Judgment.

…

And he that carryeth this Person, is called SOVERAIGNE, and said to have *Soveraigne Power*; and every one besides, his SUBJECT.

(Hobbes 1996[1651])

Spend about 10 minutes on this activity.

Discussion

Hobbes sees the solution lying in the creation of an overall ruler – the 'Leviathan' or 'Mortal God' – who can both protect people from threats from other societies (foreigners) as well as those from within ('injuries of one another'). But people can only achieve this by giving up all their power to the 'Man, or … one Assembly of men'. The contract at the heart of Hobbes' *Leviathan* is therefore the giving up of individual freedom (or 'will') and judgements to the Sovereign Power, or the state in today's terms, in return for which individuals receive a degree of protection and security.

Hobbes' views are controversial. His argument maintains that without a resolution of the problem of violence, nothing else can be resolved or built. However, the social contract on offer is a stark one – members of a political community have to give up most of their rights in order to achieve the great collective benefit of a peaceful political order. This tension between freedom and security or agency and power reappears in many contemporary settings. In the 21st century the threat from terrorism has been used in both global North and South by some politicians to argue for constraints on individual liberties in the interests of security (as you will see in Chapter 3).

Although Hobbes argued that not all rights had to be given up – for instance, a Sovereign could not take the life of subjects, otherwise this would be breaking the social contract that provides security – others, such as Hobbes' contemporary John Locke (1632–1704), argued for a different balance between liberty and security. Locke argued that the state (the Leviathan) should itself be constrained and key freedoms, such as rights to life, liberty and property, should be protected. As a result, when entering the social contract they were not sacrificing their autonomy to an authoritarian state or absolute power but conducting a deal to sacrifice a little of their liberty to secure their property. Much debate about social contracts between states and citizens revolves around the issue of what are the legitimate powers held by states vis-à-vis the rights of individuals governed by those states.

Activity 2.9

Do you agree with Hobbes that almost any kind of political order, where warfare within a country is ended, is preferable to none? Try to relate your answer to a specific example of civil war, such as the war in Mozambique or another example with which you are familiar.

Spend no more than 15 minutes on this activity.

Discussion

This is a difficult question to answer and differences in part lie behind arguments as to the justifiability of using violence against an incumbent government. On the one hand, the monopolization of violence by a state delivers a collective benefit to society as a whole by resolving the most basic problem of political order. However, remember that politics involves resolution of this question as well as the more distributional conflicts mentioned above. When the problem of order is resolved problems of inequalities of wealth, income and power remain. What if those other political questions are skewed heavily against your own interests, does that justify violence against the state? Inevitably, such issues raise the question of the legitimacy of state power. Many rebellions have argued that it does, though there are also many examples of resistance to unjust governments who have stuck resolutely to non-violent strategies, for example Gandhi's opposition to British rule in India. As it happens, non-violent strategies don't always reduce conflict –the initial non-violent protests in Egypt in 2011 in the early phases of the Arab Spring generated a very violent response from members of the state security apparatus.

One other point to note is that in 'resolving' the question of violence within states, Hobbes recreates it at the international level. As Holsti notes, 'The state of nature is universal but the states that result from the social contract are particular' (Holsti, 1995, p. 325). That is, although the problem of violence is now controlled by a state within countries, there is no means of controlling violence between states. Hobbes rejoins here the realist argument about the permanent possibility of war in the international system introduced in Subsection 2.2.1.

For many theorists, the state's monopoly of violence as understood by Hobbes is not sufficient to guarantee the possibility of development and the avoidance of civil war. The World Bank (2011, p. 2), for instance, has pointed out that 'strengthening legitimate institutions and governance to provide citizen security, justice, and jobs is crucial to break cycles of violence.' If wars are to be prevented or resolved, states need also to have **legitimacy**. But what makes state power legitimate? What makes it acceptable to the citizens of that society? How is it made part of the prevailing consensus about the rules of the game? The rules of the political game can be changed, rearranging what is dominant and subordinate, but that does not make it acceptable or legitimate unless the participants in the process acquiesce.

Beetham (1992) argues that power is legitimate when:

1   governments are formed and state power exercised according to the established rules of that society

2   the rules of society about government and the state are justifiable in terms of the values of that society

3   there is evidence of explicit consent to government and state power, typically, though not necessarily, through some form of voting.

Let's unpick this threefold definition a bit more. First, states generally try to legitimize their rule by claiming some kind of validity according to prevailing rules. Even where power is acquired by means other than the established rules (revolutions, coups d'état, and so on) power holders try to exercise this power in relation to some framework of rules if it is to be held over the longer term. Second, while these rules vary enormously from one society to the next and one time to the next, they have to be justifiable, Beetham (1992, p. 11) maintains, in relation to 'beliefs and values' of the people over whom the state rules. That is, the rules of power need to be seen as 'right' by the population as whole. Third, legitimization requires some demonstration of consent to seal the legitimacy of the state.

Remember this is a crucial difference between a political order based solely on the use of force, and political order that has some durable consent of the population. Consent may be demonstrated through electoral activity (even authoritarian regimes go through highly suspect electoral processes to try to demonstrate their legitimacy) although forms of mass mobilization seen in some communist states including China are also methods of trying to achieve similar ends. Sometimes, however, the absence of participation by citizens (i.e. apathy) can be seen as a sign of tacit consent, and that high levels of activism represents dissatisfaction with a political system.

Legitimacy is vital to sustained political order. This is so in relation to a state's ability to perform its basic duties but it is also important when considering the resort to civil war by opponents of a regime. For many people, when power is held illegitimately, the use of armed force becomes more justifiable. If the prevention and resolution of civil war is crucial to development, then the question of creating a legitimate political order is of the first importance. The problem, as the World Bank notes, is partly that '[c]reating the legitimate institutions that can prevent repeated violence is, in plain language, slow' but also that it nearly always requires some kind of action from an international community that may be ill-prepared for such a role (World Bank, 2011, p. 10).

Summary and looking forward

In this chapter you have seen how the question of war has evolved over time and increasingly how problems associated with war and political order within countries have compounded, if not replaced, the problem of warfare between states as a critical question for the international community and development policy. Two contrasting views are outlined on the relationship between different periods of warfare and development.

The first considers warfare and violent conflict to be a central barrier to development, implying that achieving peace is a necessary precondition to economic and social development in the South.

The second draws attention to the historical developmental role that warfare has played, particularly in processes around the emergence of modern states in Europe.

You then looked at more abstract ideas about the relationship between the control of violence and how states operate as the basis of political order. That discussion brings us back to the question of what is the right course of action when faced by violent conflict. There are perhaps two key questions to take away from this discussion.

First, there is a question about security. Warfare in the global South is seen as a security problem for states in the North and by the international community in general who, through the United Nations, aims to ensure international peace and security. However, the discussion of political order has also shown that this is linked closely to the question of security of people, within states. The argument in favour of a powerful Leviathan state is precisely that it claims to achieve security for individuals, possibly at the expense of their liberties.

In Chapter 4 you will see how this tension – between state security and individual or human security – has been a major issue in debates about development. Indeed, those inside and outside the societies concerned have often supported the creation of Leviathan-type states in the developing world at different times, from the modernizing authoritarianism of the Shah in Iran and the Ba-athist regime of Saddam Hussein in Iraq in the 1970s and early 1980s, to the rigid subservience to the monarchy in Saudi Arabia and the paternal dictatorship of Mubarak in Egypt. In all cases, it could be argued that protecting citizens from conflict and social breakdown was the primary objective but you also need to ask which security interests of the global North were at stake.

Second, there are questions about the actions of the international community in response to civil wars. If, following Hobbes, you take the view that any peace is better than no peace, then the job of the international community might be simply to ensure that civil wars come to an end, by any means necessary and no matter how unjust the outcome. If, however, you take the view that resolving the problem of violence within states also means addressing the overall legitimacy of the political order, then the problem facing intervention is more complex as it means becoming involved in, and helping to resolve, political conflicts within other states. Intervening in the civil disputes of other nations raises many dilemmas and issues. Most are justified on humanitarian grounds but this may conceal external interests. At the same time, civil wars can be the most savage conflicts of all for the most vulnerable citizens or minorities and many diplomats and NGO activists may feel that there is a moral justification for interventions in, for example, Bosnia, Kosovo, Rwanda, Kurdistan and Darfur, to name a few. The saddest part of these stories is that the impetus for intervention may arise from a failure to act in the past to prevent some of the worst brutalities. The legality and efficacy of such interventions will be addressed more fully in Chapter 3.

References

Beetham, D. (1992) *The Legitimation of Power*, Basingstoke, Macmillan.

Bromley, S. (2010) 'Politics and the international' in Anievas, A. (ed.) *Marxism in World Politics*, London, Routledge, pp. 231–47.

Brown, W. and Hanlin, R. (2013) 'Introducing international development' in Papaioannou, T. and Butcher, M. (eds) *International Development in a Changing World*, London, Bloomsbury Academic/Milton Keynes, The Open University.

von Clausewitz, C. 2008 ([1873]) *On War*, Oxford, Oxford University Press.

Collier, P. (2007) *The Bottom Billion: Why the Poorest Countries Are Failing and What Can Be Done About It*, Oxford, Oxford University Press.

Collier, P. and Hoeffler, A. (2002) 'Greed and grievance in civil war', *Working Paper 2002-01*, Oxford, Centre for the Study of African Economies [online] http: www.csae.ox.ac.uk/workingpapers/wps-list.html (Accessed 18 March 2011).

Cooper, R. (2004) *The Breaking of Nations: Order and Chaos in the Twenty-first Century*, London, Atlantic Books.

Council for the EU (2003) 'A secure Europe in a better world', [online] http:www.consilium.europa.eu/uedocs/cmsUpload/78367.pdf (Accessed 24 October 2011).

Cramer, C. (2006a) 'Greed versus grievance: conjoined twins or discrete drivers of violent conflict?' in Yanacopulous, H. and Hanlon, J. (eds) *Civil War Civil Peace* Milton Keynes, The Open University, in association with James Currey and Ohio University Research in International Studies.

Cramer, C. (2006b) *Civil War Is Not a Stupid Thing: Accounting for Violence in Developing Countries*, London, Hurst and Co.

Department for International Development (DfID) (2009) *Eliminating World Poverty: Building Our Common Future*. DfID White Paper, July 2009. London, The Stationary Office [online] http:www.dfid.gov.uk/Documents/whitepaper/building-our-common-future.pdf (Accessed 18 March 2011).

Doyle, M.W. (1983) 'Kant, liberal legacies and foreign affairs', *Philosophy and Public Affairs,* vol. 12, no. 3, pp. 205–35.

Held, D. (1992) 'The formation of the modern state' in Hall, S. and Geiben, B. (eds) *Formations of Modernity*, Cambridge, Polity Press, in association with The Open University.

Herz, J. (1950) 'Idealist Internationalism and the security dilemma', *World Politics*, vol. 2, no. 2, pp. 157–80.

Hobbes, T. 1996 ([1651]) *Leviathan or The Matter, Forme, and Power of a Commonwealth Ecclesiastical and Civill*, Revised Student Edition edited by Richard Tuck (1996), Cambridge, Cambridge University Press.

Holsti, J. (1995) 'War, peace and the state of the state', *International Political Science Review*, vol. 16, no. 4, pp. 319–39.

Kaldor, M. (1999) *New and Old Wars: Organized Violence in a Global Era* (2nd edn), Cambridge, Polity Press.

Kiely, R. (2013) 'Change, politics and the international system' in Papaioannou, T. and Butcher, M. (eds) *International Development in a Changing World*, London, Bloomsbury Academic/Milton Keynes, The Open University.

Laswell, H.D. 1990 ([1935]) *Politics; Who Gets What, When and How?*, London, Peter Smith Publisher.

Mann, M. (1986) *The Sources of Social Power*, Cambridge, Cambridge University Press.

Mann, M. (1987) 'The roots and contradictions of modern militarism', *New Left Review*, vol. 1, no. 162, pp. 35–50.

Morgenthau, H.J. (1948) *Politics Among Nations: the Struggle for Power and Peace*, Columbus, OH, McGraw-Hill.

Reno, W. (1998) *Warlord Politics and African States*, Boulder, CO, Lynne Rienner.

Rice, E.E. (1988) *Wars of the Third Kind: Conflict in Underdeveloped Countries*, Berkeley, University of California Press.

Teschke, B. (2003) *The Myth of 1648: Class, Geopolitics and the Making of Modern International Relations*, London, Verso.

Tilly, C. (1995) *Coercion, Capital, and European States, AD 990–1990*, London, Basil Blackwell.

US Government (2010) *2010 National Security Strategy*, Washington DC, The White House, [online] http://www.whitehouse.gov/sites/default/files/rss_viewer/national_security_strategy.pdf (Accessed 20 October 2010).

World Bank (2010) WDR 2011 Concept Note [online] http://blogs.worldbank.org/conflict/world-development-report-2011 (Accessed 18 March 2011).

World Bank (2011) *World Development Report 2011: Conflict Security and Development*. Washington, World Bank [online] http://wdr2011.worldbank.org/fulltext (Accessed 18 April 2011).

Further reading

Cramer, C. (2006) *Civil War Is Not a Stupid Thing: Accounting for Violence in Developing Countries*, London, Hurst and Co.

Jackson, R.H. and Sorensen, G. (2010) *Introduction to International Relations: Theories and Approaches*, (4th edn), Oxford, Oxford University Press.

Kaldor, M. (2006) *New and Old Wars: Organized Violence in a Global Era* (2nd edn), Cambridge, Polity Press.

Williams, P. (2011) *War and Conflict in Africa*, Cambridge, Polity Press.

You should also find it useful to consult reports from international organizations such as:

World Bank (2011) *World Development Report 2011: Conflict, Security and Development*, Washington, World Bank [online] http://wdr2011.worldbank.org/fulltext (Accessed 18 April 2011)..

Solidarity, sovereignty and intervention

Joseph Hanlon

Introduction

Earthquakes, tsunamis, major floods and droughts all trigger international assistance efforts. Our globe is alive and pulsing; we all fear the unexpected eruption that could cause havoc to our lives, so we all want to help blameless people harmed by an 'act of God' or the 'forces of nature'. Partly this is a very human desire to help, but it is also part of a much larger conception of **solidarity** – we help others because we hope, if we are in a similar circumstance, others will help us. Communities of various sorts – clans, trade unions, villages, churches and mosques – are partly built on mutual cooperation and solidarity that is a strategy to manage fear and insecurity.

Processes of globalization, the growth of mass media and international trade and travel, have made us much more aware of distant wars and disasters, and extended our sense of solidarity. This chapter looks in more detail at the support for other countries in times of upheaval, and especially at the role and impact of international interventions. In particular, the chapter has the following aims:

- to evaluate how global solidarity has grown and the structures that have evolved
- to understand the overlaps between military and civilian **interventions**, natural disasters and **peacekeeping**, and emergencies and development assistance
- to evaluate the role of international aid and how donor countries can actually cause harm as well as do good
- to understand the debate about the **right to intervene** in other countries.

The chapter starts by outlining the history of interventions, from civilian to external military intervention. Section 3.2 explores the changes in the role of humanitarian intervention through the representation of complex emergencies in the developing world. Section 3.3 turns to changes in the very notion of sovereignty, brought about by the ethical and political quandary of humanitarian intervention. Finally, it considers the effects of these debates upon aid practitioners.

3.1   From civilian to military intervention

Henry Dunant was a Swiss businessman who visited Napoleon III's headquarters near the northern Italian town of Solferino in 1859. He was stunned by the many thousands of wounded soldiers left to die on the battlefield without receiving even the most basic medical attention that might have saved them. He promoted an international covenant to protect the wounded, which became the first 'Geneva Convention', agreed in 1864. In

1863, he was also one of the founders of the International Committee for Relief to the Wounded. In the same year the committee agreed several important principles:

- it would be based on a single national relief society in each country
- volunteers would be used for relief assistance on the battlefield
- a common distinctive protection symbol would be used by medical personnel in the field, namely a white armband with a red cross.

In 1876, the committee adopted the name International Committee of the Red Cross (ICRC), and began to support prisoners of war. It accepted the existence of war, but argued that once soldiers were out of the fighting and no longer a threat in the field of battle they should be treated humanely.

Figure 3.1   Red Cross/Red Crescent

The American Red Cross was founded in 1881 and from its inception provided relief in floods and other domestic disasters within the USA, as did other national Red Cross societies. The International Federation of Red Cross and Red Crescent Societies (the Islamic equivalent), see Figure 3.1, was set up in 1919 and began actively organizing **international relief** efforts, normally coordinated through the national Red Cross society, and setting a pattern that continues today in one of the largest NGOs in the world. While the work of the Red Cross and Red Crescent societies began in war, the 20th century has seen a flourishing of government and non-government organizations concerned with mitigating insecurity and fears associated with war, natural disaster and lack of development (see Brown and Hanlon, 2013). The United Nations (UN) agencies most linked with humanitarian actions grew out of the world wars – as did the UN itself. In 1921, after World War I, the League of Nations (the precursor to the UN) established a High Commissioner for Refugees. This eventually became the UN High Commissioner for Refugees (UNHCR). UNICEF, the UN International Children's Fund, was created in 1946 to provide food, clothing and healthcare to children after World War II in Europe, and has played a key role in developing countries since. The UN World Food Programme was set up in 1962 to provide food in **emergencies**, whether these were caused by war, civil conflict or natural disasters.

This overlap between war and natural disaster, and between military and civilian activities, continues. A huge, complex and often disorganized international solidarity system has now become established. For disasters such as earthquakes and cyclones, the major international non-government organizations (INGOs) have teams that can be sent at short notice to provide water, sanitation and basic shelter, and states can also send military teams to help with initial rescue efforts. Some UN agencies have specialist disaster teams that can provide food and shelter, usually controlled by the resident representative. At its best, **humanitarian relief and aid** is well coordinated and saves tens of thousands of lives, as the case study of Mozambique highlights (see Box 3.1 and Figure 3.2). At its worst, bitter infighting between agencies can delay and diminish relief and reconstruction.

Figure 3.2   Mural near airport depicting the Independence War, Maputo, Mozambique (Source: Getty Images)

This section and Section 3.2 tries to unpack the types of interventions and authority at work during relief and disaster management operations. But it is essential to always keep in mind that the real world – especially around an emergency – is much messier and more complex than bureaucrats and development practitioners would like. Decisions are made in haste, often on the ground and by lower level officials who may be unaware of the need to integrate activities, and who do not always follow the rules. As a result, choices become subject to debate for months or years afterwards.

Box 3.1   Mozambique's war and flood

Mozambique is a UN success story, and also shows the very different ways that the international community can intervene by invitation. The UN monitoring of the 1992 ceasefire and 1994 elections worked smoothly. Even after the peace accord, with substantial distrust between the government and the rebel movement, Aldo Ajello, the UN Special Representative of the Secretary-General for the UN Operation in Mozambique (ONUMOZ), proved effective in bringing the two sides together and kept the peace process on track. A key to the success had been that the peace accord recognized the legitimacy of the existing government, and thus the UN worked through government ministries and was not seen as displacing the government.

The next test for the international community came in 2000. From September 1999 there had been forecasts of an unusually wet rainy season and the Mozambique disasters commission, Ministry of Health and Red Cross all prepared with extra training, stockpiles of medicines, etc. But an unprecedented three cyclones made the floods the worst in 150 years, and outside help was essential. Half a million people fled, including 45 000 who were rescued from the area, most by local boats although some by helicopters. But 700 people died. Nine countries provided military support, including two from the region: South Africa and Malawi. Christie and Hanlon (2001) concluded:

- International support, in the main, was timely, appropriate and effective. The UN said it was the largest air–sea rescue operation ever mounted in such a short time.

- Mozambique did prepare for rain and floods, and that preparation was essential for the success of the international response.

- The UN proved to be important and effective, particularly because it coordinated well with the national disaster management system.

- INGOs were resourceful and flexible. INGOs and other donor agencies were most effective when they worked through the Mozambican government and local agencies, such as the Red Cross.

No such operation is without problems. Out-of-date medicines were sent. NGOs and religious groups arrived unannounced and often with TV crews. One lorry killed a man as a church group, which refused to coordinate with local officials, drove through a crowd and threw sacks of food from the lorry. Infighting between UNICEF and the World Food Programme caused difficulties. Reconstruction aid was slow. But these were minor issues.

The floods showed solidarity at work. Most lives were saved because Mozambicans helped their neighbours. Nearby countries played an early and key role. The international community and the UN showed just how effective global solidarity can be in a crisis. Local leadership and organization, and the international willingness to respect that, put solidarity into practice.

3.2 Sovereignty and emergency

There is a whole range of reasons why a country cannot cope with a natural disaster or military crisis and asks outsiders to intervene (discussion on the impact of poverty on the resilience of societies and states can be found in Papaioannou and Butcher, 2013). More rarely, there are cases where states choose to intervene in another country without permission for stated reasons of humanitarian intervention (for example, the NATO intervention in Serbia in 1991). This form of international solidarity has evolved very rapidly over recent decades along with institutions and means of intervention, as well as terminology and definitions, although increasingly such actions do not fit neat categories. While legal definitions and budget lines are often very different, for example, there are supposed to be differences between military and civilian interventions, natural disasters and peacekeeping, and emergencies and development; the reality is that often there is a continuum between these categories. This section identifies the actors, their roles, the rules they operate under, and the book-keeping definitions of international intervention, while keeping in mind that these divisions are always only approximate and changing. You will see here both military and civilian intervention for two reasons: first, there are important overlaps between war and development; and second, because so many agencies are involved in both. Box 3.1 on Mozambique highlights this complexity.

Following on from previous chapters, and the discussion of the international system as a world of states with recognized borders, for the most part interventions are based on a **principle of sovereignty**, under which a state and its government have supreme authority over their territory. Help is only sent if it is asked for by the local government and if there is some degree of local control. The three UN agencies and the Red Cross network became the framework for international solidarity in the second half of the 20th century, working both in wars and (except for UNHCR) natural disasters. The role of the UN in natural disasters has evolved over time; it is not spelled out in the UN charter.

Disputes and breaches of the peace have a prominent role in the UN Charter, with the organization slowly becoming involved in peacekeeping and monitoring. War remains a major cause of suffering and, therefore, motivation for international development efforts. When intervention is requested, certain conditions must be met – most commonly some agreement is reached by the warring parties that can include a request to the UN to monitor a ceasefire, peace agreement, demobilization of the fighters, and subsequent elections, as well as to provide humanitarian and reconstruction assistance. Peacekeeping operations are individually authorized by the Security Council and organized by the Department of Peacekeeping Operations (DPKO), which is headed by an Under-Secretary-General. Early missions on the Israel–Jordan and India–Pakistan borders have continued since the 1940s. But there were only 13 such missions between 1948 and 1987, even though in the 1980s there were 40 violent conflicts raging each year (see Figure 1.4 in Chapter 1).

By 2010, there had been 63 peacekeeping missions, with 16 active, including Kosovo, Afghanistan, Côte d'Ivoire and Sudan (see Figure 3.3). These missions incorporated 124 000 personnel. The UN does not have its own soldiers but 115 countries contributed military and police resources.

Even in the UN, however, the distinctions over types of interventions can be blurred. Article 24 of the UN Charter gives the Security Council the 'primary responsibility for the maintenance of international peace and security'. But this gives the permanent members – China, France, Russia, the UK and the USA – a veto over any action relating to peace and security. Chapter VI of the Charter encourages peaceful settlement of disputes, but Chapter VII says that if the Security Council determines 'the existence of any threat to the peace, breach of the peace, or act of aggression' it can impose economic or military sanctions and take military action 'as may be necessary'. Thus Chapter VI continues to recognize sovereignty and intervention can only be by agreement, while Chapter VII is the only place in international law and practice that allows a violation of sovereignty and intervention without permission.

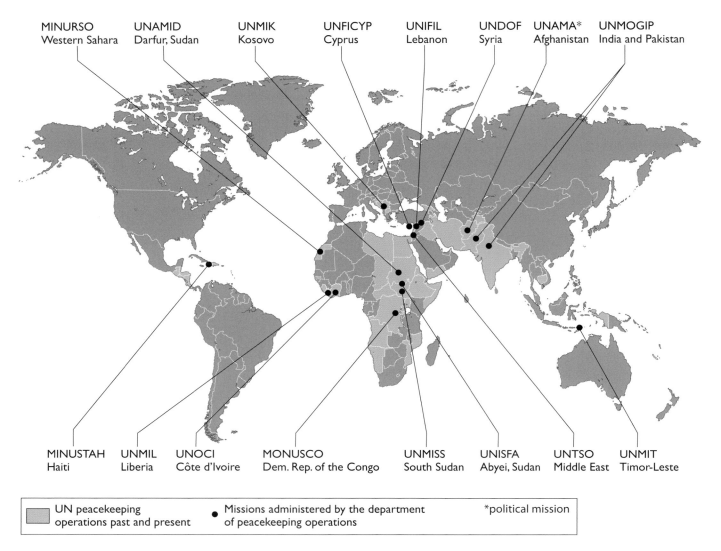

Figure 3.3 Global map of UN peacekeeping operations combined with indicators of significant past peacekeeping efforts (this map presents ongoing operations in 2008)

Africa

- United Nations Mission in the Republic of South Sudan (UNMISS)

- United Nations Interim Security Force for Abyei (UNISFA)

- UN Organization Stabilization Mission in the Democratic Republic of the Congo (MONUSCO)

- African Union–UN Hybrid Operation in Darfur (UNAMID)–

- UN Operation in Côte d'Ivoire (UNOCI)

- UN Mission in Liberia (UNMIL)

- UN Mission for the Referendum in Western Sahara (MINURSO)

Americas

- UN Stabilization Mission in Haiti (MINUSTAH)

Asia and the Pacific

- UN Integrated Mission in Timor-Leste (UNMIT)
- UN Military Observer Group in India and Pakistan (UNMOGIP)
- UN Assistance Mission in Afghanistan (UNAMA)*

Europe

- UN Peacekeeping Force in Cyprus (UNFICYP)
- UN Interim Administration Mission in Kosovo (UNMIK)

Middle East

- UN Disengagement Observer Force (UNDOF)
- United Nations Interim Force in Lebanon (UNIFIL)
- UN Truce Supervision Organization (UNTSO)

* Please note UNAMA is a special political mission, directed and supported by DPKO.

The founders of the UN did not foresee the kinds of violent conflict that are more common now, the types of civil wars discussed in Chapters 1 and 2 of this book, so the UN was not given a formal peacekeeping role. Like the UN's role in natural disasters, it is sometimes said that peacekeeping simply happened. Former UN Secretary-General Dag Hammarskjöld famously described peacekeeping as being 'Chapter 6½' of the Charter.

Peacekeeping works best when there is a peace to keep, that is, when there has been agreement among armed forces that the fighting should stop. Sometimes there are individual rebels or groups that try to keep fighting, and peacekeepers are forced to defend themselves, civilians, or even the government. In that case, Chapter VII is used to approve military actions as part of peacekeeping, as occurred in Sierra Leone, East Timor, the Congo and other places. However, in the 1990s, Chapter VII intervention in the former Yugoslavia was very different, and was explicitly intended to protect the civilian population while the war continued. Chapter VII has also been used to approve overt military intervention, notably in Korea (1950–53), Iraq (1990–91) and Afghanistan (from 2001). But the controversy about the legality of the subsequent Iraq war (2003–11) centred on whether UN resolutions under Chapter VII explicitly authorized military action, or only sanctions and actions short of military intervention.

With the end of the Cold War, half of the civil wars came to an end, particularly those with strong Cold War links, such as the one in Mozambique (see Box 3.1). But the others continued, and as Chapter 1 shows, new civil wars started. The 1990s saw 35 new peacekeeping and observer operations, from Sierra Leone to Tajikistan. By contrast there were only 11 new operations between 2000 and 2010. Linked to this was a huge jump in emergency aid (for both wars and disasters). Official emergency aid flows grew from US$738 million in 1990 to US$3.6 billion just a decade later – from 1.4% to 6.8% of the official aid flows.

3.2.1 Emergencies in context

Attempts are sometimes made to distinguish between emergency and development aid and between civilian and military intervention, but in practice there are no sharp divisions. Three terms are commonly used:

- An 'emergency' usually means an event where there is an urgent need for immediate action to provide assistance or relief.

- The Organization for Economic Co-operation and Development Development Assistance Committee (OECD DAC) then defines 'humanitarian aid' as 'assistance designed to save lives, alleviate suffering and maintain and protect human dignity during and in the aftermath of emergencies' (OECD, 2010a).

- The UN says a 'complex emergency' is 'a multifaceted humanitarian crisis … where there is total or considerable breakdown of authority resulting from internal or external conflict and which requires an international response that goes beyond the mandate or capacity of any single agency and/or the ongoing UN country program' (UN, 2003, p. 6).

(In the third bullet point, do not be confused by the use of the word 'conflict' – this quote uses diplomatic and UN language to refer to violent conflict or war.)

Here, the UN jargon does not help – a 'complex emergency' is usually not an emergency at all, but something that is ongoing and caused by war. Initial help after a natural disaster is to save lives – dig people out of the rubble and provide survivors with food, water, sanitation and shelter – but it soon moves into building and rebuilding structures, livelihoods and systems, which is normally seen as development assistance. Similarly, soldiers are often involved in emergency relief efforts, while humanitarian and development assistance has become a central part of peacekeeping operations. The same process occurs during and after a war. Saving lives quickly moves into food, housing and then rebuilding. Again, both civilian and military agencies are involved; peacekeepers are often involved in development projects. Definitions of words such as emergency, development and humanitarian aid are usually of more interest to accountants trying to find the right budget line, and of much less concern to people on the ground.

Haiti, the poorest country in the Americas, has had both kinds of interventions, humanitarian and 'complex emergency' support. After a coup and violence in 2004, the UN agreed to establish the UN Stabilization Mission in Haiti (MINUSTAH). This meant there was a force of more than 12 000 military and police in Haiti when it was hit by a devastating earthquake on 12 January 2010. The full effects of this natural disaster and the political, social and economic context in which this took place is addressed in Chapter 5. More than 20 countries sent military forces and a whole range of UN agencies and the Red Cross were involved in relief and reconstruction. There were hundreds of NGOs involved, and the 23 largest US charities collected over US $1 billion for relief efforts. However, there were complaints that infighting between agencies and governments delayed both the relief and reconstruction.

At its best, as the Mozambique case study (Box 3.1) shows, where the host government plays a central role, international intervention can be welcome and effective. But bad experiences are now causing rethinking in two areas. First, as Section 3.3 and Box 3.2 will show, aid is not always effective, and can sometimes do serious unintentional harm. Second, to be discussed in Section 3.3, the merging of security and humanitarian considerations is causing an increasing disquiet, and a fear that peacekeeping and humanitarian aid can be used as an excuse for unwelcome intervention by big powers in smaller and weaker countries, of a sort which they hoped had ended with the end of the Cold War.

Activity 3.1

Think about a recent intervention, perhaps one you have read about in the newspaper. As best you can without direct knowledge, make a list of agencies and organizations involved. See if you can distinguish between military and civilian interventions, natural disasters and peacekeeping, and emergencies and development.

Spend no more than 10 minutes on this activity.

Discussion

The Pakistan flood in July–September 2010 was the worst natural disaster in the country's history, flooding one-fifth of the country, affecting 18 million people and killing up to 2000. With a quick Web search, using the words 'Pakistan', 'flood' and '2010', it was possible to find that 76 governments, many INGOs and private donors gave more than US$1.6 billion. UN agencies and the Red Cross and Red Crescent Societies played key coordinating roles.

A more restricted Web search on 'Pakistan', 'flood, 2010' and 'military' shows that it was the Pakistani military that led the rescue and relief operations, and that several foreign military forces provided helicopters, planes and boats, as well as military personnel including doctors. But NATO caused some controversy by announced an 'air bridge' to transport in-kind donations from its member states and humanitarian organizations to Pakistan, without prior consultation with the government. Some humanitarian agencies refused to use the NATO air bridge.

3.3   Intervention and responsibility to protect

The Red Cross and the UN agencies only act when a country or national Red Cross society asks for help with a war or natural disaster that is so big it cannot cope. UN peacekeeping (see Figure 3.4) and observation missions are all based on the agreement of the combatants. Indeed the UN Charter says that 'the Organization is based on the principle of the sovereign equality of all its Members' and adds that 'nothing contained in the present Charter shall authorize the United Nations to intervene in matters which are essentially within the domestic jurisdiction of any state' (UN, 1985, Chapter I, Article 2).

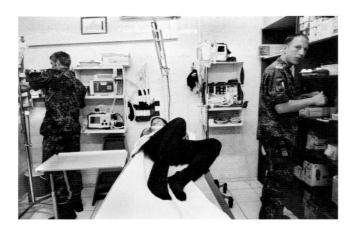

Figure 3.4   UN peacekeepers (Source: United Nations)

The Cold War strengthened the principle of sovereignty, as each of the big powers, the USSR and the USA, tried to block intervention by the other in what it saw as, or hoped would be, client states. Inevitably, there were secret interventions by security services on both sides, but, officially, state sovereignty remained the overriding principle. Even the most brutal and corrupt dictators were safe if they had East or West as a protector. But with the collapse of the Communist bloc and when the USA and its allies convinced themselves they had 'won' the Cold War with the Soviet Union, there was no longer a counterbalance. With less need to buy loyalty with aid, the powers left standing took a much more interventionist position when conflicts arose that could potentially harm their geopolitical interests or question their military and economic security. This returns to the questions raised in Chapter 1 about development as a process of change that creates fear and insecurity for some in the name of securing development (such as economic dominance) for others.

It could be argued that there was a certain degree of hubris on the part of states such as the USA, who subsequently claimed a right to intervene. Chester Crocker, a former US Assistant Secretary of State for African Affairs, talked of 'security exporting regions' (Hanlon, 2006, p. 62) which had a responsibility to intervene and even undertake '**coercive peacekeeping**', slightly misleadingly called '**peacekeeping plus**'. There were calls for 'humanitarian interventions' and even 'humanitarian wars' to prevent gross human rights violations. Nor was this interventionism just military. The Bretton Woods institutions began to impose structural adjustment and neoliberalism on developing countries, as the 'obvious' best economic policy accompanied by privatization of state industries and enterprises and cuts in public spending such as on welfare and education (Hanlin and Brown, 2013). Nicholas Wheeler's *Saving Strangers* (2000) argued that 'states which massively violate human rights should forfeit the right to be treated as legitimate sovereigns, thereby morally entitling other states to use force to stop the oppression' (Wheeler, 2000, p. 12).

Another consequence of the end of the Cold War was the breakup of Yugoslavia in 1991, which also came to exemplify the difficulties of intervention. The dissolution of the country led to a series of wars and seven different UN peacekeeping operations, one of which, in Kosovo, was still in operation 20 years after the crisis started. The European Union, the USA and NATO also intervened. In Chapter 1, it was noted that civil wars have a special brutality and ferocity, in part because the fighting is between families, neighbours and co-workers. Because the 'enemy' may be standing next to you in the market and you do not know, and because they look just like you, it is sometimes argued that the only way to create security is to force them out. The breakup of Yugoslavia into its constituent states was given an ethnic overtone by respective leaders, and so Croatians drove out Serbian neighbours and Serbs drove out Muslims. This came to be known as 'ethnic cleansing', which was defined in 1994 by a UN commission as 'a purposeful policy designed by one ethnic or religious group to remove by violent and terror-inspiring means the civilian population of another ethnic or religious group from certain geographic areas' (UN, 1994).

The most extreme example was the massacre in the town of Srebrenica in Bosnia and Herzegovina. Serbs had besieged the largely Muslim area and in April 1993 the UN declared the enclave a 'safe area' under UN protection. However, in July 1995, a 400-strong contingent of armed Dutch UN peacekeepers failed to prevent the town's capture and the subsequent massacre by the Bosnian Serbs of more than 8000 civilians, mostly men and boys. The violent events that took place in Srebrenica and elsewhere, such as the Siege of Sarajevo, it was argued morally legitimated the intervention in the war, and later interventions such as in Kosovo in 1999.

Perhaps the key event, however, which has caused the most heart-searching debate was a failure to intervene in 1994 in Rwanda. The UN, and the international community as a whole, failed to prevent a genocide that killed an estimated 800 000 people. The UN's small peace-monitoring force in Rwanda was withdrawn instead of strengthened. It has been argued that there was more than adequate warning and extensive television coverage of the massacres themselves, but in what was widely seen as perhaps the most significant failure in UN history, the international community did little at the key moments of the processes involved. It is arguable that there were limits on what it could do within the constraints of peacekeeping missions at that time and, with the benefit of hindsight and witness testimony, the highly organized manner of the genocidal activities that followed. However, as DesForges (1999) highlighted, information about the systematic killing of Tutsis as well as opposition Hutu citizens flowed without obstruction to the UN and other nation states right from the start. It is possible that sheer disbelief played a part and, rather than 'genocide', the terms used were ethnic rivalries, tribal killings and tribal resentments in public statements, followed by references to Rwanda as a 'failed state'. More critical commentators suggest that cultural prejudice also played a part in international inaction (ibid). As a result, by the time the full implications of the genocide were taken seriously, for most of the victims it was already too late.

Interventions in Yugoslavia and Iraq combined with the failures to anticipate massacres in Srebrenica and Rwanda showed that the choices by the powerful countries about when and how to intervene were proving deeply problematic (see Figure 3.5).

The debate about intervention led the Canadian government to convene the International Commission on Intervention and State Sovereignty (ICISS), which reported in 2001. It was co-chaired by Gareth Evans, a former Australian foreign minister, and Mohamed Sahnoun, a senior Algerian

Figure 3.5 Impact of war on civilian population. Taken from the English language news service of Al Jazeera, highlights a new development in the regional reporting of conflict. This news channel presents a much more graphic and less sanitized account of the effects of war and conflict in the Middle East compared to Western-based news such as CNN and the BBC (Source: Aljazeera.com)

diplomat who had been deputy director general of both the Organisation for African Unity (OAU) and Arab League. The ten members included a former chair of the military committee of NATO, a former president of ICRC, and human rights and peace activists. One of their starting points was an analysis of four failures:

- Rwanda in 1994, which 'laid bare the full horror of inaction'
- Bosnia in 1995, where the UN failed to protect civilians sheltering in UN-declared safe areas
- Somalia in 1992, when an intervention was botched by flawed planning, poor execution and an excessive dependence on military force
- Kosovo, 1999.

The ICISS concluded that sovereignty does still matter.

> In a dangerous world marked by overwhelming inequalities of power and resources, sovereignty is for many states their best – and sometimes seemingly their only – line of defence. But sovereignty is more than just a

functional principle of international relations. For many states and peoples, it is also a recognition of their equal worth and dignity.

(ICISS, 2001, p. 7, para. 1.32)

But the ICISS also concluded that:

> sovereign states have a responsibility to protect their own citizens from avoidable catastrophe – from mass murder and rape, from starvation – but that when they are unwilling or unable to do so, that responsibility must be borne by the broader community of states.

(ICISS, 2001, p. viii)

Perhaps the most important decision of the ICISS was to not talk about a 'right to intervene' but rather to create a new '**responsibility to protect**' (R2P). This is discussed in Box 3.2. It argued that a right to intervene is unhelpful because:

- it focuses on the rights and claims of the intervening state rather than the potential beneficiaries of the action
- it focuses narrowly on the act of intervention
- it is 'intrinsically more confrontational' (ibid, p. 7, para. 2.29)
- 'at the outset of the debate it loads the dice in favour of intervention' (ibid, p. 16, para. 2.28)

Box 3.2   Operationalizing R2P

The following has been adapted from a paper written by Gareth Evans of the ICISS.

It is a central characteristic of the responsibility to protect that it should only involve the use of coercive military force as a last resort: when no other options are available, this is the right thing to do morally and practically, and it is lawful under the UN Charter. If such force from outside has to be used, as the only way to protect people from genocide and mass atrocity crimes, then it is far better for this to happen with the consent of the government in question. This poses very difficult problems for military planners because it is not the kind of role in which militaries have been traditionally engaged, where they have well-developed doctrine and for which they can draw on a large body of experience. What is involved here is neither traditional war fighting (where the object is to defeat an enemy, not just to stop particular kinds of violence and intimidation) nor, at the other extreme, traditional peacekeeping concerned essentially with monitoring, supervision and verification.

The new task is partly what is now described as 'peacekeeping plus' or 'complex peacekeeping', where it is assumed from the outset that the mission, while primarily designed to hold together a ceasefire or peace settlement, is likely to run into trouble from spoilers of one kind or another; that military force is quite likely to have to be used at some stage, for civilian protection purposes as well as in self-defence. The other part of the task is that which may arise in a Rwanda-type case, where there is the sudden eruption of conscience-shocking crimes against humanity, beyond the capacity of any existing peacekeeping mission to deal with, demanding a rapid and forceful 'fire brigade' response from a new or extended mission to quash the violence and protect those caught up in it. Together, these 'peacekeeping plus' and 'fire brigade' operations are appropriately described as 'coercive protection missions', which is as useful a terminology as any to use in addressing what is needed to create the capability to operate them effectively. Operational effectiveness in practice depends on getting a number of other things right:

- force configuration (what kind of force structure, and quantities of personnel and equipment, do militaries have to have to be able to mount these kinds of operations, individually or collectively)

- deployability (how rapidly can the necessary forces get to whatever theatre is involved)

- preparation (ensuring that doctrine and training are matched to these operations)

- mandates and rules of engagement (ensuring that they are appropriate for the particular mission proposed)

- military–civilian cooperation (ensuring that structures and processes are in place to maximize the effectiveness of each).

The distinctiveness of coercive protection operations from more familiar military tasks – and the need to tread a line that involves something short of a full-scale war-fighting mind-set but more than an observing and monitoring one – makes it crucial that forces be properly prepared for them. That in turn means much attention to training but also to ensure that the training is properly focused. UN-mandated human protection operations should be based on the following:

- the operation must be based on a precisely defined political objective expressed in a clear and unambiguous mandate, with matching resources and rules of engagement

- the intervention must be politically controlled, but be conducted by a military commander with authority to command to the fullest extent possible, who disposes of adequate resources to execute his mission, and with a single chain of command which reflects unity of command and purpose

- the aim of the human protection operation is to enforce compliance with human rights and the rule of law as quickly and as comprehensively as possible, but it is not the defeat of a state; this must be properly reflected in the application of force

- the conduct of the operation must guarantee maximum protection of all elements of the civilian population

- strict adherence to international humanitarian law must be ensured

- force protection for the intervening force must never have priority over the resolve to accomplish the mission

- there must be maximum coordination between military and civilian authorities and organizations.

Mandates and Rules of Engagement are the legally binding instructions for particular missions, describing at different levels of generality not only what their basic tasks are but when, where and to what extent their members may use force. For example, in the case of the UN Mission in the Democratic Republic of the Congo (MONUC), the mandate spelled out in Security Council Resolution 1565 of 2004 included paragraphs making clear that the Security Council was acting 'under Chapter VII of the Charter of the United Nations'; that it was mandating (that is, instructing) MONUC, among a number of other tasks, 'to ensure the protection of civilians, including humanitarian personnel, under imminent threat of physical violence'; and that it was authorizing the mission, in carrying out this among other tasks 'to use all necessary means, within its capacity and in the areas where its armed units are deployed'. The rules of engagement (ROEs) for this mission made clear, in turn, exactly what 'all necessary means' meant, that is 'Forces may use up to deadly force to protect civilians when competent local authorities are not in a position to do so.' If we want to ensure that coercive peace operations carried out under the umbrella of the R2P norm are, in their conceptualization, detailed planning and on-the-ground execution, absolutely consistent with international humanitarian law, we still have a long way to go.

(Source: Evans, 2008)

In contrast to a 'right to intervene', the 'responsibility to protect' examines the issues from the viewpoint of those needing support. It becomes a shared responsibility of a state for its own citizens and of outside interveners. Most importantly, the ICISS said it also entailed a 'responsibility to prevent' and a 'responsibility to rebuild'. The 'responsibility to prevent' meant reversing the decline in international aid, tackling the debt crisis in the developing world, reversing unfair trade policies and taking other actions to help countries 'meet the social and economic development needs of their populations' (ICISS, 2001, p. 20, para. 3.8).

It also meant addressing political needs including support, and pressure if required, for building democratic institutions, power sharing, improved legal protection, and other social and political changes needed to reduce possible causes of war. The most important aspect of the 'responsibility to protect' was its recognition that security depends on development.

Hanlon (2006, p. 66) notes that the Commission warned: 'too often in the past the responsibility to rebuild has been insufficiently recognized.' Interveners leave too quickly, and the country is 'still wrestling with the underlying problems that produced the original intervention'. What is needed, then, is 'a genuine commitment to helping to build a durable peace, and promoting good governance and sustainable development'.

On the fraught issue of intervention, the Commission stressed the need to try measures short of military action, particularly sanctions, and set six criteria for military interventions: right authority, just cause, right intention, last resort, proportional means, and reasonable prospects (ICISS, 2001, p. xii).

On just cause, it drew a very narrow window, allowing military intervention only to prevent 'large scale loss of life' or 'large scale ethnic cleansing'. In particular, military intervention would not be permitted simply to reverse the overthrow of a democratically elected government – where sanctions are called for instead.

Activity 3.2

Go back to the UN Charter Chapter VII interventions mentioned earlier – Sierra Leone, East Timor, Congo, former Yugoslavia, Iraq and Afghanistan – and pick two examples. How might those interventions have been different if R2P in its initial formulation in 2001 had been applied. You may want to make a note of the main elements of R2P and how it differed from the earlier right to intervene.

Discussion

Each country with a UN intervention had its own history, different from the others. And hindsight has the advantage that we now have much more information than decision makers did at the time. For Sierra Leone, problems began in the 1980s when a collapse in state services, notably education, brought a response from youth, which claimed the 'West' (still in the Cold War era) was backing the government because it was imposing structural adjustment policies. In retrospect, then, the 'responsibility to prevent' could have involved more international support for job creation and maintaining the education system – and perhaps limiting corruption. The early 1990s saw a series of military coups and a growing civil war; aid did increase, but a condition of aid was an IMF stabilization programme that led to 30 000 people losing their jobs and weakened the army – which only fuelled the civil war. In many ways this was a civil war triggered by young people feeling they had been excluded from development, and where aid may have done harm. Finally, as the civil war escalated and the population opposed military governments, could the international community have done more to end the war?

R2P remains controversial, and was on the UN agenda for the next decade, but the international community backed away from the implications of the broad definition. The 2005 World Summit, a heads-of-state-level meeting of the UN General Assembly, accepted only a limited version of R2P in just two paragraphs of the final statement. R2P applied only to four specific crimes and violations, namely genocide, war crimes, ethnic cleansing and crimes against humanity. It also stressed that 'each individual state has the responsibility to protect its populations', dropping the original phrase 'primary responsibility' (UN, 2005). All reference to responsibilities to prevent and to rebuild disappeared; Bellamy notes that 'the idea that R2P implied responsibilities –

even obligations – on the part of international society and especially the Security Council was all but removed' (Bellamy, 2008, p. 623).

Nevertheless, the Summit stated that intervention can only be authorized under Chapter VII of the UN Charter, which requires Security Council approval. The discussion homed in on military intervention, just what Commission chairs Gareth Evans and Mohamed Sahnoun had hoped to avoid by using the terminology of responsibilities to prevent, protect and rebuild. The 'revolt against R2P was in large part fuelled by the continuing association of the principle with humanitarian intervention and fears that it could be abused to justify self-interested unilateral interventions such as Iraq', explains Bellamy (2009, p. 125). Influential states such as India, the Philippines, China and Russia expressed 'deep seated scepticism towards armed intervention – only reinforced by the use of humanitarian language to justify the 2003 invasion of Iraq' (Bellamy, 2009, p. 113). Such suspicions can be seen in the 2008 veto by China and Russia of French attempts in the Security Council to authorize the forcible distribution of humanitarian assistance in Burma after Cyclone Nargis, and a two-day General Assembly debate in 2009 refused to expand R2P. Similar debates and opposition have been seen in response to the NATO intervention in Libya (2011) that led to the overthrow of its leader, Colonel Gaddafi, and in arguments for and against intervention in Syria's civil unrest in 2011–12. As Bellamy ruefully concludes, 'it is not hard to see why many governments continue to suspect that R2P is simply a "Trojan horse" for the legitimization of unilateral intervention' (Bellamy, 2008, p. 617).

The uses of words and their framing is important. Later in Chapter 4 we will explore the security–development nexus, and address concern about the way development assistance is increasingly being framed partly in security terms, and the way terms like 'fragile' and 'failing' states are used to justify intervention. Even the original proposal of the International Commission on Intervention and State Sovereignty (ICISS) used the phrase 'state failure'. Despite genuine concern by emerging powers such as China about armed conflict and genocide, the distrust of the USA and Europe simply remains too great to give them any licence for intervention. But the narrow framing of R2P in the debates meant that the link between development and security, which had been built into R2P by Evans and Sahnoun – with responsibility to prevent and to rebuild – was lost. The suspicions that policies of intervention, such as R2P, could do harm can also be seen in arguments that even development aid may not be a good thing, as the following section examines.

3.4 Donors can do harm

Florence Nightingale worked in British military hospitals in the Crimean war of 1855–56 and contributed to the improved treatment of wounded soldiers and the development of the nursing profession in Britain. Yet she was strongly opposed to the founding of the Red Cross on the grounds that it would simply 'render war more easy', because states knew someone else would take responsibility for the wounded. In effect, the Red Cross would become an ally of the armies. Hugo Slim calls this 'Nightingale's risk' – the risk that humanitarian action is coopted and actually assists a warring party or promotes war (Slim, 2001).

It took two writers in the late 1990s, Uvin and Anderson, to shock the aid community into finally accepting that in some cases aid did more harm than good, reducing security and even encouraging violence. Uvin's 1998 book about the Rwanda genocide was titled, explicitly, *Aiding Violence*. According to Uvin:

> Rwanda was usually seen as a model of development in Africa, with good performance on most of the indicators of development, including the usual indicators, such as growth in gross national product (GNP), manufacturing, or services; the more social indicators, such as food availability or vaccination rates; and the new bottom-up indicators, such as number of non-governmental organizations (NGOs) and cooperatives in the country.
>
> *(Uvin, 1998, pp. 1–2)*

But the aid community was fooled by its own indicators and did not see what was happening on the ground. Thus:

> the process of development and the international aid given to promote it interacted with the forces of exclusion, inequality, pauperization, racism, and oppression that laid the groundwork for the 1994 genocide. … Aid financed much of the machinery of exclusion, inequality, and humiliation [and] provided it with legitimacy and support.
>
> *(Uvin, 1998, p. 231)*

A closer study of aid projects showed that most of the benefits went to the elite, not the poor, through salaries, houses, land, contracts, etc. Uvin notes that in the four years before the genocide, there was 'widespread violence and massive human rights abuses'. This included the killing and harassment of aid agency and partner NGO staff. Yet there was no protest from the agencies. Indeed, aid increased sharply in this period, in part to support a World Bank Structural Adjustment Programme (SAP).

> As Rwanda's farmers were facing crises without precedent, as inequality and corruption reached endemic proportions, as hope for the future was extinguished, and as violence, hatred, and human rights abuses became government policy, the international community was congratulating Rwanda.
>
> *(Uvin, 1998, p. 89)*

Significant amounts of the increased aid were used to import weapons and increase military spending. For one commentator, far from using that power to prevent genocide, the aid industry was an 'active and willing partner' (ibid, p. 231) in creating the conditions for the genocide.

Recognizing that 'aid can reinforce, exacerbate and prolong the conflict', development economist Mary B. Anderson elaborated the concept of 'do no harm'. The phrase comes from the longstanding guidance to doctors. Hippocrates, originator of the doctor's oath, wrote in *Epidemics* (Book I, Section XI) that doctors should 'help, or at least do no harm'. The Roman physician, Galen, is said to have written that doctors should 'first, do no harm'. Anderson's impact was dramatic and unexpected. Despite all that had been written, bilateral aid agencies and NGOs were first shocked by the suggestion that they might be doing harm and then became even more disturbed by the proposal that analysis of possible harm should be part of their planning process. However, field experience of harm done by aid was persuasive, and agencies did change. Yet this also caused a dilemma because some agencies became overly cautious in some situations, refusing to work where they might do harm. This forced Anderson in *Do No Harm* to note that 'It is a moral and logical fallacy to conclude that because aid can do harm, a decision not to give aid would do no harm' (Anderson, 1999, p. 2). Anderson sets out how aid can feed into, reinforce and prolong conflict as well as peace:

1   Aid resources are often stolen by warriors and used to support armies and buy weapons.

2   Aid affects markets by reinforcing either the war economy or the peace economy.

3   The distributional impacts of aid affect intergroup relationships, either feeding tensions or reinforcing connections.

4   Aid substitutes for local resources required to meet civilian needs, freeing them to support conflict.

5   Aid legitimizes people and their actions or agendas, supporting the pursuit of either war or peace.

(Anderson, 1999, pp. 37, 39)

Aid often distorts local markets, and if aid organizations are not careful, when they are hiring staff, buying goods and distributing assistance, they can be benefiting some groups in preference to others, which may actually increase tension. Aid also tends to give increased credibility to those in power, sometimes the government but at other times the local armed group claiming to represent a specific community, as was seen in the conflict in the Democratic Republic of the Congo at the beginning of the 21st century. And just as Nightingale argued, Anderson also shows that if aid agencies take responsibility for civilians, then this reduces the burden on the fighters, and can 'render war more easy'.

Claims to 'do no harm' and 'Nightingale's risk' are both examples of how the narrow humanitarian approach may do more harm than good in some circumstances. Aid does not always aid. A 1993 handbook for practitioners of 'humanitarian action in times of war' actually has the exhortation: 'Don't just do something, stand there!' (Minear and Weiss, 1993). It argues that, particularly in an emergency, it is necessary to stop and think carefully about the implications of any action, rather than jumping in without analyzing the consequences.

Activity 3.3

'Don't just do something, stand there!' does not mean do nothing. As we noted above, the ICISS based its thinking on four failures: Rwanda in 1994, Bosnia in 1995, Somalia in 1992 and Kosovo in 1999. Take *one* of these. If you do not have enough information, take 10 minutes (no more) to look up some basic details of one of these cases on the internet. Then think about two questions:

First, before the crisis – how could aid have been restructured to not do harm? How might aid have been reconfigured to reduce the likelihood of conflict becoming violent?

Second, think about the crisis, when innocent people are under attack and when, arguably, there was too much 'standing there', and faster thinking and a shorter pause was required. How might the UN have intervened, but in a better way?

Spend no more than 20 minutes on this activity.

Discussion

These four cases are still debated, so there is no right answer. But as the best minds in the international community failed in these instances, so your answers may be no worse than theirs were.

The ICISS, in producing the R2P charter, tried to bring development and international relations components together. It defined a responsibility to prevent conflict and stressed that the international community had to address the root causes, including developmental ones. The unwillingness of the UN diplomats to accept this did not make those development issues go away, and the group of donor nations, the OECD DAC, commissioned an important study on how to support statebuilding in what it defined as fragile states and those affected by violent conflict. That study came with a harsh warning:

> Donors can inadvertently do harm when the resources they deliver or the policy reforms they advocate exacerbate rather than mitigate the conditions for violent conflict, or weaken rather than strengthen the state as a site of decision making and policy formation over the deployment of public resources. They can do harm when aid is delivered in such a way as to act as a disincentive to states to consolidate their own revenue base. By not understanding the history and power dynamics in a partner country, donor actions can disrupt the political settlement that underpins the state, weakening the incentive for powerful elites to buy in to statebuilding processes and increasing their incentives to opt out.

(OECD, 2010b, p. 9)

The report goes on to say:

> The central message that comes out of Anderson's work is as applicable to statebuilding as it is to peacebuilding: donors must be sensitive to the specific context in which they are intervening; that is, universal templates

seldom can make an effective contribution to statebuilding; and donors need to develop deeper knowledge of the history and diversity of a country. ... Donors need to look for both intended and unintended consequences linked to their interventions.

(OECD, 2010b, p. 28)

The OECD study effectively restates the messages above, harking back to the claim by Chang et al. (2013) that culture and situated knowledge needs to be taken into account in development interventions. No matter how serious or urgent the crisis seems, it is too easy to do more harm than good, and essential to think and learn more about the country and the crisis before intervention. Of course, real-life situations do not always allow this. Intelligence reports of situations in other countries, especially authoritarian regimes, can be partial and fragmented. In addition, what is known is often shaped by the lenses of self-interest and the immediate security concerns of the state that is gathering intelligence. Often the key actors that emerge in attempts to replace a regime may be barely on the radar of intelligence organizations or aid agencies. There may also be uncertainty about the intentions of some if not all actors involved, such as in the Libyan civil war of 2011; although in that case UN-sanctioned military activity was carried out by NATO member countries. Similarly, the distribution of aid may contribute towards unanticipated outcomes and even control of food aid can become a kind of weapon for manipulating specific populations (as seen in the Somali famine of 2011). 'Generally, donors lack the knowledge of local politics, of the balance of power between locally contending groups and elites or how they are linked to the centre, so support in this area is often blind and therefore in danger of provoking unintended outcomes' (OECD, 2010b, p. 11). Nevertheless, as Anderson herself warned, it is not an invitation to do nothing, but rather to think and analyse before acting. As the report's introduction says, donor interventions can positively contribute to statebuilding in 'fragile situations', by focusing on:

- the endogenous political processes that drive statebuilding
- the legitimacy of the state in society
- the relations between state and society
- the expectations society has of the state
- the capacities of the state to perform its basic functions (security, the rule of law, taxation, management of economic development and the environment, and the delivery of essential services).

(OECD, 2010b, p. 11)

The study is important because, in trying to bridge development and international relations, it explicitly recognizes the roles and interests of the state. Note, in particular, the use of the phrase 'fragile situations' instead of the more common 'fragile states', making the point that it is not the state which is fragile, but rather the situation it finds itself in and for which it requires support. The report notes that donors are not just intervening through humanitarian motives, but have their own goals:

Donors are often faced with the difficult task of reconciling their government's strategic objectives in-country with statebuilding and development objectives. In the past the former have usually trumped the latter. Geopolitical objectives remain primary, including international security (today marked by the 'war on terror' and regional conflicts), global economic integration and problems of global warming as well as strong ideological commitments around the defence of human rights and the propagation of democratic politics. While there are endless efforts to suggest how all these goals are interconnected and sit easily together, reality demonstrates that they are often contradictory.

The strategic dilemmas confronting donors will not disappear and statebuilding objectives will not always trump other strategic objectives. In such situations, it may be impossible for donors to avoid 'doing harm' to statebuilding, from the vantage point of actors within a given state. Understanding these strategic dilemmas is arguably the first step in undertaking an assessment of the impact of donor intervention on statebuilding.

(OECD, 2010b, pp. 35–6)

The report underlines that donor priorities, such as elections, decentralization, technical assistance and support for NGOs, may not be local priorities and may not be the most useful things to do. Economic and development support may be much more urgent:

Ensuring livelihoods and employment opportunities for the population at large remains a central source of state legitimacy in all fragile states where people often live on the margins of subsistence. Donor programmes that contribute to livelihood protection can enhance state legitimacy providing they keep track of the impact these have on the informal economy. ... Donors risk doing harm to statebuilding by failing to provide support for the creation of capacity within fragile states to expand productive activities.

(OECD, 2010b, pp. 58, 117)

Analysis is also important in determining the type of aid that causes problems, such as financial instruments in the form of loans that become very difficult to pay back if, as a result of weak economic conditions or food shortages (see Figure 3.6), the country in question has defaulted on interim payments. In other cases, it could be aid linked to development of a specific cash crop or new agricultural product, only for the developing country government to discover that global market demand has made the crop uneconomic or even that the crop completely fails due to not understanding the ecological conditions of a country or region. More selfishly, it could be the provision of technologies such as vehicles that are difficult to repair and maintain within existing infrastuctures and where only the donor countries gain in the expensive imports of spare parts. All of these examples relate to ensuring that the form of aid is suited to context and increasing the capacities of the developing society to meet changes in conditions. In short, aid needs to be connected to capacity building and promoting resilience (see Johnson and Farooki, 2013; Chang et al., 2013).

Figure 3.6   Picture of aid distribution (Source: AFP/Getty Images)

Summary and looking forward

Solidarity with those suffering natural disaster or war is a strong human motivation. Global solidarity systems have developed through the UN and INGOs. An enduring question remains, however, on when, and how, the international community should intervene. This is an ongoing debate, with some countries anxious that humanitarian intervention should not be used as an excuse for a violation of sovereignty.

The language of 'humanitarianism' and 'failed states' has been questioned as part of a hegemonic discourse that perpetuates a relationship between stronger and weaker states in the global North and South. However, in some situations, as we saw in Rwanda, an overly cautious approach could prove disastrous. As a result, debates also continue on the circumstances in which intervention, like aid, does not always help. This has led to an understanding that it is not sufficient to just rush in and 'do something'. Rather, actions of external states or INGOs must be guided by an overriding mandate of 'do no harm', with an emphasis on understanding the context of the conflict and the country.

These arguments will be extended in Chapters 4 and 5, which will examine the impact of intervention at both the individual level (in relation to human trafficking) and in the case studies of Haiti and Trinidad.

References

Anderson, M.B. (1999) *Do No Harm: How Aid Can Support Peace – or War*, Boulder, CO, Lynne Rienner.

Bellamy, A. (2008) 'The responsibility to protect and the problem of military interventon', *International Affairs*, vol. 84, issue 4, pp. 615–39.

Bellamy, A. (2009) 'Realizing the responsibility to protect', *International Studies Perspectives*, vol. 10, pp. 111–28.

Brown, W. and Hanlon, J. (2013) 'International action to reduce poverty development' in Papaioannou, T. and Butcher, M. (eds) *International Development in a Changing World*, London, Bloomsbury Academic/Milton Keynes, The Open University.

Chang, D., Farooki, M. and Johnson, H. (2013) 'Culture, livelihoods and making a living' in Papaioannou, T. and Butcher, M. (eds) *International Development in a Changing World*, London, Bloomsbury Academic/Milton Keynes, The Open University.

Christie, F. and Hanlon, J. (2001) *Mozambique and the Great Flood of 2000*, Oxford, James Currey.

DesForges, A. (1999) *Leave None to Tell the Story: Genocide in Rwanda*, Washington DC, Human Rights Watch, [online] http://www.hrw.org/legacy/reports/1999/rwanda/index.htm#TopOfPage (Accessed 17 November 2011).

Evans, G. (2008) 'Operationalising R2P in coercive peace operations', Paper presented to Working Group on Peace Operations and the Protection of Civilians, *ICRC and IIHL Conference on International Humanitarian Law, Human Rights and Peace Operations*, San Remo, 5 September 2008, [online] http://www.gevans.org/speeches/speech304.html (Accessed 17 November 2011).

Hanlin, R. and Brown, W. (2013) 'Introducing international development' in Papaioannou, T. and Butcher, M. (eds) *International Development in a Changing World*, London, Bloomsbury Academic/Milton Keynes, The Open University.

Hanlon, J. (2006) 'Intervention' in Yanacopulos, H. and Hanlon, J. (eds) *Civil War, Civil Peace*, Milton Keynes, The Open University.

International Commission on Intervention and State Sovereignty (ICISS) (2001) *The Responsibility to Protect: Report of the International Commission on Intervention and State Sovereignty*, [online] http://responsibilitytoprotect.org/ICISS%20Report.pdf (Accessed 5 December 2011).

Johnson, H. and Farooki, M. (2013) 'Thinking about poverty' in Papaioannou, T. and Butcher, M. (eds) *International Development in a Changing World*, London, Bloomsbury Academic/Milton Keynes, The Open University.

Minear, L. and Weiss, T.G. (1993) *Humanitarian Action in Times of War: a Handbook for Practitioners*, Boulder, CO, Lynne Rienner.

Organization for Economic Co-operation and Development (OECD) (2010a) DAC Statistical Reporting Directive, DCD/DAC(2010)40/REV, 12 November 2010, p. 38, para. 184, [online] http://www.oecd.org/dataoecd/28/62/38429349.pdf (Accessed 19 December 2011).

Organization for Economic Co-operation and Development (OECD) (2010b) *Do No Harm: International Support for Statebuilding*, Paris, OECD, [online] http://www.oecd.org/dataoecd/8/32/44409926.pdf (Accessed 5 December 2011).

Papaioannou, T. and Butcher, M. (eds) (2013) *International Development in a Changing World*, London, Bloomsbury Academic/Milton Keynes, The Open University.

Slim, H. (2001) 'Violence and humanitarianism: moral paradox and the protection of civilians', Security Dialogue, vol. 32, issue 3, pp. 325–39.

United Nations (UN) (1985) *Charter of the United Nations and Statute of the International Court of Justice*, United Nations, [online] http://www.un.org/en/documents/charter/ (Accessed 5 December 2011).

United Nations (UN) (1994) Final report of the Commission of Experts established pursuant to the Security Council Resolution 780 (1992), Annex to 'Letter Dated 24 May 1994 from the Secretary-General to the President of the Security Council',

Security Council Document S/1994/674, dated 27 May 1994, [online] http://www.un.org/ga/search/view_doc.asp?symbol=S/1994/674 (Accessed 19 December 2011).

United Nations (UN) (2003) *Glossary of Humanitarian Terms in relation to the Protection of Civilians in Armed Conflict*, New York, Office for the Coordination of Humanitarian Affairs Policy Development and Studies Branch, United Nations.

United Nations (UN) (2005) 'Resolution adopted by the General Assembly 60/1', *2005 World Summit Outcome*, adopted 16 September 2005, [online] http://daccess-dds-ny.un.org/doc/UNDOC/GEN/N05/487/60/PDF/N0548760.pdf?OpenElement (Accessed 19 December 2011).

Uvin, P. (1998) *Aiding Violence: the Development Enterprise in Rwanda*, Bloomfield, Kumarian Press.

Wheeler, N.J. (2000) *Saving Strangers: Humanitarian Intervention in International Society*, Oxford, Oxford University Press.

Further reading

Bellamy, A., Williams, P. and Griffin, S. (2010) *Understanding Peacekeeping* (2nd edn), Cambridge, Polity Press.

Carey, S.C., Gibney, M. and Poe, S.C. (2010) *The Politics of Human Rights: the Quest for Dignity*, Cambridge, Cambridge University Press.

Hehir, A. (2009) *Humanitarian Intervention: an Introduction*, Basingstoke, Hampshire, Palgrave Macmillan.

Klein, N. (2007) *The Shock Doctrine: the Rise of Disaster Capitalism*, New York, Picador.

Weiss, T.G. (2007) *Humanitarian Intervention: Ideas in Action,* Cambridge, Polity Press.

Human security and human development in a world of states

4

Claudia Aradau

Introduction

> People are the real wealth of a nation. The basic objective of development is to create an enabling environment for people to live long, healthy and creative lives. This may appear to be a simple truth. But it is often forgotten in the immediate concern with the accumulation of commodities and financial wealth.
>
> *(UNDP, 1990, p. 9)*

This is how the first United Nations *Human Development Report* (*HDR*) introduced the notion of **human development** in 1990. Since then, the UN has been issuing yearly reports that are centred on its Human Development Index (HDI), combining indicators of life expectancy, educational attainment and income (Johnson and Farooki, 2013). But the language used is not new. The notion of human development can be traced back to at least the 1970s, when it emerged as a reaction to state-led development plans inspired by structuralism, and the aim of promoting human wellbeing as the goal of development (Brown and Hanlon, 2013). It can also be traced back to debates in the 1980s about the restrictive focus on economic growth and the need to devise a more comprehensive notion of development. The 20-year anniversary *HDR* (2010, see Figure 4.1), titled *The Real Wealth of Nations: Pathways to Human Development* further reinforced the need for people-centred development.

Yet, as Hanlon (2013a) shows, in 1994, just four years after the first *HDR*, a new concept became central for the UN understanding of development: 'human security'. Although the UN body in charge of international peace and security is the UN Security Council, the concept of human security came from the UN Development Programme (UNDP), as it was felt to be an important supplement to human development, not only to national security. What do these changes mean and why are they important for development theory and practice?

To answer this question, this chapter is structured in three main sections. Section 4.1 is an analysis of the concept of human security and the differences between human security and human development. Here the argument is that human security and human development have different meanings: the former implies negative freedom, survival and **protection** and the latter positive freedom, empowerment and wellbeing. Section 4.2 introduces one of the most difficult global problems today, **human trafficking**, in order to understand whether it raises questions of human development or human security or both. What we do about human trafficking globally is shaped by whether we

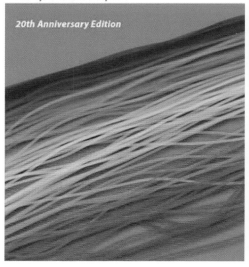

Figure 4.1   Cover of the 2010 *Human Development Report*

understand human trafficking to be primarily a question of security or development and the meanings associated with this. Section 4.3 offers an evaluation of the constraints that the international system, understood as a 'world of states', poses for both human security and human development. Given these constraints, it can be argued that the meaning of human development is transformed to fit security concerns within the international system. In summary, this chapter aims to:

- understand how human security transforms development ideas and practices
- discuss the problem of human trafficking and the challenges it poses for security and development
- identify the constraints that the international system poses for human security and development policies.

4.1   Human security: what does it mean?

Activity 4.1

The UNDP provides rankings of countries according to their HDI. Have a look at the countries listed in Figure 4.2, with very high HDI.

Are you surprised by the listing of any countries in this category? If so, why?

Spend no more than 15 minutes on this activity.

At first sight, it appears hardly surprising that countries like the USA, Singapore, Italy, the UK and Israel are all on the list of countries with very high HDIs. So you may not have found much to challenge you in this hierarchy. Now read the following media headlines about the countries just mentioned.

> USA: 'New border fear: violence by a rogue militia' (McKinley and Wollan, 2009)
>
> Singapore: '"Textbook example" of a repressive state' (Human Rights Watch, 2010)
>
> Italy: '"Nomad plan" to evict 6000 Roma people into new camps could leave hundreds homeless, says new report' (Amnesty International, 2010)
>
> Israel: 'Israeli strike on Gaza Strip amid tensions' (BBC, 2010)
>
> UK: 'Raped, beaten and helpless: UK's sex slaves' (Roberts, 2006)

HDI Rank	Human Development Index (HDI) value	Life expectancy at birth (years)	Mean years of schooling (years)	Expected years of schooling (years)	Gross national Income (GNI) per capita (PPP 2008 $)	GNI per capita rank minus HDI rank	Non-income HDI value
1 Norway	0.938	81.0	12.6	17.3	58 810	2	0.954
2 Australia	0.937	81.9	12.0	20.5	38 692	11	0.989
3 New Zealand	0.907	80.6	12.5	19.7	25 438	30	0.979
4 United States of America	0.902	79.6	12.4	15.7	47 094	5	0.917
5 Ireland	0.895	80.3	11.6	17.9	33 078	20	0.936
6 Liechtenstein	0.891	79.6	10.3	14.8	81 011	-5	0.861
7 Netherlands	0.890	80.3	11.2	16.7	40 658	4	0.911
8 Canada	0.888	81.0	11.5	16.0	38 668	6	0.913
9 Sweden	0.885	81.3	11.6	15.6	36 936	8	0.911
10 Germany	0.885	80.2	12.2	15.6	35 308	9	0.915
11 Japan	0.884	83.2	11.5	15.1	34 692	11	0.915
12 Korea, Republic of	0.877	79.8	11.6	16.8	29 518	16	0.918
13 Switzerland	0.874	82.2	10.3	15.5	39 849	-1	0.889
14 France	0.872	81.6	10.4	16.1	34 341	9	0.898
15 Israel	0.872	81.2	11.9	15.6	27 831	14	0.916
16 Finland	0.871	80.1	10.3	17.1	33 872	8	0.897
17 Iceland	0.869	82.1	10.4	18.2	22 917	20	0.928
18 Belgium	0.867	80.3	10.6	15.9	34 873	3	0.888
19 Denmark	0.866	78.7	10.3	16.9	36 404	-1	0.883
20 Spain	0.863	81.3	10.4	16.4	29 661	6	0.897
21 Hong Kong, China (SAR)	0.862	82.5	10.0	13.8	45 090	-11	0.860
22 Greece	0.855	79.7	10.5	16.5	27 580	8	0.890
23 Italy	0.854	81.4	9.7	16.3	29 619	4	0.882
24 Luxembourg	0.852	79.9	10.1	13.3	51 109	-18	0.836
25 Austria	0.851	80.4	9.8	15.0	37 056	-9	0.859
26 United Kingdom	0.849	79.8	9.5	15.9	35 087	-6	0.860
27 Singapore	0.846	80.7	8.8	14.4	48 893	-19	0.831

Figure 4.2   Human Development Index (Source: UNDP, 2010)

The inclusion of these countries amongst those having a very high HDI raises the question of what these indicators – such as life expectancy, schooling or GNIpc (Gross National Income per capita) – say about people's everyday security? It would seem not much. The people that some of the headlines talk about – irregular migrants, victims of human trafficking or the Roma – would most likely not even be counted when HDI calculations are made. Overall, the headlines show that HDI indicators do not adequately capture the qualitative character of contemporary realities for many groups of people, and may be an insufficient measure of human wellbeing as a result. Insecurity and violence are rife in areas of some of the countries that rank high on the UNDP HDI list, although as with other measures of inequality (see Hanlon, 2013b), some people are affected more than others. As Chapter 1 showed, security relates not only to warfare and conflict, but also to everyday vulnerabilities and fears. Insecurity is not necessarily located in particular parts of the world, but more widely. Insecurities and vulnerabilities are widely dispersed and unevenly distributed, although in some developing societies the combined effects of multiple vulnerabilities can lead some parts of a society to experience more than their fair share.

Insecurities can be the result of ordinary violence, everyday policies of authoritarian governments, and the legal measures of democratic ones. In the case of the USA, the *New York Times* headline draws attention to violence against immigrants perpetrated by vigilante groups that deem the state security policies to be flawed. In the case of the UK, the headline draws attention to the global problem of human trafficking, which is often spoken about as a new form of slavery. These insecurities are different from both state survival and the protection of territory. They point, rather, to insecurities that take place in times of peace, and raise questions of the security of individuals within and beyond states.

In the UN's 1994 *HDR*, entitled *Human Security*, the term was a supplement to human development. It did not simply replicate the people-centred development approach, but rather attempted to change the ways in which we think about security *and* development at the same time. Human security is thus a challenge to existing understandings of national security, which had been too focused on war and the survival of states. While such an understanding of international security appeared self-evident in the conditions of the Cold War, with its end it became increasingly difficult not to consider other insecurities and vulnerabilities. At the same time, human security drew attention to the everyday violence that many traditional understandings of human development had tended to marginalize. Countries affected by violent conflict or other forms of insecurity and vulnerability confronted challenges that were not envisaged by development measures such as the Millennium Development Goals. For the UN, the security–development nexus needed to be expanded beyond war and violent conflict on the one hand and beyond the exclusive focus on income and economic indicators on the other. Drawing on the questions raised by these headlines, Section 4.1.1 develops an argument about the differences between human security and human development. As you have seen in Chapters 1 and 2, development and security are interrelated in many ways. Security can be a condition of development, for instance. But what do security and development mean in these instances? Is security the absence of war or absence of fear? Three concepts enable our understanding of a particularly powerful meaning of human security that can be contrasted with existing definitions of human development: negative freedom, protection and survival.

4.1.1 Positive and negative freedom

Look again at the newspaper headline about the UK: 'Raped, beaten and helpless: UK's sex slaves' (Roberts, 2006). Victims of trafficking experience fear and insecurity, but the headline also evokes questions of a lack of freedom. Had the women in question been free, one can imagine they wouldn't be faced with these specific insecurities (even if they were to be confronted with different insecurities, such as unemployment or poverty, for instance). On the basis of this argument, if security is linked with freedom, then so is (human) development. The concept of human development, enshrined in the UN *HDR*s, was inspired by Amartya Sen's capabilities theory and his definition of development as freedom (Johnson and Farooki, 2013). A later *HDR* (2007) explains what this conception of development means: 'All development is ultimately about expanding human potential and enlarging human freedom. It is about people developing the capabilities that empower them to make choices and to lead lives that they value' (UNDP, 2007). Sen himself includes protective security among the instrumental freedoms necessary to development (Sen, 1999). So what is the difference between the understanding of freedom in human security and in human development, if both are about freedom?

The capabilities approach as formulated by Sen and taken up in the *HDR* is based on the distinction between 'freedom to' and 'freedom from'. This distinction between 'freedom to' and 'freedom from' or between positive and negative freedom is credited to the political theorist Isaiah Berlin. These two forms of freedom can be used to draw out a first differentiation between the logic of human security and that of human development. For Berlin, **negative freedom** referred to the absence of obstacles, interference or coercion. People are free to the extent that they are not coerced or interfered with:

> I am normally said to be free to the degree to which no human being interferes with my activity. Political liberty in this sense is simply the area within which a man can act unobstructed by others. If I am prevented by other persons from doing what I could otherwise do, I am to that degree unfree; and if this area is contracted by other men beyond a certain minimum, I can be described as being coerced, or, it may be, enslaved.
>
> *(Berlin, 1969, p. 233)*

Berlin's definition of negative freedom captures the negative effects that insecurity and fear can have on human development projects. Fear, in Berlin's understanding, would restrict what one could do – and would make us 'unfree'. Moreover, coercion and enslavement can seriously deny possibilities for agency. **Positive freedom** on the other hand is about the possibility of acting in the world:

> The 'positive' sense of the word 'liberty' derives from the wish on the part of the individual to be his own master. I wish my life and decisions to depend on myself, not on external forces of whatever kind. I wish to be the instrument of my own, not of other men's acts of will. I wish to be a subject, not an object; to be moved by reasons, by conscious purposes which are my own, not by causes which affect me, as it were, from outside. I wish to be somebody, not nobody; a doer – deciding, not being decided for, self-directed and not acted upon by external nature or by other men as if I were a thing, or an animal, or a slave incapable of playing a human role, that is, of conceiving goals and policies of my own and realizing them.
>
> *(Berlin, 1969, p. 238)*

Following Berlin's distinction, human security and human development appear clearly differentiated. Human security is about keeping fear at bay and also about preserving an area in which the individual can act freely, not coerced by somebody else. For victims of human trafficking, this would mean freeing them from traffickers and the conditions that led to them being trafficked in the first place. Human development focuses on the actions that people can pursue or their 'capabilities' for choice and a good life. In the case of trafficking, this would entail policies to ensure that victims of trafficking can pursue their own understandings of a 'good life'.

Activity 4.2

In this activity we would like you to start thinking about human trafficking.

Is human security solely about negative freedom? Think of victims of human trafficking – who acts to deliver them from exploitation?

Spend no more than 10 minutes on this activity.

Discussion

The concept of human security can in fact be expanded to encompass a positive understanding of freedom. The fact that security is focused on negative freedom doesn't mean that there is no freedom to act. Who acts to keep this area free of coercion or interference from enemies? In the case of victims of trafficking, you may have thought of the state, the police, or even NGOs and charities. Bear in mind that as 'victims' they are not likely to be in a position to exercise such agency, although former victims often become involved in NGOs, charities and support groups themselves. In addition, there are state bodies involved in intervention, such as the police force and the border agency.

The distinction between human security and human development is a bit more complicated than positive versus negative freedom. It is also about who has freedom and who doesn't. To clarify this, let us return to one of the most influential stories about security, that of Hobbes' Leviathan. You have seen in Chapter 2 that Hobbes' main concern is to protect people by eliminating the war of all against all in the state of nature and reducing it to relations between states. War is eliminated from the domestic realm by the force of government – which is now regulated by the social contract and hierarchical relations – and relegated to the international realm. In Hobbes' story, this shift is possible only on condition of limiting freedom of action with nation states. In the state of nature, however, there is no overarching authority and everybody has the freedom to act: the result of too much freedom to act is insecurity. In this story, positive freedom can actually lead to insecurity. Therefore, Hobbes argues, a sovereign is needed to limit the freedom to act and thereby create a space for freedom from others' actions.

Negative freedom shifts the power to act to a third party, a mediator or a protector. It is the Leviathan – the state – that will have the 'freedom to', the liberty to act. This can mean that the state may reduce freedom, rights and the scope for civil liberties – or even worse, that it can become an authoritarian state. Ultimately, the state can be both coercive and destructive of people's positive freedoms. Yet, even in the happy situation in which the state fulfils its mandate to ensure negative freedom, that is, the absence of coercion, and limit positive freedoms only in accordance with the law, the fear of war and the need for protection still means that there is an unequal relationship at stake, that somebody else can decide about your freedom on your behalf.

Freedom needs limits, Hobbes argues, because, left to their own devices, individuals can harm each other. Therefore, based on the need to protect and limit freedom, human security is further differentiated from human development. To have human security – or any form of security for that matter – a protector is needed. Therefore, human security is not only about the many areas in which we should be free of insecurity. It is also essentially about who will fulfil the role of protector and what happens when the state takes on that role. To have human development, however, what is needed is **empowerment**. There are many understandings of this term but a good definition has been offered by Rowlands (1995) to encompass not only the inclusion of powerless groups in decision making, but also the process through which individuals and groups perceive themselves and are able to act in the world and influence it. Section 4.1.2 looks more in depth at the difference between protection and empowerment.

4.1.2   Protection and empowerment

Activity 4.3

What does protection mean? According to the *Oxford English Dictionary*, 'to protect' means 'to defend or guard from danger or injury; to preserve from attack, persecution, harassment; to shield from attack or damage'. The feminist philosopher Iris Marion Young brings out more troublesome aspects of protection than the dictionary meaning indicates. Read the following excerpt from her article, and write down the main elements that she sees as defining protection.

Security as protection

To the extent that citizens of a democratic state allow their leaders to adopt a stance of protectors toward them, these citizens come to occupy a subordinate status like that of women in the patriarchal household. We are to accept a more authoritarian and paternalistic state power, which gets its support partly from the unity a threat produces and our gratitude for protection. …

The 'good' man is one who keeps vigilant watch over the safety of his family and readily risks himself in the face of threats from the outside in order to protect the subordinate members of his household. The logic of masculinist protection, then, includes the image of the selfish aggressor who wishes to invade the lord's property and sexually conquer his women. These are the bad men. Good men can only appear in their goodness if we assume that lurking outside the warm familial walls are aggressors who wish to attack them. The dominative masculinity in this way constitutes protective masculinity as its other. The world out there is heartless and uncivilized, and the movements and motives of the men in it are unpredictable and difficult to discern. ...

Central to the logic of masculinist protection is the subordinate relation of those in the protected position. In return for male protection, the woman concedes critical distance from decision-making autonomy. When the household lives under a threat, there cannot be divided wills and arguments about who will do what, or what is the best course of action. The head of the household should decide what measures are necessary for the security of the people and property, and he gives the orders that they must follow if they and their relations are to remain safe. ...

Feminine subordination, in this logic, does not constitute submission to a violent and overbearing bully. The feminine woman, rather, on this construction, adores her protector and happily defers to his judgment in return for the promise of security that he offers. She looks up to him with gratitude for his manliness and admiration for his willingness to face the dangers of the world for her sake. That he finds her worthy of such risks gives substance to her self. It is only fitting that she should minister to his needs and obey his dictates.

(Young, 2003, pp. 16, 18)

Spend no more than 25 minutes on this activity.

Discussion

Are you surprised by Young's account of protection and security? We often associate security with a desirable state of protection, where we see no danger or fear and where we can enjoy our freedoms. Young, however, challenges us to revisit our ideas about security. In her view, there are three characteristics of protection that we need to be aware of: subordination, benevolence and masculinity.

Subordination refers to the exchange in which the sovereign state limits the citizens' liberty to act in return for protection against fear. Think, for instance, of how European states have justified the limits on civil liberties and erasure of human rights in the fight against terrorism. In order to counter the fear of terrorism, governments have argued for the need to suspend or change the law. In the UK, for instance, successive governments have passed laws on surveillance, stop and search powers, speech offences and private data collection. Some of these laws unequally and differentially affected members of particular ethnic and racial communities, for instance Asian and black youths. These measures have been justified in the name of averting the threat of terrorism and reducing fear. Moreover, the measures were supposed to affect only a minority, those suspected of terrorism. Yet, not only were these protective measures affecting large communities, they ended up affecting everybody's freedoms. Freedoms of speech, of protest and even of taking photographs were limited.

The second characteristic of protection for Young is that of **benevolence**: the state does not need to exert violence or coercion, but responds to our desire for protection. Who wouldn't want to be free from fear and insecurity? Faced with growing insecurities in the world, many people would like to see states tackle associated problems. Yet, protection comes at a cost too, as noted above.

Thirdly, protection is characterized by **masculinity**. Protection is imagined on the model of the household, in which 'good' men protect and provide for the household members. Young argues that masculine protection divides people between 'good' and 'bad men' on the one hand and 'protector-men' and 'vulnerable women and children' on the other. The protection against fear and danger comes, therefore, at a high price – that of the freedom of choosing how to act. Citizens, for instance, are protected only as long as they are 'good' citizens, those who obey the state and do not rebel against it. Understood through the logic of protection, security is not only about fear and freedom from fear, but it is about a triad: victim, aggressor and protector. If you think of victims of trafficking – some states offer them temporary residence only if they testify against their traffickers and do not return to sex work (Aradau, 2008). These women are asked to act as 'good citizens'.

So ultimately, what makes security so powerful and desirable? Why are we ready to concede (some of) our freedoms for the promise of security in the future? This brings us to the final distinction drawn between human security and human development, namely that between survival and wellbeing.

4.2   Survival and wellbeing

As shown in Section 4.1, we tend to think of security as a state of protection in which the state wards off danger and violence. Yet, there is another way in which International Relations scholars understand security: as **survival**. While security is often thought of in relation to everyday concerns, from health to unemployment and from peace of mind to children's welfare, security is also about the fear of death. In this sense, security is the opposite of development, which foregrounds the goal of **wellbeing**.

Unlike the goal of developing the resources and capabilities that enable people to lead the lives they choose, security is about 'existential challenges, which endanger the survival of the political order' (Huysmans, 2006, p. 25). What is at stake in security threats is our existence as individuals or as a community, that is, our survival. It not only means violent death, but also the destruction of values, the effacement of a community, of nature or particular ethnic groups, nations, and so on. Therefore, security has priority over other non-security questions. It is reasoned that if we don't survive, we won't be able to deal with other problems. Similarly, if the values and identity of a community are destroyed, then other problems can no longer be dealt with. Without a state or a political community to make decisions, other social and political problems lose their importance. This implies that some problems need to be tackled urgently and have absolute priority.

Security, therefore, changes how we understand particular problems and in so doing, also changes debates about priorities. When faced with life-threatening war, education, for instance, can appear as less of a priority. It is then not surprising that when governments want to prioritize a particular policy, the language of security, threat and danger may be used. For instance, both terrorism and drugs have been incorporated in phrases like the 'war on terror' or the 'war on drugs'. The USA had its 'war on crime', 'war on poverty' and even 'war on cancer' (Simon, 2007).

Activity 4.4

Take a look at the cartoon depiction of the 'war on terror' and 'war on drugs' in Figure 4.3. What do you note about the similarities and differences between the two policies?

Figure 4.3   Andy Singer, 'War on terror' and 'War on drugs'

Spend no more than 10 minutes on this activity.

Discussion

In listing the same policies under both the 'war on drugs' and the 'war on terror', the cartoonist draws attention to the fact that there is something specific that is linked with the power of the word 'war' rather than primarily with 'terror' or 'drugs'. Indeed, security experts emphasize the interconnectedness of terrorist networks and drug cartels as well as other forms of organized crime, such as money laundering and smuggling. Sometimes, in the prevalent conditions of moral panics over social threats and dangers, the language used to characterize criminals, terrorists, hackers and other perceived dangers (including some vulnerable marginal sections of the population such as migrants, asylum seekers, refugees, trafficked sex workers, and so on) is largely the same. The language of war, which prospers in times of moral panic, is primarily about survival in the face of violence. It also implies urgency. When we face the prospect of war, we need to act with immediacy. Although poverty can also kill, it is not necessarily seen as immediate or violent, as Hanlon (2013a) has argued. Instead, poverty is more often seen by government and non-government organizations as a question of responsibility, and in particular accepting duties and obligations for providing international and humanitarian aid as well as creating the conditions for sustainable and equitable economic growth. While aid staves off insecurities and immediate fears such as starvation or, as in Haiti following the 2010 earthquake (see Chapter 5), lack of shelter, it is the commitment to sustainable and equitable longer-term solutions that will promote security.

So, although human security has at times been seen as a subcategory of human development (Alkire, 2010), the two concepts can have very different meanings. This implies that we need to think of the *security–development nexus* as a tension between human security and human development rather than simply an extension or reinforcement of one by the other.

What difference does it make if we think of human security and human development as very different concepts? First, it means that we cannot have both at the same time, that one concept needs to come first. For instance, Martha Nussbaum, who has developed Sen's theory of capabilities for human development to include the needs of women across the world, has also argued that the provision of security and the fight against violence comes first – before human development can be pursued:

> No woman in the world is secure against violence. Throughout the world, women's bodies are vulnerable to a range of violent assaults that include domestic violence, rape within marriage, rape by acquaintances or dates, rape by strangers, rape in wars and communal conflicts, honour killing, trafficking and forced prostitution, child sexual abuse, female infanticide, female genital mutilation, and sex-selective abortion. Other practices that are not as obviously violent also contribute to the atmosphere of threat in which all women live the entirety of their lives: sexual harassment, stalking, threats of violence, deprivation of bodily liberty, the under nutrition of girls.
>
> *(Nussbaum, 2005, p. 167)*

Nussbaum accepts that security is the priority, given the urgency of survival over wellbeing and the elimination of violence over empowerment. In her view, security needs to come first, development second. To speak of different issues in terms of war or security mean that they receive priority, as Ken Booth highlights.

> It makes all the difference in the world to potential victims whether rape is defined as a security issue/war crime as opposed simply to a problem to be dealt with by 'women's studies' or 'sociology'. Equally, it matters whether global poverty is categorized as a security issue/global challenge rather than an item on the agenda of 'development studies'. Rape and poverty provoke

more insecurity, day by day, for most people across the globe, than do the movements of a neighbour's army.

(Booth, 2007, p. 159)

While Booth and Nussbaum are quite optimistic about putting security first, the account of security developed in this chapter so far suggests that security changes the meaning of development. So when we finally think that the time of human development has come, given the emphasis now on the HDI and terms such as wellbeing, we may have a very different state of affairs. This is the second point about the tension between human security and human development. The meanings associated with human security and human development can change and be quite subjective. You may have started reading this chapter with different experiences of what security and development mean. The next two sections will explore this tension between human security and human development in a concrete policy context but first is a summary of the argument.

We have argued that human security and human development are different. When the language of security is used, three elements are usually associated with it: negative freedom ('freedom from'), protection and survival. Human development, on the other hand, is based on people's capacity for action, or agency ('freedom to'), self-empowerment and wellbeing. While people can be actors for their own development, security implies that a protector is needed, somebody who acts to keep us free from fear. In his assessment of the development of human security, the UN Secretary General Ban Ki-moon made clear the role of governments as protectors against threats:

> Human security is based on a fundamental understanding that governments retain the primary role for ensuring the survival, livelihood and dignity of their citizens. It is an invaluable tool for assisting Governments in identifying critical and pervasive threats to the welfare of their people and the stability of their sovereignty.

(UN, 2010)

Table 4.1 gives an overview of the differences between human security and human development.

Table 4.1 Differences between human security and human development

Human security	Human development
'Freedom from'	'Freedom to'
Protection	Empowerment
Survival	Wellbeing

Section 4.3 examines how the meanings of human security and human development influence what can be done about global problems, looking specifically at human trafficking.

4.3 Human trafficking: a global problem of development or security?

4.3.1 Developmental causes of human trafficking

> Slowly and painfully a picture is emerging of a global crime that shames us all. Billions of dollars are being made at the expense of millions of victims of human trafficking. Boys and girls who should be at school are coerced into becoming soldiers, doing hard labour or sold for sex. Women and girls are being trafficked for exploitation: forced into domestic labour, prostitution or marriage. Men, trapped by debt, slave away in mines, plantations, or sweatshops.
>
> *(UNODC, 2008, p. v)*

According to the US Annual State report, which takes up research conducted by the International Labour Organization (ILO), out of the 12.3 million adults and children in forced and bonded labour, 1.39 million are victims of commercial sexual servitude, both transnational and within countries (US Department of State, 2009). TV series, media news and even Hollywood movies have taken on the problem of trafficking. Human trafficking for sexual exploitation has received most public attention, even as it became evident that more and more people – women, men and children – are trafficked for forced labour. *Lilya 4-Ever*, one of the most celebrated films about human trafficking, tells the story of a sixteen-year old Lithuanian girl trafficked to Sweden (Figure 4.4).

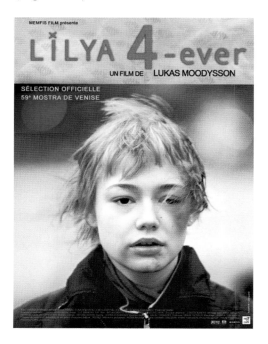

Figure 4.4   Lilya 4-Ever (Source: Venice Film Festival)

The film depicts a bleak unnamed post-socialist town in the former Soviet Union and a young destitute girl who is driven to prostitution through both poverty and deception. Stories like Lilya's, alongside reports about the numbers of trafficked persons worldwide, have drawn international attention to the problem of human trafficking since the 1990s. In 2000, the UN codified the definition of human trafficking in a protocol to the UN Convention against Transnational Organized Crime, adopted by the UN General Assembly, to mean:

> The recruitment, transportation, transfer, harbouring or receipt of persons, by means of the threat or use of force or other forms of coercion, of abduction, of fraud, of deception, of the abuse of power or of a position of vulnerability or of the giving or receiving of payments or benefits to achieve the consent of a person having control over another person, for the purpose of exploitation.

> Exploitation shall include, at a minimum, the exploitation of the prostitution of others or other forms of sexual exploitation, forced labour or services, slavery or practices similar to slavery, servitude or the removal of organs.

> *(UN, 2000)*

Activity 4.5

Figure 4.5 shows the main countries of origin and destination for victims of human trafficking. The so-called 'rising powers' (Brazil, Russia, India and China), as well as most of Eastern and Southern Europe, are areas of origin for trafficked persons.

1   What do you think would be some of the causes of human trafficking? Write down two or three answers.

2   Why do you think some countries become both the origin and destination of human trafficking? Is this just coincidence or is there something distinctive about such countries?

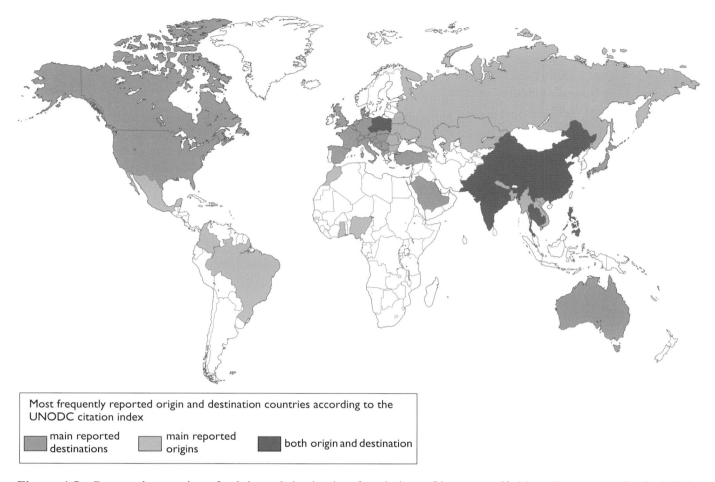

Figure 4.5   Reported countries of origin and destination for victims of human trafficking (Source: UNODC, 2006)

Spend about 10 minutes on this activity.

Discussion

1   You may have thought of poverty, inequality, conflict, gender discrimination or even authoritarian policies. These are some of the main causes of human trafficking that NGOs and international organizations have started to identify. In brief, it is a lack of human development.

2   In some of the cases highlighted in Figure 4.5, such as China, India and Thailand, trafficking can be seen in terms of outward and incoming flows. These countries have booming economies (see Mohan, 2013) that are attractive to traffickers, but also high levels of economic and social inequality, which can provide a supply of vulnerable people for trafficking to wealthier countries.

According to Pangsapa (2009), some societies become sending and receiving nations of exploitable migrant and largely undocumented workers as a result of a variety of push and pull factors of migration. For example, Thai migrants move to work in destinations as diverse as fruit picking in Scandinavia, sex work in such countries as Japan and Holland, domestic labour throughout the

Middle East, construction in Dubai and other Gulf states as well as the Iraq green zone (although in the latter case, they did not know they would be working in central Baghdad during US occupation with all the danger that implied).

Figure 4.6 Report by Anti-Slavery International (Source: Kaye, 2008)

At the same time, this migration has impacts in the originating society, causing labour supply problems in certain areas of the employment market, such as domestic labour, fisheries and factory work. Simultaneously, in conditions of global economic recession, transnational private corporations and intra-regional companies in the Southeast Asian mainland want to secure ever cheap labour in their global supply chains. Faced with labour shortages, local and national companies in these supply chains then turn to migrant and often 'stateless migrant' labour to fill these gaps at lower wages, especially in smaller subcontracting firms. For example, Pangsapa and Smith (2008) highlight how the Thai state facilitated a series of special economic zones using Burmese refugees as cheap labour in factories along the Burmese–Thai borderlands, manufacturing in areas such as the garment and leather goods trades.

A report by the World Bank defines the causes of human trafficking as residing in 'common development dimensions, such as poverty, gender inequality, unemployment, a lack of education, weak rule of law, and poor governance accompanied by socio-economic factors' (World Bank, 2009). The cover of a report by Anti-Slavery International, an NGO involved in counter-trafficking and promoting new measures to tackle trafficking and slavery internationally, conveys a similar message – *Arrested Development* (see Figure 4.6). Arrested development can mean that human trafficking is not just caused by poverty and lack of development, but it also stalls or even stops development, as victims of trafficking are caught in a cycle of exploitation.

The US Agency for International Aid (USAID) depicts a gripping and very bleak picture of the causes of human trafficking:

> Human trafficking thrives in the dark shadows of poverty, desperation, discrimination, corruption, dashed hopes and broken dreams, deceit, trickery, violence, political conflict and criminality. The victim may be female or male, child or adult, any race or ethnicity, from a country in any region of the world. Poverty and the lack of economic opportunities provide fertile ground for traffickers. Often the families of victims are deceived, but sometimes a family member is complicit in the victim's fate. In other places where the economy has collapsed, education is no protection from vulnerability and may even create false illusions of opportunities abroad. Political instability, community-sanctioned discrimination, corruption and weak rule of law shelter those who play by their own rules of deceit, trickery, and criminality. Violence in the community, crises in the home, and the low value placed on women and children can push many into the arms of waiting traffickers.

(USAID, 2006, p. 3)

Activity 4.6

Do you associate the causes described by USAID with lack of development or lack of security (or both)?

Spend about 5 minutes on this activity.

Discussion

The causes of human trafficking are largely described as developmental. Yet, alongside social and economic conditions, violent conflict, individual vulnerability and criminality could also be causes of human trafficking, which are particularly related to security and the need for protection. As men and women attempt to escape violence, they can enter trafficking rings in an attempt to cross borders and search for better lives.

Although some researchers have pointed out the agency of women and men in this movement as a form of trying to better their lives and be empowered (Agustin, 2007; Doezema and Kempadoo, 1998), most analyses of the causes of trafficking convey a rather different image of its victims. They appear passive, lacking initiative, having been coerced, constrained or deceived by their traffickers. Even if victims of trafficking may have given their consent to go abroad (be it irregularly) or even to work in the sex industry, their consent was considered to be irrelevant. For instance, the UN has identified six different ways in which victims of trafficking can be coerced and constrained and thereby have their capacity for agency reduced or destroyed (UNODC, 2008, p. 12):

- complete coercion through abduction or kidnapping
- selling a person, typically a child
- deception by promises of legitimate employment and/or entry
- deception through half-truths
- deception about working conditions
- abuse of vulnerability.

This image of helpless, young, passive victims of trafficking, which films like Lilya 4-Ever have also promoted, has triggered a different response to human trafficking. Victims of trafficking need to be protected because they lack the capacities or resources to act, are confronted with constraints on their freedoms and can even have their survival at stake. A lack of security, as Nussbaum would argue, appears as an even more acute problem than the lack of development. This has led to human trafficking becoming a global security issue.

4.3.2 Dangers of human trafficking

For many states, human trafficking appeared as 'the most menacing form of irregular migration due to its ever-increasing scale and complexity involving, as it does arms, drugs, prostitution and so on' (Laczkó and Thompson, 2009, p. 19). In this definition, human trafficking is seen as a security threat for states globally, as suggested earlier, involving as it does links with organized crime, illegal migration and drug trafficking. In the midst of a political context defined by the global threat of terrorism, where, for example, the security of the EU and its member states has acquired a new urgency (Council of the European Union, 2004), human trafficking has also been connected with concerns about terrorism. 'High profits from labour and sexual exploitation,' a report by the European Commission pointed out, 'are often subject to money laundering and may enable traffickers to engage in other criminal activities and to achieve economic, social or even political power' (European Commission, 2005, p. 4).

The EU Hague Programme on the area of freedom, security and justice spelled out the need for a more effective approach in 'cross-border problems such as illegal migration, trafficking in and smuggling of human beings, terrorism and organized crime, as well as the prevention thereof' (Council of the European Union, 2004, p. 3). Human trafficking is often placed in the top-three hierarchy of profits from international organized crime, after arms dealing and drugs. According to an ILO report by Belser (2005), the profits that are generated annually from forced commercial sexual exploitation as a result of trafficking were US$27.8 billion. As a result of these understandings of human trafficking as the danger of irregular migration, connected with organized crime and even terrorism, many states have adopted a blanket criminalization approach, focused on the deportation and even incarceration of trafficked persons, no matter what adverse circumstances forced them to become mobile.

Yet, throughout the 1990s, and particularly in preparation for the UN Protocol in 2000, many organizations and academics increasingly argued that human trafficking is not a problem of migration, crime or terrorism that concerns national security, but it is about women's (human) security. Human trafficking, it was argued, strips victims of their rights to liberty, dignity, security of person, the right not to be held in slavery, the right to be free from cruel and inhumane treatment' (OSCE, 1999). In other words, it reduces their capacity for positive freedoms. At the same time, being involved in trafficking, regardless of how they had been coerced, made these same actors criminal, pathological, subversive and dangerous. Rather than viewed as statistics, these organizations argued, human trafficking needed to be seen from the everyday lens of human life to calibrate the suffering of the actors involved and to set as a marker the complicity of factors in developed societies as contributing to the suffering of women and children in other countries.

This approach tried to promote understanding and sympathy for the situation of victims of trafficking and focused on personal stories and explanations of the pain and suffering trafficking causes. Many reports point out that victims of trafficking are subjected to violence, rape, battery and extreme cruelty as well as other types of pressure and coercion (European Commission, 2002). Amnesty International, like many other NGOs involved in anti-trafficking, has provided evidence that women are 'systematically subjected to torture,

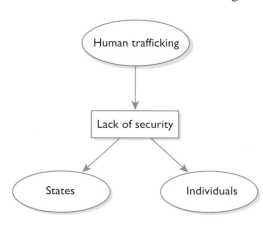

Figure 4.7   Human trafficking and the double lack of security

including rape and other forms of cruel, inhuman and degrading treatment' (Amnesty International, 2004).

The main purpose of these accounts is to promote our imaginary identification with victims of trafficking and compassion for their suffering (Aradau, 2008). Rather than potentially dangerous and involved in organized crime, illegal border crossings, falsification of papers and prostitution rings, trafficked persons were increasingly understood as vulnerable. This description nicely illustrates the arguments of international relations experts that security should be about '*real people in real places*' and not only about the state (Booth, 1995, p. 123). It also allows us to understand human trafficking not just as a lack of development but also as a lack of security. Negative freedom is limited through coercion and constraint, victims of trafficking lack agency and therefore need a protector and their survival can be at stake. Protection, freedom from coercion and survival become the defining elements of fighting the threat that human trafficking poses to women (see Figure 4.7).

Who would therefore protect victims of trafficking? The answer to this question proved to be quite a complicated one. Was it states of origin or was it states of destination? Was it international organizations or NGOs? The reason the answer was quite complicated was that states of destination were keen to deal with the problem of trafficking by returning women to their countries of origin. Even if not taking up legal procedures against them and accepting that victims of trafficking had to be freed from their traffickers and protected, states around the world – despite having ratified the UN protocol – were keen to return victims of trafficking through what they labelled as 'voluntary repatriation'. Only when victims of trafficking would testify in court against their traffickers would they be allowed to temporarily remain in the country. Such reprieves often only occur after sustained NGO lobbying with the secured statements of affected women and children, often against expert witnesses and academic specialists who had little real experience (outside the court) of the impacts of offences.

States found it difficult to change their understanding of human trafficking as largely a problem of cross-border movement and illegal migration, which could be solved by returning women to their countries of origin. The work of the USAID, the agency charged with anti-trafficking support to more than 70 countries around the world, had also facilitated the signing of agreements with the USA under which countries of origin promise to help trafficked victims safely return. This approach led to an outcry among anti-trafficking campaigners who argued that returning victims of trafficking to the same conditions they had fled would only lead to re-trafficking. Victims could not be protected, they argued, by being returned, but needed to be helped to regain their capacity to act. In many cases, returning female victims of slavery are stigmatized as outcasts and viewed as unmarriageable by their families and communities. Many are likely to have been exploited in their originating country. In addition, deportees and voluntary returnees tend to have no or few transferable skills. Women, particularly if exploited in sex work, are thus condemned to a life of ostracism and hardship just by virtue of being a victim of trafficking and slavery.

This double 'lack of security' led to two-track measures to tackle human trafficking. On the one hand, women are to be rescued in raids by benevolent police and protected from the violence of traffickers. On the other, different measures are needed to protect women as well as to bring good governance and fight corruption in the countries of origin. These measures are also likely to dissuade women from migrating or make it more difficult for them to do so. Both women and states need the intervention of a third party, an external actor, be those other states, international organizations or NGOs.

Understanding human trafficking as a global security issue – be it for states, individuals or both – also changes what needs to be done about the lack of development. It effaces the ways in which women may see mobility and migration as a possibility for human development, for empowerment and wellbeing. Protection, survival and negative freedom through the mediation of Western states and international NGOs trump positive freedom, empowerment and wellbeing as defined by women themselves. So why do security meanings and policy measures take over and transform the measures to tackle the developmental causes of trafficking? Section 4.4 offers an answer to why particular concepts are more powerful than others and therefore constrain what we can do about human trafficking.

4.4 Living in a world of states

As you have seen in Chapter 2, the international system has been dominated by states, even as other categories of actors – transnational corporations, social movements, international organizations, courts and even individual citizens – increasingly make claims at the international level and interact with other actors. States continue to hold a privileged position in both theories and practices of international politics. For Hobbes, security could only be achieved within the state and the international system was equivalent to the 'state of nature', where insecurity and anarchy reigned. Living in a state was, according to him, the only form of civilization. So for Hobbes being human was essentially linked with living in a state.

Today, the states in the international system still limit the provision of security to those who live within their borders and are deemed to be worthy of state protection. Even if membership within a particular state and national community can be obtained by some people – particularly the highly mobile and affluent – the function of the international system as a 'world of states' defined by national sovereignty limits these possibilities. Moreover, those who are thought to be dangerous to the state, its citizens or the values of the national community are to be excluded and kept at a distance. This is the case, paradoxically, for most victims of trafficking. However, there are moves to break down such narrow conceptions of responsibility tied to national territory so that states recognize their duty of care for victims of trafficking and slavery, and more broadly that citizens in countries that enslave migrants have obligations to the enslaved in their own and other societies. We can see this in campaigns to end child slavery involved in some global supply chains for Western retailers as well as the messages developed by NGOs such as Free the Slaves and Anti-Slavery International. Such a move would be analogous to citizens of developed countries recognizing that their actions have climate change implications for people elsewhere in the world and thus they have obligations beyond borders.

Activity 4.7

Nandita Sharma, a feminist academic who interviewed trafficked women in Canada, describes the situation they encountered to show the role that states play in their lives, not as a source of protection but as a source of vulnerability. Read the following excerpt and make notes on how her description of insecurity is different from the one discussed in the previous section.

> All 24 women I interviewed were ultimately deported from Canada. The last time I spoke to any of them, all were distraught at being sent to the places where they hold citizenship ... (Significantly, most of the respondents (18 of 24) declared their intent to try again even though their last attempt did involve varying degrees of coercion, deceit, and even abuse. Angry at having been captured before reaching their desired destination of New York City and now owing large sums of money, they stated that only by hiring another group of smugglers could they achieve their goals of being rid of debt and supporting themselves and their families. Thus, contrary to the idea that women who experience some form of coercion, abuse, or deception while partaking in dangerous and illegal migration routes are passive victims of trafficking, many of these women expressed their desire to live and work in the United States (or Canada) and saw the smugglers as the only people who could help them to achieve this. From the standpoint of these women migrants, then, the smugglers (or traffickers) were not the source of the exploitation they faced or their greatest danger.
>
> Thus, while they readily acknowledged the difficult and dangerous nature of their journeys, not one of the women I interviewed saw herself as a 'victim of trafficking'. Instead, their self-identity was informed largely through their courage in seeking new homes and new livelihoods across borders. None articulated the demand to 'end trafficking' but wanted cheaper, safer, and more reliable migration routes. Without exception, the demands they most often articulated were to stay in Canada (or, even better, the United States) without fear of deportation, to work, make and save money, and to be reunited with the significant people in their life.
>
> From their perspective, the biggest problem they faced was the Canadian state, most especially its immigration officials, who wanted to return them to their point of departure and, thus, force them to start anew their search for new livelihoods, this time even greater in debt. Being rescued from the smugglers/traffickers by the Canadian state – the very thing anti-trafficking campaigns advocate for – was the last thing these women wanted. They wanted to avoid the Canadian state – not be seen by it, for this meant the loss of everything for which they had worked

(Sharma, 2005, p.12)

Spend no more than 15 minutes on this activity.

Discussion

Section 4.3 highlighted that women who migrate may get entrapped in situations of violence, exploitation and insecurity. Their insecurity is seen to be either the result of developmental causes in their countries of origin or of immoral and exploitative traffickers. Sharma offers a different perspective on women's lack of security, as she argues that this is neither the result of traffickers' actions nor simply of women's vulnerability and bad governance in the developing world. The most important cause of insecurity emerges out of Canada's immigration policies. Sharma's description is valid for Europe too. Women who have been rescued by the police from brothels or massage parlours in anti-trafficking 'rescue' actions have often been incarcerated in detention centres or deported. Even when women testify against their traffickers, they are given at most 'temporary stay'. In most cases, they are returned to their countries of origin. Even if instead of 'deportation', organizations like the International Organization for Migration (IOM) speak euphemistically about 'voluntary return', irregular migrants are still returned to their countries of origin. This is the situation of most trafficked persons.

The understanding of the international as a world of states effaces both the need for transnational mobility (to escape poverty, for example) and the role that borders play in causing vulnerability and insecurity. Human trafficking is, therefore, an unintended consequence of restrictive migration policies and of the efforts to curb illegal entry and illegal employment of migrants. Koser (1998) has pointed out that the activities of smugglers and traffickers have flourished in the context of tightening political restrictions on migration. Given that legal channels of migration are more and more reduced or restricted to specific categories such as highly skilled migrants, other types of migrants need to have recourse to mediating parties. Visa regimes and restrictive immigration regulation also work in favour of the third-party organizers of trafficking as a supplementary or alternative migration system (Andrijasevic, 2003).

Holding the passport of a European Union country gives one rights to mobility and freedom of action within the EU that a holder of a Chinese passport, for instance, may not enjoy. Those who do not hold citizenship do not enjoy the same protection as citizens. In brief, human security applies to citizens differently from others who are labelled as simply human. Krause and Williams (1997) have suggested that there are different understandings of human beings implied by the category of human security:

1   *Individuals as citizens*

    This is the usual understanding of the 'human' in 'human security'. It assumes a traditional definition of the social contract, according to which the state provides security to its citizens by protecting its borders and territory. Of course, history shows there have been many cases in which protection has been withdrawn from particular individuals or categories of people: 'internal enemies' for instance or even whole categories of people such as Jews or the Roma.

2   *Individuals as persons*

This category emerges out of the limitations of the first category. As argued, there is little security for persons who move irregularly across borders. States enforce border policies and visa regimes designed to keep non-citizens at a distance. Yet, these very policies and border governance make millions of people around the world more insecure and restrict the possibilities for development if development is understood as enabling capacities or agency. For example, a report by the International Fund for Agricultural Development in 2007 showed that remittances exceeded international aid given to developing countries (BBC, 2007). Many scholars have argued that restrictive migration policies benefit developed states as it allows them to receive flexible and cheap labour. Without recognition of legal status, migrants are not able to claim labour rights, which exacerbates their insecurity.

3   *Individuals as 'members of a transcendent human community with common global concerns'*

This understanding of the 'human' makes it possible to think about global threats that do not stop at state borders. Human trafficking is one such global problem – rather than stopping at borders, it is also caused by border regimes. Another global problem that ignores borders, and is increasingly influencing migration, is environmental degradation, discussed in Chapter 5.

In an international system dominated by the state, the 'human' in 'human security' is often only regarded as the 'citizen'. Although statelessness is still one of the most insecure conditions in the world (think of the fate of European Jews in the 1930s and 1940s or that of Palestinians since 1948), states are also sources of vulnerability and insecurity. According to Krause and Williams (1997), if human security is to have any real political impact, it needs to expand the understanding of the human to encompass individuals as persons as well as members of a global community. This may entail challenging some of the meanings of security more radically. Understanding people as agents of their own empowerment may challenge the ideals of the protector, be it the state or the NGO in charge of the 'rehabilitation and reintegration' of trafficked persons. Moreover, if the actors of development are not constrained to the citizens of particular countries, but start including mobile men and women and 'world citizens', it may also entail changes in how we understand human development too.

Summary and looking forward

This chapter has shown that human security is not only a subcategory or addition to human development but its meanings are in tension with how human development is understood, respectively: negative freedom, protection and survival through the mediation of a third-party; and positive freedom, empowerment and well-being through self-organization and collective action.

When human development and human security are brought together in answer to global problems, security often appears as priority. Security comes with a sense of urgency, that is, if we don't act now it will be too late. In this interpretation, development can only happen once insecurity has been eliminated. Moreover, a lack of development becomes a source of insecurity that needs to be dealt with first. However, the question of what to prioritize as important for survival is also a question of whom to prioritize for the purposes of protection.

It is argued that a particular understanding of the 'human' in human security is prioritized in the international system, namely, that citizens are prioritized over non-citizens. In the case of human trafficking, this understanding of security effaces the insecurities created by state actions, transnational border governance and restrictive migration policies. The insecurity of victims of trafficking is, therefore, also the result of security policies. As irregular migrants, people who are trafficked are made insecure by the very states that claim to protect them in order to stop human trafficking. If we are to respond more effectively to global developmental problems, such as trafficking, we need to redefine both the 'human' of human security and human development and the meanings that prioritize survival, negative freedom and protection.

References

Agustin, L. (2007) S*ex at the Margins: Migration, Labour Markets and the Rescue Industry*, London, Zed Books.

Alkire, S. (2010) 'Human development: definitions, critiques, and related concepts', *Human Development Research Paper 2010/11*, UNDP, [online] http://hdr.undp.org/en/reports/global/hdr2010/papers/HDRP_2010_01.pdf (Accessed 31 October 2010).

Amnesty International (2004) '"So does it mean that we have the rights?" Protecting the human rights of women and girls trafficked for forced prostitution in Kosovo', [online] http://www.amnesty.org/en/library/info/EUR70/010/2004 (Accessed 5 August 2006).

Amnesty International (2010) '"Nomad plan" to evict 6000 Roma people into new camps could leave hundreds homeless, says new report', 11 March 2010, [online] http://www.amnesty.org.uk/news_details.asp?NewsID=18663 (Accessed 10 January 2011).

Andrijasevic, R. (2003) 'The difference borders make: (il)legality, migration and trafficking in Italy among Eastern European women in prostitution' in Ahmed, S., Castaneda, C., Fortier, A. and Sheller, M. (eds) *Uprootings/Regroundings: Questions of Home and Migration*, Oxford, Berg.

Aradau, C. (2008) *Rethinking Trafficking in Women: Politics Out of Security*, Basingstoke, Palgrave Macmillan.

BBC (2007) 'Remittance cash "Tops world aid"', *BBC News*, 18 October 2007, [online] http://news.bbc.co.uk/1/hi/business/7047304.stm (Accessed 10 January 2011).

BBC (2010) 'Israeli strike on Gaza Strip amid tensions', *BBC News*, 21 December 2010, [online] http://www.bbc.co.uk/news/world-middle-east-12047342 (Accessed 11 January 2011).

Belser, P. (2005) 'Forced labour and human trafficking: estimating the profits', Working Paper, Geneva, International Labour Organization, [online] http://www.ilo.org/wcmsp5/groups/public/—ed_norm/—declaration/documents/publication/wcms_081971.pdf (Accessed 13 October 2011).

Berlin, I. (1969) 'Two concepts of liberty' in Warburton, N. (ed.) *Philosophy: Basic Readings*, Abingdon, Routledge.

Booth, K. (1995) 'Human wrongs and international relations', *International Affairs*, vol. 71, no. 1, pp. 103–26.

Booth, K. (2007) *Theory of World Security*, Cambridge, Cambridge University Press.

Brown, W. and Hanlon, J. (2013) 'International action to reduce poverty development' in Papaioannou, T. and Butcher, M. (eds) *International Development in a Changing World*, London, Bloomsbury Academic/Milton Keynes, The Open University.

Council of the European Union (2004) *The Hague Programme: Strengthening, Freedom, Security and Justice in the European Union*, [online] http://www.eu.int/comm/justice_home/doc_centre/doc/hague_programme_en.pdf (Accessed 16 January 2006).

Doezema, J. and Kamala, K. (eds) (1998) *Global Sex Works: Rights, Resistance, and Redefinition*, London, Routledge.

European Commission (2002) *Trafficking in Women. The Misery Behind the Fantasy: From Poverty to Sex Slavery. A Comprehensive European Strategy*, Directorate General Justice and Home Affairs, [online] http://europa.eu.int/comm/justice_home/news/8mars_en.htm#b1 (Accessed 12 November 2004.)

European Commission (2005) *EU Action against Trafficking in Human Beings and the Sexual Exploitation of Children*, [online] http://europa.eu.int/comm/justice_home/fsj/crime/trafficking/fsj_crime_human_trafficking_en.htm# (Accessed 30 June 2007).

Hanlon, J. (2013a) 'Fear and development' in Butcher, M. and Papaioannou, T. (eds) *New Perspectives in International Development*, London, Bloomsbury Academic/Milton Keynes, The Open University.

Hanlon, J. (2013b) 'Inequality – does it matter?' in Papaioannou, T. and Butcher. M. (eds) *International Development in a Changing World*, London, Bloomsbury Academic/Milton Keynes, The Open University.

Human Rights Watch (2010) '"Textbook example" of a repressive state', [online] http://www.hrw.org/en/news/2010/01/20/singapore-textbook-example-repressive-state (Accessed 10 January 2011).

Huysmans, J. (2006) *The Politics of Insecurity: Fear, Migration and Asylum in the EU*, London, Routledge.

Johnson, H. and Farooki, M. (2013) 'Thinking about poverty' in Papaioannou, T. and Butcher, M. (eds) *International Development in a Changing World*, London, Bloomsbury Academic/Milton Keynes, The Open University.

Kaye, M. (2008) 'Arrested development: slavery and discrimination in the 21st century', London, Anti-Slavery International, [online] http://www.antislavery.org/includes/documents/cm_docs/2009/a/arresteddevelopment.pdf (Accessed 1 November 2011).

Koser, K. (1998) 'Out of the frying pan and into the fire: a case study of illegality amongst asylum-seekers' in Koser, K. and Lutz, H. (eds) *The New Migration in Europe: Social Constructions and Social Realities*, London, Macmillan Press.

Krause, K. and Williams, M.C. (1997) 'From strategy to security: foundations of critical security studies' in Krause, K. and Williams, M.C. (eds) *Critical Security Studies: Concepts and Cases*, London, UCL Press.

Laczkó, F. and Thompson, D. (eds) (2009) *Migrant Trafficking and Human Smuggling in Europe: a Review of the Evidence with Case Studies from Hungary, Poland and Ukraine*, Geneva, IOM.

McKinley, J. and Wollan, M. (2009) 'New border fear: violence by a rogue militia', *New York Times*, 26 June 2009.

Mohan (2013), p. 99.

Nussbaum, M. (2005) 'Women's bodies: violence, security, capabilities', *Journal of Human Development and Capabilities*, vol. 6, no. 2, pp. 167–83.

OSCE (1999) *Osce Anti-Trafficking Guidelines*, [online] http://www.osce.org/documents/odihr/2001/06/1563_en.pdf (Accessed 25 January 2006).

Pangsapa, P. (2009) 'When battlefields become marketplaces: migrant workers and the role of civil society and NGO activism in Thailand', *International Migration*, [online] doi: 10.1111/j.1468-2435.2009.00559.x.

Pangsapa, P. and Smith, M.J. (2008) 'The political economy of Southeast Asian borderlands: migration, development and developing-country firms', *Journal of Contemporary Asia*, vol. 38, issue 4, pp. 485–514.

Roberts, Y. (2006) 'Raped, beaten and helpless: UK's sex slaves', *The Guardian*, 2 April 2006, [online] http://www.guardian.co.uk/uk/2006/apr/02/ukcrime.humantrafficking (Accessed 10 January 2011).

Rowlands, J. (1995) 'Empowerment examined', *Development in Practice,* vol. 5, no. 2, pp. 101–7.

Sen, A. (1999) *Development as Freedom*, Oxford, Oxford University Press.

Sharma, N. (2005) 'Anti-trafficking rhetoric and the making of global apartheid', *NSWA Journal*, vol. 17, no. 3, pp. 88–111.

Simon, J. (2007) *Governing through Crime: How the War on Crime Transformed American Democracy and Created a Culture of Fear*, New York, Oxford University Press.

United Nations (UN) (2000) *Protocol to Prevent, Suppress and Punish Trafficking in Persons, Especially Women and Children, Supplementing the United Nations Convention against Transnational Organized Crime*, New York, United Nations, [online] http://www.uncjin.org/Documents/Conventions/dcatoc/final_documents_2/convention_%20traff_eng.pdf (Accessed 20 August 2003).

United Nations (UN) (2010) *Human Security: Report of the Secretary General*, UN General Assembly, New York, United Nations.

United Nations Development Programme (UNDP) (1990) *Concept and Measurement of Human Development*, New York, United Nations, [online] http://hdr.undp.org/en/reports/global/hdr1990/chapters/ (Accessed 1 November 2011).

United Nations Development Programme (UNDP) (2007) 'Fighting climate change: Human solidarity in a divided world', *Human Development Report 2007/2008*, New York, United Nations.

United Nations Development Programme (UNDP) (2010) *The Real Wealth of Nations: Pathways to Human Development,* United Nations, [online] http://hdr.undp.org/en/reports/global/hdr2010/chapters/ (Accessed 26 November 2011).

United Nations Office on Drugs and Crime (UNODC) (2006) *Human Trafficking: Global Patterns*, New York, United Nations, [online] http://www.ungift.org/doc/knowledgehub/resource-centre/UNODC_TIP_Global_Patterns_2006.pdf (Accessed April 2006).

United Nations Office on Drugs and Crime (UNODC) (2008) *Human Trafficking: An Overview*, New York, United Nations, [online] http://www.ungift.org/docs/ungift/pdf/knowledge/ebook.pdf (Accessed 30 October 2011).

US Department of State (2009) *Trafficking in Persons Report*, Washington, DC, Department of State.

US Agency for International Development (USAID) (2006) *Trafficking in Persons: USAID's Response*, USAID, [online] http://pdf.usaid.gov/pdf_docs/PDACH052.pdf (Accessed March 2006).

World Bank (2009) 'Human Trafficking: An Overview', Social Development Notes, *Conflict, Crime and Violence*, vol. 122, [online] http://siteresources.worldbank.org/ EXTSOCIALDEVELOPMENT/Resources/244362-1239390842422/6012763- 1239905793229/Human_Trafficking.pdf (Accessed 1 November 2011).

Young, I.M. (2003) 'The logic of masculinist protection: reflections on the current security state', *Signs*, vol. 29, no. 1, pp. 1–25.

Further reading

Aradau, C. (2004) 'The perverse politics of four-letter words: risk and pity in the governance of human trafficking', *Millennium: Journal of International Studies*, vol. 33, no. 2, pp. 251–77.

Columba Peoples and Vaughan-Williams, N. (2010) *Critical Security Studies: an Introduction*, London, Routledge.

Duffield, M. (2007) *Security, Development and Unending War*, Cambridge, Polity Press.

Huysmans, J. (2006) *The Politics of Insecurity: Fear, Migration and Asylum in the EU*, London, Routledge.

Sjoberg, L. (ed.) (2010) *Gender and International Security: Feminist Perspectives*, London, Routledge.

You should find academic journals such as *Security* useful for more demanding further reading.

Vulnerability in a world risk society

Mark J. Smith

Introduction

The previous chapters have shown we live in a world of insecurities, risks and conflicts, and that these pose problems for achieving development goals. However, these impacts are unequally shared and, in some contexts, specific groups of people will be more likely to experience a wider range of insecurities, and experience them in much more substantive ways (for example, victims of human trafficking, Chapter 4). This is expressed by the concept of **vulnerability**. All of us have vulnerabilities but their form and intensity will depend on such factors as our place in the life course (being young or old, for example), conditions that create impairments whether by birth or through injury, income and wealth (being poor or rich, for example), cultural or national contexts (where harm is sanctioned in some way, such as vulnerabilities for women), or structural location in the global supply chain which shape how those affected negatively by change, specific events or disasters (such as droughts and earthquakes) can respond to adverse circumstances (also see Chang et al., 2013).

Risks associated with vulnerabilities are also unevenly distributed and widely dispersed. For example, while all of us face possible negative consequences because of our vulnerability to climate change, some people will encounter greater risks according to their situation. Chapter 1 describes how security is often defined as the absence of fear, threat and war. For Ulrich Beck, a key figure in the discussions in this chapter, risks emerge not only from conflict but also in conditions of peace. They 'thrive in the centres of rationality, science and wealth, and enjoy the protection of those responsible for law and order' (Beck, 2009, p. 25–6). Such risks are not always the result of deliberate attempts to harm for they have a systematic quality; they result from the way things are organized, and are manifest in patterns and tendencies. As a result, in a sense they can be seen as politically calculable (just like the likelihood of traffic accidents, criminal activity, epidemics, famines and shortages). The way such risks are calculated is dependent on how we understand the vulnerabilities we face (as well as how we deal with the **vagaries** of market cycles and the **vicissitudes** of disasters).

Given the stakes involved, it is important to first identify the kinds of vulnerability that create such problems and then specify which vulnerabilities exist in each context. As a result, this chapter aims to:

- develop context dependent and flexible frameworks for analyzing risks, insecurities and vulnerabilities
- understand the theories of risk and vulnerability that have arisen in the 21st century

- examine the usefulness of these theories in explaining risks, insecurities and vulnerabilities in both developed and developing societies.

The chapter focuses on how theories of risk and vulnerability take account of political, economic and cultural forces that operate locally, nationally and internationally. It provides a snapshot of the complex problems the human species is likely to face in the light of discussions on security and vulnerabilities, Section 5.1 focuses on food insecurities.

Section 5.2 turns to theory. Theories of risk and vulnerability have been based on scenarios in the global North. Therefore, on the one hand, they can serve as a useful benchmark to assess the kinds of issues that can arise in societies that are currently developing and experiencing the effects of processes such as industrialization, modernization and urbanization. On the other hand, these theories may need to be modified to speak to the realities in the global South. For example, while the West experienced development at the same time as being able to draw upon the resources and peoples of the rest of the world in a relatively unfettered way, the current context places ever stricter limits on the use of resources and the extent to which labour costs can be kept low over time.

The chapter concludes by reassessing these theories in the light of such evidence. Even in the same region, with relatively similar conditions, the extent and intensity of vulnerabilities may vary considerably, as demonstrated by the contrast between Haiti and Trinidad in Section 5.4.

5.1 Food insecurities

Chapter 1 drew attention to fear in framing our understanding of security and vulnerability. How risks are framed may generate significant fears even when the likelihood of adverse events is slim and the effects manageable. To illustrate, consider the issue of **food security**. For a citizen in a developed country, food security questions are more likely to be focused on shortages in some products as part of a wider mix of dietary needs or possibly the effects of food price hikes in commodities such as meat or grain. In some developing societies, it may be essential food stuffs that are frequently in short supply, such as rice or corn, perhaps as a result of excessive exports to developed societies, causing personal suffering, economic dislocation and political conflict (see Box 5.1). Figure 5.1 provides four examples of protests and conflicts generated across the world during a period of food price hikes in 2007–10.

So we should be careful to treat risks as relative to actual conditions. The response to natural forces and rising world prices in some countries has been to restrict exports of basic food stuffs, such as Brazil and Egypt's rice exports in 2008, India's non-Basmati rice, corn and wheat exports since 2008, and Russia's wheat exports in 2010. This highlights the important national and international dimension to the management of insecurities and vulnerabilities by government intervention in the context of global food markets. In all these cases, there was an attempt to maintain availability and keep domestic prices lower than they would otherwise be to avoid social unrest.

The pressures on food security are neatly highlighted in the *Population: One Planet, Too Many People Report* (IME, 2011) that argues such pressures are exacerbated by population growth and changing dietary intakes, such as the increased consumption of meat and dairy products in emerging economies such as China. In addition, the report highlights the links between this and water security in relation to agriculture and food production (accounting for 70 per cent of global water usage) at the same time as there is increased pressure on water sources as a result of urbanization, such as in sanitation processes. Even here one of the important characteristics of vulnerabilities can be seen; they tend to cluster in the same location. The people who experience vulnerabilities to food shortages are likely to experience water shortages, if only as a result of increased localized demand and inadequate infrastructures. You will notice that we focus on insecurities and vulnerabilities here in the plural to reflect the experiences of people, especially in developing societies.

Box 5.1 The impact of rising food prices

This article was published in The Guardian on 25 October 2010.

Global food crisis forecast as prices reach record highs: cost of meat, sugar, rice, wheat, and maize soars as World Bank predicts five years of price volatility

Rising food prices and shortages could cause instability in many countries as the cost of staple foods and vegetables reached their highest levels in two years, with scientists predicting further widespread droughts and floods. Although food stocks are generally good despite much of this year's harvests being wiped out in Pakistan and Russia, sugar and rice remain at a record price. Global wheat and maize prices recently jumped nearly 30% in a few weeks while meat prices are at 20-year highs, according to the key Reuters–Jefferies commodity price indicator. Last week, the USA predicted that global wheat harvests would be 30 million tonnes lower than last year, a 5.5% fall. Meanwhile, the price of tomatoes in Egypt, garlic in China and bread in Pakistan are at near-record levels.

'The situation has deteriorated since September,' said Abdolreza Abbassian of the UN food and agriculture organization. 'In the last few weeks there have been signs we are heading the same way as in 2008. We may not get to the prices of 2008 but this time they could stay high much longer.' However, opinions are sharply divided over whether these prices signal a world food crisis like the one in 2008 that helped cause riots in 25 countries, or simply reflect volatility in global commodity markets as countries claw their way through recession. 'A food crisis on the scale of two or three years ago is not imminent, but the underlying causes [of what happened then] are still there,' said Chris Leather, Oxfam's food policy adviser. 'Prices are volatile and there is a lot of nervousness in the market. There are big differences between now and 2008. Harvests are generally better, global food stocks are better.'

But other analysts highlight the food riots in Mozambique that killed 12 people last month and claim that spiraling prices could promote further political turmoil. They say this is particularly possible if the price of oil jumps, if there are further climatic shocks – such as the floods in Pakistan or the heatwave in Russia – or if speculators buy deeper into global food markets. 'There is growing concern among countries about continuing volatility and uncertainty in food markets,' said Robert Zoellick, president of the World Bank. 'These concerns have been compounded by recent increases in grain prices. World food price volatility remains significant and in some countries, the volatility is adding to already higher local food prices.' The bank last week said that food price volatility would last a further five years, and asked governments to contribute to a crisis fund after requests for more than US$1bn (£635m) from developing countries were made.

'The food riots in Mozambique can be repeated anywhere in the coming years,' said Devinder Sharma, a leading Indian food analyst. 'Unless the world encourages developing countries to become self-sufficient in food grains, the threat of impending food riots will remain hanging over nations. The UN has expressed concern, but there is no effort to remove the imbalances in the food management system that is responsible for the crisis.' Mounting anger has greeted food price inflation of 21% in Egypt in the last year, along with 17% rises in India and similar amounts in many other countries. Prices in the UK have risen 22% in three years. The governments of Kenya, Uganda, Nigeria, Indonesia, Brazil and the Philippines have all warned of possible food shortages next year, citing floods and droughts in 2010, expected extreme weather next year, and speculation by traders who are buying up food stocks for release when prices rise.

Food prices worldwide are not yet at the same level as 2008, but the UN's food price index rose 5% last month and now stands at its highest level in two years. World wheat and maize prices have risen 57%, rice 45% and sugar 55% over the last six months and soybeans are at their highest price for 16 months. UN special rapporteur on the right to food, Olivier de Schutter, says a combination of environmental degradation, urbanization and large-scale land acquisitions by foreign investors for biofuels is squeezing land suitable for agriculture. 'Worldwide, 5m to 10m hectares of agricultural land are being lost annually due to severe degradation and another 19.5m are lost for industrial uses and urbanization,' he says in a new report. But the pressure on land resulting from these factors has been boosted in recent years by policies favouring large-scale industrial plantations. According to the World Bank, more than one-third of large-scale land acquisitions are intended to produce agrofuels.

Source: Vidal, 2010

(a)

(b)

(c)

(d)

Figure 5.1 Food protests and riots 2007–10: (a) Haiti; (b) Philippines; (c) Mexico; (d) Mozambique (Source: Worldpress.com, AFP/Getty Images, PA Photos)

Activity 5.1

Look at the images in Figure 5.1 and read the extract in Box 5.1, then make notes on the causes of food protests. List these causes in the first column of Table 5.1.

In the second column list countries that have been affected by the causes in the first column.

Please bear in mind that you can do a search for country cases and complete this activity when you have finished reading this chapter.

Table 5.1 Causes of food protests

Causes of food protests	Country cases

Spend about 15 minutes on this activity.

Discussion

The causes that you may have highlighted could include: natural disasters, climate change effects on food crops, food stockpiles falling, fuel price increases, fertilizer price increases, increased meat consumption impacting on grain supplies, national overdependence on specific kinds of food, land taken out of food production due to biofuels and urban growth, population increases, commodity price speculation on global financial markets, export of food commodities despite local shortages, and restrictions in exports for domestic reasons affecting global prices and causing shortages elsewhere. Vidal's report (Box 5.1) also highlights a crucial element of contemporary discussions on security. In particular, measures to increase energy security, such as converting agricultural land or woodlands used for both household fuel and food into biofuel production, can create new food insecurities.

In addition, food security can be impacted by political decisions by one's own and other governments seeking to maintain the social solidarity necessary to manage internal conflict. In some societies, the social tensions generated by food shortages provoke not only protests against politicians but also civil strife and war (see Chapter 2), on occasion contributing to revolutionary situations such as those in Tunisia, Egypt (Figure 5.2), Yemen, Bahrain, Libya and Syria in 2011.

Figure 5.2 Tahrir Square demonstration (Cairo, Egypt, 2011) demanding political change as a consequence of food and economic insecurities (Source: Flickr.com

At this stage, it is useful to remind ourselves that theories of security and vulnerability have been strongly influenced by experiences and social research traditions in developed societies, which are sometimes referred to as the core societies in the world system. This is discussed further in Section 5.2.

5.2   Theorising risk and vulnerability

The benchmark study of risk has been the '**risk society**' (*Risikogesellschaft*) by Ulrich Beck, subsequently developed in the 1990s (Beck, 1992, 1995). Beck argued that while the risks and hazards generated by technological knowledge, that is, development, can be anticipated, they present problems that cannot be easily addressed and for which technical solutions on their own are likely to be inadequate. He argued that the hazards of development in the 19th and early 20th centuries generated risks that were localized and calculable. As a result, the causes of a specific problem could be identified and blame appropriately attached to the cause, particularly if that was a company or industrial sector. For example, this was particularly evident for carbon-based carcinogens where it became increasingly recognized that regular contact with some materials increased the likelihood of cancer. This was apparent as early as the 18th century with chimney sweeps, later with bladder cancer following exposure to chemical dyes, through to the effects of radium, x-rays and smoking in the last 100 years.

Over time, the effects of industrial processes in polluting water and air became widely associated with cancers, respiratory diseases, immune disorders, digestive diseases, liver damage and birth deformities. In many cases, direct involvement in the productive processes or proximity to industrial sites provided a tangible basis for linking cause and effect, so maintaining clearer lines of responsibility. On environmental risks, for example, the fuel economy was regulated to ensure smokeless fuels were used in urban areas, addressing the problem of urban 'smog'. Similarly, in policy areas such as welfare and private insurance, a 'safety state' emerged by the mid-20th century where clear rules of conduct existed for attributing causal responsibility for harm, support in the face of a disaster and awarding compensation for those who experience the harsh effects of the vagaries of the market system (see Box 5.2). The reserve army of unemployed in this period was sustained through benefits so that adequate labour supplies were available for low-skilled and temporary employment and the few periods of full employment.

However, by the last two decades of the 20th century, it had become apparent that harm and risk were increasingly un-attributable and that many negative effects on people's lives were the culmination of several processes working together without necessarily identifying a single actor as a cause. For example, incidences of cancer in the vicinity of Sellafield power station in the UK could be seen as the product of natural sources of radiation, the side effects of contaminated rainfall following the Chenobyl disaster or the consequence of personal lifestyles rather than the direct result of the activities of a nuclear plant. Similarly in Japan, nuclear contamination following the 2011 earthquake and tsunami outside the vicinity of the exclusion zone in Fukushima could be attributed to the widespread use of nuclear power throughout the country and the residual effects of two nuclear explosions in 1945 (in Hiroshima and Nagasaki) at the end of World War II. Even when the cause may seem obvious to many of those concerned, proving it definitively in scientific and legal terms is always problematic.

Box 5.2 Unpredictable negative effects – the '3 Vs'

Vulnerability, associated with risks – susceptibility to injury and harm (physical and psychological), possibly even attack or wounding; openness to censure and criticism (assailable), implies some need for protection (being precarious, off-guard or exposed) and involves in some cases anticipation.

Vagaries, associated with crises – unexpected or inexplicable changes in situations (such as vagaries of the markets or climate) or behaviour, possibly including erratic wild, capricious or unusual forms of agency such as mass migration, mass protest and economic depressions.

Vicissitudes, associated with disasters – a hardship or difficulty associated with changeable conditions or characteristics; social and/or natural changes that can be favourable (fortune) or unfavourable (even neutral such as fluctuation and succession), but more likely to be associated with difficulties or hardships in common usage.

Activity 5.2

Consider which of the '3 Vs' in Box 5.2 have affected you the most – vulnerability, vagaries or vicissitudes.

Spend no more than 10 minutes on this activity.

Discussion

You will probably find that your own experiences in regard to these have been shaped by your geographical location(s), your position in terms of life span, your economic assets, whether your government has implemented policies to protect you from unusual natural events or even your proximity to sources of pollution. The key point to bear in mind is how your susceptibility to the '3 Vs' is your own context.

Initially, Beck focused on environmental impacts, arguing that their complexity, fluidity and unanticipated consequences means that even for scientific management no guarantees exist, that 'victims cannot be specified or determined in advance' (Beck, 1995, p. 10). He develops this into a critique of political decision makers in contemporary developed societies for 'organized irresponsibility' – the subtle ways in which elite groups fail to acknowledge the seriousness of the problems they face as well as how scientific knowledge leads to the treatment of danger as normal. Beck makes here the opposite argument from the one in earlier chapters: rather than using fears in order to provide protection, elites and leaders attempt to downplay risks that they cannot control.

In short, the enormous risks associated with economic production, such as in the agricultural and food sectors noted above, are translated into acceptable costs. His argument is based on a distinction in types of risks:

- *old risks*, which can include the types of conflicts that emerge from industries that have direct effects on local populations, such as contaminated water supplies

- *new risks*, which are often unanticipated, and, to the extent that they often result from many acts or activities in different places (such as in the case of air pollution), are perceived as less controllable. Most notably, these risks are associated with nuclear waste, toxic chemicals and acid rain where trans-boundary spread generates problems in international coordination and acceptance of responsibility.

This latter argument can be questioned in two ways.

- There is considerable evidence that developed societies still have numerous localized causes of harm. For example, there are over 100 years' worth of landfill sites that have since been built upon, often with public housing. In addition, the dumping and transportation of harmful materials (LULUs – locally unwanted land uses, such as the storage facilities for toxic waste) has often followed the line of least resistance. Hence it is often the communities with the least active citizenry that are the most vulnerable to insidious and creeping local forms of pollution.

- The most damaging forms of industrial pollution have not been eliminated but merely moved elsewhere, into developing countries; so the West or developed nations can only be described as post-industrial in the sense that the negative effects of industry have been redistributed on a global basis. Countries that specialize in capital goods production, financial services, microelectronics and cultural industries still need raw materials transformed into goods first.

5.3   Old risks and the rustbelt

A good example of the ongoing legacy of old risks can be seen in the remaining waste from industrial development in the Great Lakes Region of the USA and Canada (Figure 5.3).

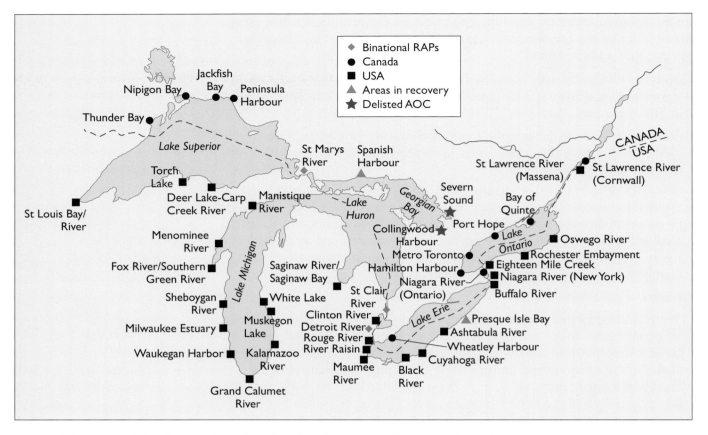

Figure 5.3   Map of the Great Lakes, Canada/USA (Source: Environment Canada)

This example raises questions about the long-term effects of development and what kinds of development are appropriate. The toxic dumps on the US side of the Great Lakes Region around Chicago, Detroit, Cleveland and Buffalo highlight the important role of cities that linked the extraction of raw materials across the Midwest and in western New York State, USA, with shoreline manufacturing processes and easy access to maritime transportation through the lakes and canal systems to the St Lawrence river and the Atlantic Ocean. As a result the industrial zones of the Midwest were responsible for a significant proportion of the USA's economic growth and development. Today these manufacturing areas are more often described as the 'Rustbelt'.

Cities like Detroit, Cleveland and Buffalo were founded on manufacturing, in particular chemical processing and automotive construction, as well as a range of industries tied to the export of resources from the Midwest, such as grain milling in Buffalo. In 1910 Detroit and Buffalo were respectively the ninth and tenth largest cities in the USA. Detroit would continue to prosper as a result of the car industry but by the 1980s, deindustrialization was generating similar effects in each city. With the movement of industries elsewhere, especially with outsourcing to developing countries, the knock-on effects to supply companies ensured that employment rates fell significantly, resulting in depopulation and high levels of unemployment. By 2000 each city had an infrastructure constructed for at least twice the current population levels and an inadequate tax base to maintain crumbling transport routes and sanitation systems, built in more prosperous times. In the 2009 *American Community Survey* (US Census Bureau, 2009), these three cities were cited as the three poorest in the USA in terms of the percentage of the population living below the official poverty rate – Detroit (36.4%), Cleveland (35.0%) and Buffalo (28.8%). The effects of deindustrialization have been called '**development in reverse**' but there is an additional factor. As well as the social problems that result from these processes, such as high crime, urban blight and poverty, these cities have a mammoth task in coping with 80 years of industrial waste (Glauber and Poston, 2010). This is particularly evident in Buffalo and surrounding districts (see Figure 5.4).

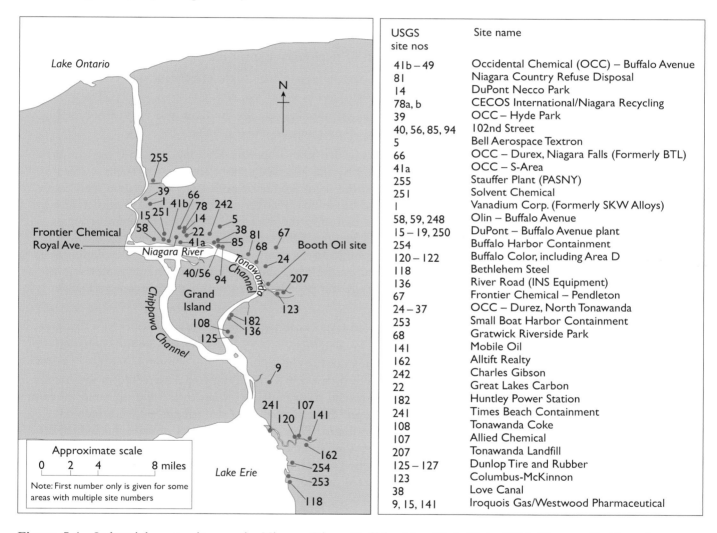

USGS site nos	Site name
41b – 49	Occidental Chemical (OCC) – Buffalo Avenue
81	Niagara Country Refuse Disposal
14	DuPont Necco Park
78a, b	CECOS International/Niagara Recycling
39	OCC – Hyde Park
40, 56, 85, 94	102nd Street
5	Bell Aerospace Textron
66	OCC – Durex, Niagara Falls (Formerly BTL)
41a	OCC – S-Area
255	Stauffer Plant (PASNY)
251	Solvent Chemical
1	Vanadium Corp. (Formerly SKW Alloys)
58, 59, 248	Olin – Buffalo Avenue
15 – 19, 250	DuPont – Buffalo Avenue plant
254	Buffalo Harbor Containment
120 – 122	Buffalo Color, including Area D
118	Bethlehem Steel
136	River Road (INS Equipment)
67	Frontier Chemical – Pendleton
24 – 37	OCC – Durez, North Tonawanda
253	Small Boat Harbor Containment
68	Gratwick Riverside Park
141	Mobile Oil
162	Alltift Realty
242	Charles Gibson
22	Great Lakes Carbon
182	Huntley Power Station
241	Times Beach Containment
108	Tonawanda Coke
107	Allied Chemical
207	Tonawanda Landfill
125 – 127	Dunlop Tire and Rubber
123	Columbus-McKinnon
38	Love Canal
9, 15, 141	Iroquois Gas/Westwood Pharmaceutical

Figure 5.4   Industrial waste sites on the Niagara River, Buffalo, New York State, USA (Source: Smith and Pangsapa, 2008)

These 'brown field' sites (i.e. previously developed sites) include materials as lethal as dioxins, PCBs (polychlorinated biphenyl) and even nuclear waste left over from parts of the Manhattan military project in the 1940s. In one infamous case, a working class housing estate and a school were built on top of 21 000 tons of dioxins. Love Canal is a neighbourhood of Niagara Falls,

New York. The canal from which it takes its name was an 1890s project intended to produce hydroelectric power from the Niagara River. However, the canal site was abandoned and used as a general dumping ground for petrochemical and military wastes, until it was bought in the 1940s by the Hooker Chemicals and Plastics Corporation (later a subsidiary of Occidental Petroleum). Between 1942 and 1952, Hooker used the canal as a waste disposal landfill site for toxics, including the following chemicals:

- dioxin – a toxic chemical known to cause cancer, birth defects, mutations and foetal death in laboratory animals
- tetrachloroethylene – a carcinogen that also exhibits adverse effects on the central nervous system and liver
- chloroform – a carcinogen that also causes narcosis of the central nervous system, destruction of liver cells, kidney damage and cardiac problems
- dichloroethane – a carcinogen whose toxic effects include central nervous system disorders, depression, anorexia, and kidney and liver dysfunction
- lindane – a carcinogen that also attacks the liver and central nervous system and causes adverse reproductive effects.

Once full, the site was sealed with impermeable clay. In 1953, the site was compulsorily purchased by the Niagara School Board against the wishes of Hooker Chemicals and the legal advice of both sides (who were well aware of the potential for future litigation). Hooker set the notional price of US$1 for the deal and secured a clause in the contract that absolved them of legal liability. During the 1950s and 1960s, an elementary school and affordable housing projects were built on and around the site with the foundation work damaging the clay seal on the toxic dump. Thus the contamination was a result not of poor storage but of subsequent building, drainage and sewer construction.

In the 1970s, reports on health problems, water contamination and chemical residues prompted an investigation into the area. The first environmental assessment, in 1976, resulted in the Environmental Protection Agency (EPA) conducting its own investigation in 1978. With toxics detected in the homes in 'Ring 1', the area nearest to the canal site, New York State declared a health emergency and evacuated those residents whose properties were located immediately above the dump. This alarmed residents outside the immediate evacuation area, who initiated a campaign through the Love Canal Homeowners' Association (LCHA) led by Lois Gibbs, to have the whole neighbourhood evacuated and for those responsible for the problems to be held accountable. However, the area was not fully evacuated until 1980, when the area was declared a national emergency by President Carter.

The LCHA highlighted the potential risks of various toxics produced by Hooker Chemicals. The company was involved in the manufacture of both plastics and pesticides, such as DDT and mirex (both of which are listed in the 'dirty dozen' chemicals covered by the Stockholm Convention on persistent organic pollutants, which came into force in 2004). Resulting toxic materials included dioxins and PCBs (also listed under the Stockholm Convention), as well as benzene and chemicals with solvent properties or uses in the extraction of oils from plants, such as chloroform, trichloroethane and tetrachloroethane. These and other toxics were believed to have had detrimental health effects on residents and also on the children who attended the 99th Street elementary school, which was in close proximity to the waste storage site.

However, the slow official response to the situation resulted from contradictory scientific evidence. The New York State Department of Health did not find convincing evidence to suggest that residents' health was being affected. Ad hoc community research conducted by campaigners in conjunction with health experts from the local university nevertheless highlighted a range of symptoms among residents that contradicted this advice. By collating evidence from residents, they observed effects in the community including higher than average birth defects and miscarriages, a range of illnesses, short stature in children and some indications of borderline nerve exposure effects (Steegman, 2001). However, this research was not conducted in terms of the established procedures of epidemiology (the study of factors affecting the health and illness of populations). As Steegman indicated, 'Science here was a long way from the clinic and laboratory, with all their securities. It was rough, fast field work at a low level toxic exposure site – a situation designed to promote borderline results and disagreements' (ibid, p. 181). The evidence produced by local activists was challenged on the basis that it came from an overly difficult questionnaire and unsystematic blood tests (some of which were lost), and that data collectors were not trained and there was no control group. There were also difficulties in acquiring the medical records of residents, inhibiting medical condition verification.

In response to questions about the miscarriage and birth defect rates outside 'Ring 1', Lois Gibbs developed the 'swale hypothesis'– that the health effects of the dump appeared to be concentrated along filled-in stream beds and wet areas (swales and ponds). However, this hypothesis was also rejected to begin with, on the grounds that it was initially tested on residents who knew about it and thus might have over-reported their symptoms (contrary to the double-blind methodology of epidemiology). The swale hypothesis was accepted by the Department of Health in 1979, resulting in a partial evacuation of children and pregnant women. In 1980, the EPA highlighted the possibility of chromosomal damage; this alarmed the community, who took two EPA investigators hostage. The EPA chromosomal study remains uncorroborated, but it generated a greater sense of urgency for political actors. By October of that year, the homes in the neighbourhood outside 'Ring 1' had been bought by the state authorities and the evacuation was completed.

It later emerged that voles – a potential indicator of the toxic effects – were largely absent from the area in the vicinity of the dump and that those present had lindane in their tissues (Christian, 1983), suggesting that the activists' findings had been correct. However, the debate did not end there. Subsequent medical studies cast doubts on the reasons for the evacuation; for example, one finding showed that the cancer rates of Love Canal residents matched those of other New York State residents outside New York City. In addition the Lewis Thomas Panel, appointed by the state governor to establish a basis for reconciling scientific disagreement on Love Canal, announced that the EPA chromosome study was 'a paradigm of administrative ineptitude' (Thomas et al., 1980, p. 13). The panel criticized activist research for using small samples, using anecdotal evidence and assuming that health problems were present without clear proof, and claimed that causal attribution had not been demonstrated.

Further questions have since been raised about the qualifications of this panel for assessing field research in a community environment and, given the potential vulnerabilities of residents, the pressures to come up with policy-relevant information and explanation makes lengthy peer-review processes inapplicable. As a result of the dispersal of the residents following the evacuation, the generation of conclusive scientific evidence was no longer feasible and by the 1990s the Love Canal Revitalization Agency (LCARA) was able to initiate the sale of housing projects in the outer ring of the evacuation area.

As this case study shows, even in the context of a developed society, **scientific uncertainty** raises considerable problems in relation to anticipating and devising appropriate responses to vulnerabilities and risks. The complexities of conducting epidemiological studies within the context of the presence of various environmental hazards ensure that, even if correlations can be identified, the plausibility of a particular explanation depends on a number of factors:

- the strength of the association
- the presence of consistent empirical findings in different situations
- specificity (that a specific source is the likely cause of a particular health effect)
- evidence of a temporal relationship (that the cause is followed by the effect)
- presence of a biological gradient or dose–response curve (that where there is greater exposure to an identifiable cause, this generates a greater effect on the health of those affected).

Clearly, causal attribution for pollution associated with old as well as new risks can be difficult to establish. Much depends on the plausibility of existing scientific knowledge, its coherence with existing explanation of the pathogenic causes of illness, and the support of experimental and/or other evidence. In the end, all the actors involved discovered they bore responsibility. The company that placed the waste in storage did not want the site to be subject to redevelopment, and in its land-sale negotiations with the Niagara School Board attempted to limit its liabilities as part of the contract of sale. However, in 1995, after 16 years of litigation about the relationship between ownership and negligence, Occidental Petroleum finally agreed to pay the EPA US$129 million to cover the costs of the clean-up of the site within the terms of the 'Superfund' law.

Yet Hooker Chemicals/Occidental Petroleum were not the only responsible actors. The legal advisors for both parties indicated that the development project should not go ahead, given the risks involved for residents and the possibilities of future litigation, but the Niagara School Board went ahead with its development plans for the area despite this advice. The political authorities in New York State and at the federal level in the USA procrastinated on the need for action, on the grounds that the evidence of contamination was insufficient or fell short of epidemiological procedures. Ultimately, the full evacuation ordered by President Carter was initiated not on the grounds of a comprehensive public health analysis but as a result of media reports of the possibility of chromosomal damage amongst residents.

This one case among many in developed societies indicates the persistence of vulnerabilities associated with development, especially as a result of heavy industry and manufacturing. Moreover, it highlights the longevity of established risks and hazards, even if they are not added to in the same way in the present. So in developed societies there are some inaccuracies in Beck's idea that old risks are giving way to new ones. While environmental regulation in developed countries ensures that certain forms of productive processes no longer take place or impose strict measures on toxic waste in terms of storage and disposal, that is, attempting to reduce risk, there remains a long legacy of toxic materials in landfills, many of which have since been subject to redevelopment. In addition, many products in Western markets can only be produced through lax regulation of the same toxics and hazardous materials in countries outside developed societies. In short, localized risks in the developed world have been exported as part of outsourcing production. And developing societies must manage these risks and vulnerabilities differently, as the negative effects of these development processes combine with the generation of new, insidious trans-boundary risks such as the negative effects of climate change. In addition, the emergence of the international trade in e-waste (electronic waste, such as redundant computers, mobile phones, televisions, and so on) makes risks more mobile than hitherto experienced, intensifying the burden for countries in the global South. It is to these situations we will direct our attention in the next section.

5.4   Vulnerabilities in Haiti and Trinidad: 'small is dangerous, small is vulnerable'

The adoption of the promise of neoliberalism, that development will meet all social needs through the opening up of markets to free competition and capital mobility, has helped generate new lifestyle aspirations in developed countries. The desire to acquire ownership of comfortable homes, high-performance luxury vehicles, air conditioning and central heating and readily available fast food or to consume meat and milk as a significant part of dietary intake is not simply restricted to the emerging middle classes. When 15 per cent of the world's population have enjoyed these benefits for so long, you might even consider it to be hypocritical to deny such things to the other 85 per cent. Iain Wilkinson captures the dilemmas faced by the majority of the world's people in the following extract.

> For the majority of the 85 per cent of the world's population living in developing societies, everyday life consists of a bitter struggle for existence under conditions where a combination of hard physical labour, malnutrition and disease are always threatening to bring their lives to a premature end. ...

> Almost half of the world's population live on less than US$2 a day, while a fifth live in absolute poverty on less than a US$1 a day. The life expectancy of a child born in sub-Saharan Africa is less than half that for that of a child born in the United States (World Bank, 2006). In developing societies, a third of all children suffer from malnutrition and it is estimated that 30,000 die each day from preventable causes (UNDP 2000/2001, 2003). ... In developing societies, 21 per cent of all deaths and 70 per cent of childhood deaths are caused by pneumonia, diarrhoea, malaria, measles and malnutrition. The vulnerability of the poorest populations to such diseases is understood to be largely attributable to the fact that 1.1 billion people lack access to safe drinking water and 2.6 billion lack adequate sanitation facilities.
>
> *(Wilkinson, 2010, p. 4)*

Added to this misery, there has also been a significant change in the organization of international trade due to the industrialization and technological development of countries like India and China, generating a resource grab on a scale not seen before. For Jonathan Fenby, 'China is rich in people but short of resources and wants to have stable supplies of its own rather than having to buy on the open market' (cited in Arnott, 2010). If resources disappear from the open markets, this potentially reduces supply (resulting in higher prices) and increases vulnerability to market fluctuations for all those still dependent on open markets, developed and developing alike.

The export of labour exploitation, environmental degradation and questionable technologies from the developed to a less regulated developing world still means that old risks are relevant, again raising a question over Beck's analysis. In addition, rapid development and modernization in some developing countries without an equitable distribution of the benefits of development can raise its own difficulties and possibly generate major social and political conflicts (see Chapter 1).

However, while Beck's distinction between old and new risks may be debatable, his subsequent work (1999, 2005, 2009) does usefully explore the meaning of **global risks**. In the *World at Risk* p. 13, he distinguishes *three logics or types of global risk* that together interact to shape the world as we understand it in the early 21st century – 'environmental crises, global financial risks and terrorist threats' (Beck, 2009, p. 13). He distinguishes terrorism from the other two because he argues that it occurs as a result of deliberation and purpose rather than by chance. It need not concern us here as it was discussed in earlier chapters, that some states have used international cooperation on security with Western countries concerned with terrorist threats as additional leverage in environmental and economic negotiations.

Environmental crises, such as those associated with climate change, and financial risks are portrayed as the 'contingent side effects of decisions in the process of modernization' (ibid, pp. 13–14). In addition, Beck seems to increasingly accept that older risks such as industrial hazards and war as well as natural disasters such as earthquakes are becoming more intertwined with these new forms of global or world risk. These are bold and interesting claims about the forces at work in processes of development so this section will examine these ideas in concrete circumstances, where old risks, natural disasters and new global risks interact and possibly intensify the effects of each.

It is impossible to cover all kinds of risks and vulnerabilities so instead this section will focus on the cases of Haiti and the twin island nation of Trinidad and Tobago in the same region, the Caribbean. These two contexts face many common problems but their specific circumstances and development pathways have created different outcomes, impacted by their small size (Griffith, 2003; McGregor et al., 2009). In global politics, the size of a country is important; as Anthony Payne argues, 'small states have been largely unsuccessful in asserting their own interests in global politics … vulnerabilities rather than opportunities are the most striking consequence of smallness in global politics' (Payne, 2004, p. 623).

5.4.1   Haiti

The Republic of Haiti occupies the Western side of the island of Hispaniola, shared with its neighbour the Dominican Republic (see Figure 5.5).

Haiti was the first independent Caribbean nation to emerge and did so through revolutionary action inspired by French Jacobinism and revolutionary fervour in Europe (James, 1963; Granger, 2003). However, the resulting republic reinforced the inequalities of the sugar plantation system and suppressed autonomous movements. In the words of C.L.R. James, 'no economic regime has had so demoralising an effect as the sugar estates' (cited in Henry and Buhle, 1992, p. 163). The resulting history of Haiti has authoritarianism interspersed by periods of foreign occupation by the USA. The Marron Inconnu statue in Port-au-Prince indicates the potential for self-governance, but remained only an inspiration to a call to arms as metaphorically depicted in the use of the conch shell (see Figure 5.6; Mohammed, 2009, pp. 336–69).

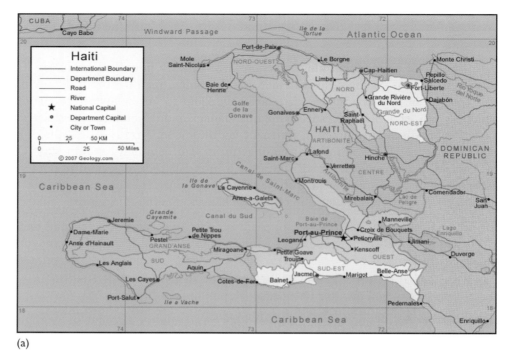

Figure 5.5 (a) Haiti's political departments; (b) the impact of the 2010 earthquake (Source: Travelinghaiti.com)

(a)   (b)

Figure 5.6 Marron Inconnu, Port-au-Prince, Haiti: (a) pre-earthquake and (b) post-earthquake (Source: Google Images)

Haiti has been understood in both negative and positive ways in relation to development. Certainly, it has significant problems and remains at the bottom of the Human Development Index (HDI) in the Americas, with specific practical difficulties that result from multiple vulnerabilities clustering in one location. In fact, Haiti has been unfortunate to witness a difficult convergence of vulnerabilities, vagaries and vicissitudes (see Box 5.2) in the 21st century.

Historically, poor governance was a part of the rule of the Duvalier regimes of 'Papa Doc' (1957–71) and 'Baby Doc' (1971–86), where power was wielded through a militia, the 'Tonton Macoutes'. This generated human rights violations and created a culture of political corruption to the extent that Haiti has been described as a kleptocracy, a political system based on systematic and organized theft from the people. Following a period of coups and conflicts between contending successors, René Préval and Jean-Bertrand Aristide, the latter came to dominate a corrupt political regime with an interest in the income from narcotics. As a result, an international peacekeeping force was deployed in 2004 and Préval came to power in 2006. Political instability, embedded corruption and a tendency towards rights abuses alongside intervention from other governments, such as the USA, provide a particularly difficult context for social and economic development (see Chapter 3 on the role of peacekeeping).

When we examine the experiences of Haitian citizens we can identify a range of vulnerabilities in their lives. Haiti has a poor record in terms of life expectancy, adult literacy and living standards as well as high levels of morbidity and mortality, as a result of severe poverty. The country also has a record of being involved in the illegal transnational narcotics trade, sex tourism and trafficking, plus it became one of the earliest to experience HIV/AIDS infections on a substantial scale in the mid-1980s. In this case we can see evidence of a range of vulnerabilities, especially for women and children, in a society with few signs of political accountability and transparency. The Food and Agriculture Organization also designated the country as economically vulnerable.

So, on top of deep-seated vulnerabilities, Haiti was probably least able to cope with the vagaries generated by the effects of the transatlantic banking crisis in 2007–9 and the severe vicissitudes of the 2010 earthquake, although some of the negative effects could have been mitigated through alternative development strategies and more effective support from international aid. In this context, the disaster of January 2010 came as a significant blow. The 7.0 magnitude earthquake on the Western outskirts of the administrative capital, Port-au-Prince, which was followed by a series of over 60 aftershocks, had an impact not seen since the 18th century. There remains the prospect of additional quakes in the near future, including another seismological event of a similar magnitude. The long-term potential for disasters in the region is a constant issue, whether these are severe weather events (such as hurricanes), earthquakes or tsunamis.

On the day of the earthquake, 12 January 2010, many of the key members of the government and the UN stabilization taskforce were still in their offices. As a result of poor construction and regulatory failure, many buildings collapsed in a concertina manner or, worse still, with a pancake effect, and the chances of survival were very slim (Figure 5.7). Consequently, the death toll was very high and a high proportion of the over 200 000 estimated victims included many of the civil servants, business managers and a range of other professionals, such as teachers and doctors, who would have been crucial actors in reconstruction. A quarter of government administrators died in the event and the emerging commercial sector in the capital was devastated. The loss of both public and private sector expertise will take many years to replace. In addition, collapsed concrete buildings cannot be salvaged, so vast areas of the city could only be rebuilt from scratch after the rubble was cleared. Even one year after the earthquake, between 15 and 20 million cubic metres of debris awaited removal or recycling in Port-au-Prince.

Figure 5.7   The devastation of the 2010 earthquake and its aftermath (Source: Ideal Stock/Alamy)

Activity 5.3

To aid consolidation of the material on Haiti, summarize the major factors generating vulnerability in Haiti based on the above information. Now try to list them in order of priority – which factors would you consider the most significant for the citizens of Haiti?

You may also find it useful to consider whether Haiti's difficulties are caused by vulnerabilities, vagaries and/or vicissitudes (see Box 5.2).

Spend no more than 10 minutes on this activity.

The humanitarian and relief NGO sector already had a sizable presence due to the long-term vulnerabilities of many in the country and the cycle of vagaries through a succession of crises. Many NGOs survive on natural disaster relief funding from governments and the general public. As a result it has been estimated that around 10 000 NGOs have been operating in Haiti since the disaster, roughly one NGO for every 1000 Haitian citizens. Most are doing essential work, providing medical care (including support for the many amputees), educational skills and temporary housing, and laying pipes for water supplies. Some pursue less selfless goals such as religious conversion and dubious child adoption programmes.

A new problem emerged, however, as NGOs became a de facto government service but lacked the capacity to coordinate effectively even at a basic level, such as ensuring the water pipes of one project could fit onto the well construction equipment of another. Inevitably, the sanitation system, such as it was, collapsed, and the combination of human waste in cramped camps and the human bodies remaining un-retrievable in many former buildings, created the conditions for disease, most evident in the cholera outbreak in 2010–11. As a result, with over one million homeless in an environment with a heavy rainfall season and in a hurricane zone, the camp dwellers faced the greatest challenges. In addition, women and children in the camps were particularly vulnerable to rape, abuse and other forms of exploitation.

The combination of political, social and natural factors in accounting for the dire situation of many Haitians is remarkable. Yet the conditions that led to this situation are not unique and hence the need for a comparison with another Caribbean society that has developed more successfully, following a different pathway involving higher levels of political agency.

5.4.2 Trinidad

The 'two island' Republic of Trinidad and Tobago (see Figure 5.8) also exists in an earthquake zone; in this case over the faults from the southern edge of the Caribbean plate and South America, with the larger island Trinidad being 14 miles from Venezuela. The focus here is on Trinidad, which has a major advantage over Haiti in that it is located just outside the hurricane zone and has the biodiversity of both a Caribbean island and the mainland (Trinidad was joined to the mainland in the last ice age). The major economic difference for this country is the existence of oil and gas fields as well as largely untapped oil flats and asphalt lakes.

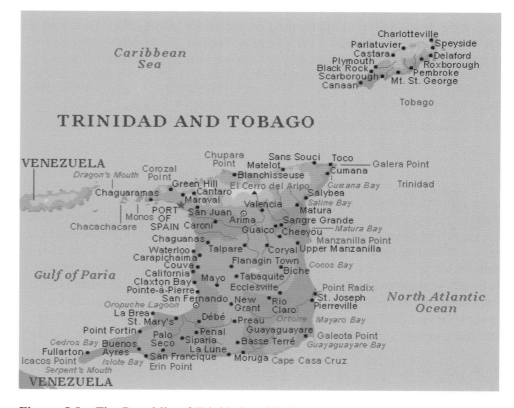

Figure 5.8 The Republic of Trinidad and Tobago

The effects of this can be seen in the relative GDP of Caribbean islands (see Figure 5.9), although it should be emphasized that the majority of Trinidadians have incomes well below this average.

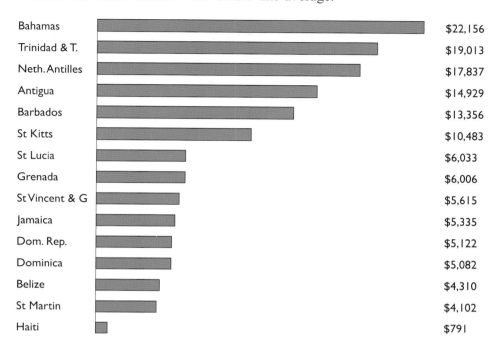

Bahamas	$22,156
Trinidad & T.	$19,013
Neth. Antilles	$17,837
Antigua	$14,929
Barbados	$13,356
St Kitts	$10,483
St Lucia	$6,033
Grenada	$6,006
St Vincent & G	$5,615
Jamaica	$5,335
Dom. Rep.	$5,122
Dominica	$5,082
Belize	$4,310
St Martin	$4,102
Haiti	$791

Figure 5.9 GDP per capita in the Caribbean region (Source: IMF World Economic Outlook Database, 2009; cited in Nickenig, 2010)

Until the earthquake, both Haitian and Trinidadian citizens demonstrated common occupational patterns with many citizens holding down a range of occupations, usually a combination of paid work and self-employment. In both societies, educational processes have a key role in providing opportunities for social mobility, although the range of occupations for graduates in Trinidad was wider even before the disaster. This is especially important for the social mobility of women, in that there is a significant gender imbalance in education throughout Caribbean countries. At the University of the West Indies in Trinidad, 80 per cent of graduates are female and in the region it is often higher (85 per cent in Jamaica). Aspirations for men are largely tied to the motor trade, electronics and music. The scale of a small island places certain limits on professional advancement in the public sector, with a low turnover of staff. This generates two options: migration or self-employment.

Both Haiti and Trinidad have high emigration levels and many families in each country are in part dependent on the regular remittances from family members working overseas, especially from those in the USA. According to Nurse (2004), this tendency towards emigration often includes a disproportionate share of citizens with tertiary education qualifications, leading to a Caribbean brain-drain. For those that stay, it is common for a household to become a place of work drawing on the range of skills of its members. A typical example would be a house offering sewing, typing and children's language classes. Other examples include home dental practices, where patients queue on the front porch, 'Roti' or 'Doubles' bar (making local street-food delicacies along with beer), and car parts specialist. Families typically build the lower floor of a house in stages, moving into back rooms and setting up shop in the front, building a second floor for living and expanding the commercial premises as the ventures generate income. This adds to the vulnerability factor in housing construction, since the foundations are rarely adequate for the form of multi-floor dwelling that eventually results. Many take years to move from concrete frames to full use (see Figure 5.10) but, as in Haiti, these often hazardous buildings are also testimony to enormous efforts of people with limited resources to provide their own families with material wellbeing and improve their social status as a result of their own efforts and hard work. This highlights how inaccurate some stereotypes of the citizens of developing societies can be. In both cases, they face considerable obstacles (based on different and similar vulnerabilities) but at the same time deploy personal and collective resources to considerable effect.

Figure 5.10   Warren Street grocery and prospective new home above

In Trinidad, as in Haiti, environmental degradation is common and for the most part unregulated. Environmentally, Haiti's natural resources have been pillaged and tropical forest is now only between one and four per cent of land area, resulting in soil erosion. Ecological restoration would be a long-term solution. In Trinidad, encroachment of its remaining of the remaining wild areas is increasing, especially near the major cities as homes are constructed up the mountain sides and across the savannah in the north. Elsewhere, deforestation is a major problem due to clearance for agriculture, quarrying and hunting, producing a proliferation of forest fires in the dry season. While quarrying in sites of 150 acres or above would be subject to regulation through the Environmental Management Authority, no quarries are currently on that scale – so, in the words of one community activist, 'De whole island is a quarry!'

This is where Trinidad's development pathway differs in remarkable ways from that experienced in Haiti, enabling protection against some of the same vulnerabilities and risks. In the context of parliamentary democracy and some circulation of power, a vibrant and active **civil society** has also developed that can act as a break on some of the more negative aspects of development and create opportunities for exposing political corruption and holding the government accountable. As a result, there are many campaigns for social reform (see Figure 5.11) and environmental protection, and some willingness in the government to offer public consultation mechanisms ranging from stakeholder meetings to public events. One possible conclusion that can be drawn here is that the presence and continued robustness of civil society action generates a degree of social solidarity that avoids some of the distress and alienation resulting from social exclusion, as seen in the obstacles to capacity building in Haiti. This also provides mechanisms that mitigate against risk.

(a)   (b)

Figure 5.11 (a) News coverage of the La Brea coalition campaign against the La Brea Aluminium Smelter project; (b) generating responsibility through civil society: break the silence campaign on child abuse, incest and HIV infection (Source: Trinidad & Tobago Guardian)

In addition, the 'People's Partnership Government' elected in 2010 is seeking to develop a greater measure of regulatory oversight in certain policy areas, such as initiating fines for talking on the phone while driving, in conjunction with corporate sponsored activities, such as Digicel's 'On de road, off de phone' public information campaign. Other areas, for example conservation measures, are reinforced by partnerships between NGOs and communities, such as Nature Seekers and the replacement of the turtle egg (supposedly an aphrodisiac) and turtle meat trade with ecotourism revenues in Matura Natural Park. The problem of excessive hunting of wild animals for bush meat has been acknowledged recently for the first time by NGOs as a significant problem in terms of both biodiversity loss and the cause of forest fires that are used to drive the animals towards the recreational hunters from Port of Spain. The species most under threat are usually the most popular in wild meat dishes that are available at 'the best calypso parties' and celebrated in soca parang music in songs such as 'Wild meat riddem' and 'Want ah piece ah pork' (such as Quenk or the Agouti rodent which is considered to have the taste of pork and is popular in celebrations from November through to Christmas), as well as in the rapso parties leading into carnival. On water issues and beach conservation, partnerships between academics, research institutes and NGOs have been especially important in informing policy on pollution and deforestation problems (which also have an effect on water quality).

Figure 5.11(a) shows civil society groups such as 'Citizens for Social Justice' and the 'Square Deal Resident Association' successfully overturning a planning decision to construct a major aluminium smelter plant (by the transnational company Alcoa) in the south-east at La Brea. The residents who had farmed the land there and developed community livelihoods based on forest resources were evicted from the land in 2004, only later discovering that they should have been consulted, compensated and re-housed. The campaign they launched drew together civil society organizations in a broad alliance which discovered that an Environmental Impact Assessment (EIA) had been invented as part of the process of approval. This campaign generated pressure on the government to take more care to follow the rule of law rather than to seek shortcuts in the name of development, and later contributed to a change in government at the subsequent election. In the words of Anslym Carter, community spokesman, 'we fought a good fight, to bring the smelter to where it is now, buried, it is dead' (Smith and Pangsapa, forthcoming). However, they were still fighting for compensation six years on from the first eviction and had lost a great deal in terms of community livelihoods.

Trinidad has not yet had to cope with the vicissitudes associated with disasters experienced by Haiti or for that matter, the other small island nations that are in the hurricane zone for half of the year. They have, however, had to deal with the vagaries associated with economic crises at different times, such as the international financial crisis. Hence their main concern is the vulnerabilities created by these conditions. Unlike Haiti, Trinidad and Tobago's international links with the Commonwealth (the product of its colonial history) helped focus attention on the political conditions that generate risks and vulnerabilities. As a member of the Commonwealth, this has been a focus since the 1977 meeting of Commonwealth Finance Ministers and subsequently at CHOGM 1979. The *Overcoming Vulnerability Report* in 1997 and initiatives such as the Commonwealth/World Bank task force focused on how to address vulnerable developing countries in terms of insularity, diversification, disasters, capacity building, investment and the role of trade. Trinidad also has considerable multi-cultural and multi-faith diversity, with European, African and Asian minorities (based on waves of migration – colonial, African, South Asian Indian and Chinese), and anglophone roots as a military base. Its relationship to the USA, as a business opportunity for trade and investment, is quite different to that of Haiti where the USA has been primarily concerned with security and the drugs trade. In addition, the English language in Trinidad may have proved to be advantageous regionally, compared to the francophone orientation of Haiti, particular when considering trade and investment.

In Trinidad, transnational business involvement has primarily been concerned with the oil and gas sector, with the revenues channelled into state-sponsored industrial infrastructure projects and state enterprises. This has created some social inequalities but crucially has established a 'multi-cultural middle class' which, in conjunction with an active civil society, has led to the emergence of a fairly open political class as opposed to an **oligarchic political class** or elite. In addition, governments have tried to ensure some distribution of the benefits of development throughout society and heavily subsidize some basics, such as fuel for cars. As a result, when there have been crises there is an orderly succession based on elections rather than military intervention and street riots. Moreover, the 2010 coalition government led by Kamla Persad-Bissesar seeks to encourage private responsibility (alongside state regulation) as an answer to vulnerabilities. Nevertheless, dangers remain. In August 2011, the prime minister declared a state of emergency and an economically damaging curfew, until November, as a result of a crime spree in some areas. Maintaining an active and free civil society is not a pre-given certainty, when governments decide other forms of security should take precedence.

Activity 5.4

To aid consolidation of this material on Haiti and Trinidad, note down the conditions that you think generate vulnerability in each country. What are the key differences between the two? These could be related to physical geography, history, politics, relationships with other countries, etc. Incorporating your study of other chapters, why do you think Trinidad has been able to develop a stronger civil society than Haiti to manage risks and conditions of vulnerability?

Spend no more than 10 minutes on this activity.

Haiti clearly lacks some of the advantages found in Trinidad, and remains volatile but it is useful to examine its options. Without oil and gas, the alternatives are minerals, with some copper and gold deposits, and agricultural exports. However, given the decline in soil quality and low prices in many fruit and vegetable crops suited to the Caribbean, then the latter are unlikely to be transformative and much of the environment will need nurturing for a generation before it returns to former levels of productivity. With a population of over ten million there is the potential for opting for the 'outsourced manufacturing development pathway' although this will depend on very large external investments in infrastructure for transport, power and water. It will also depend on subsidies for transnational corporate investment and guarantees of security. One individual measure that the international community could contribute is to continue to subsidize gas and oil imports to reduce production costs in Haiti.

The solution would be a raft of measures probably combined with the expectation that a significant proportion of the population will migrate overseas. The success of all of the above depends on political stability and control of corruption, especially since many economic projects in the past 20 years turned out to be scams, such as pyramid schemes. Internal and external investments will probably need to be underwritten by the international community until trust is restored. So long as the richest one per cent of the population owns half the country's wealth then resentments and the feeling of injustice are likely to undermine post-disaster reconstruction. Successful development depends then on the perception of a fair distribution of its benefits and awareness of its costs alongside protection of vulnerable people and habitats.

Summary and looking forward

As this chapter has shown, the risk society and the emerging idea of global risk highlight some important processes. Certainly in cities such as Detroit, Cleveland and Buffalo in the USA's 'Rustbelt', old risks and new ones are clearly interconnected, demanding new kinds of development strategies such as creating post-industrial entrepreneurialism as well as maintaining state intervention. This has been achieved to a limited extent in Buffalo where some of the worst aspects of urban blight have been avoided through investment in the cultural industries in areas such as the renovation of Canal Side. In developing societies, such as Haiti, we can also see the close connections between old and new risks (Hillman and D'Agostino, 2009; McGregor et al., 2009). In Trinidad, the combination of old and new risks are mitigated by political development, plus the economic benefits of oil and gas exploration. These factors ensure that some of the worst effects on the most vulnerable, which have been witnessed in Haiti, have been avoided. However, there are plenty of vulnerabilities that still need to be addressed in terms of who bears a disproportionate share of the costs of industrial development, and addressing the urgent problems of water and air pollution as well as protecting the remaining ecological reserves.

This chapter has proposed a different way of analyzing these vulnerabilities, risks and development. Rather than thinking about development as a linear process, we propose to recognize its diversity and context dependence. Instead of considering the story of risk as a transition between manageable old risks and difficult to contain new risks we need to start from the assumption that both are likely to be present but their combined effects may vary depending on the context. As a result, we can assess multiple vulnerabilities and how they can converge in some situations, which can produce humanitarian crises as well as more focused problems that emerge in the unique conditions of each place. The story of risk and vulnerability that has emerged in the West also needs to be supplemented by an account of institutional formation and the political as well as the socio-economic conditions for development. In this way, policy formation is likely to be able to take account of the contingencies in risk susceptibility, the range of vulnerabilities in both developed and developing societies and how to build institutional capacity that is more resilient in the face of uncertainty and unexpected change.

References

Arnott, S. (2010) 'Fears of Chinese land grab as Beijing's billions buy up resources', *The Independent*, 2 October 2010.

Beck, U. (1992) *Risk Society: Towards a New Modernity*, London, Sage Publications.

Beck, U. (1995) *Ecological Politics in an Age of Risk*, Cambridge, Polity Press.

Beck, U. (1999) *World Risk Society*, Cambridge, Polity Press.

Beck, U. (2005) *Power in a Global Age*, Cambridge, Polity Press.

Beck, U. (2009) *World at Risk*, Cambridge, Polity Press.

Chang, D., Farooki, M. and Johnson, H. (2013) 'Culture, livelihoods and making a living' in Papaioannou, T. and Butcher, M. (eds) *International Development in a Changing World*, London, Bloomsbury Academic/Milton Keynes, The Open University.

Christian, J.J. (1983) 'Love Canal's unhealthy voles', *Natural History*, vol. 00, issue 8, pp. 8–16.

Glauber, B. and Poston, B. (2010) 'Milwaukee now fourth poorest city in nation', *Journal Sentinel*, 28 September 2010, [online] http://www.jsonline.com/news/wisconsin/103929588.html (Accessed 28 November 2011).

Granger, D. (2003) 'Deye mon gen mon: the Haitian Revolution and the discourse on race and slavery' in Barrow-Giles, C. and Marshall, D.D. (eds) *Living at the Crossroads: Issues in Caribbean Sovereignty and Development*, Kingston, Jamaica, Ian Randle Publishers.

Griffith, I.L. (2003) 'Security and sovereignty in the contemporary Caribbean: probing elements of the local–global nexus' in Barrow-Giles, C. and Marshall, D.D. (eds) *Living at the Crossroads: Issues in Caribbean Sovereignty and Development*, Kingston, Jamaica, Ian Randle Publishers.

Hillman, R.S. and D'Agostino, T.J. (eds) (2009) *Understanding the Contemporary Caribbean* (2nd edn), Boulder CO, Lynn Rienner.

Institution of Mechanical Engineers (IME) (2011) *Population: One Planet, Too Many People Report*, London, Institution of Mechanical Engineers, [online] http://www.imeche.org/knowledge/themes/environment/Population (Accessed 29 October 2011).

James, C.L.R. (1963) *The Black Jacobins: Toussaint L'Ouverture and the San Domingo Revolution*, New York, Random House.

McGregor, D., Dodman, D. and Barker, D. (eds) (2009) *Global Change and Caribbean Vulnerability: Environment, Economy and Society at Risk*, Kingston, Jamaica, University of the West Indies Press.

Mohammed, P. (2009) *Imagining the Caribbean: Culture and Visual Translation*, Oxford, Macmillan.

Nickenig, 2010.

Nurse, 2004.

Payne, A. (2004) 'Small states in the global politics of development', *The Round Table*, vol. 93, no. 376, pp. 623–35.

Smith, M.J. and Pangsapa, P. (2008) *Environment and Citizenship: Integrating Justice, Responsibility and Civic Engagement*, London, Zed Publications.

Smith, M.J. and Pangsapa, P. (forthcoming) *Environment and Citizenship in the Caribbean*.

Steegman, A.T. Jr. (2001) 'History of Love Canal and Suny at Buffalo's response: history, the university role, and health research', *Buffalo Environmental Law Journal*, vol. 8, no. 2, pp. 174–94.

Thomas, L., Farber, S.J., Doherty, R.A., Kappas, A. and Upton, A.A. (1980) *Report of the Governor's Panel to Review Scientific Studies and the Development of Public Policy on Problems Resulting from Hazardous Wastes, October, 1980*, Albany, New York Department of Health.

United Nations Development Programme (UNDP) (2000/2001) *Human Development Report 2000/2001: Attacking Poverty*, New York, UNDP.

United Nations Development Programme (UNDP) (2003) *Millennium Development Goals: a Compact Among Nations to End Human Poverty*, New York, UNDP.

US Census Bureau (2009) *American Community Survey*, [online] http://factfinder.census.gov (Accessed 30 October 2010).

Vidal, J. (2010) 'Global food crisis forecast as prices reach record highs', *The Guardian*, 25 October 2010, [online] http://www.guardian.co.uk/environment/2010/oct/25/impending-global-food-crisis (Accessed 29 October 2011).

Wilkinson, I. (2010) *Risk, Vulnerability and Everyday Life*, London, Routledge.

World Bank (2006) *World Development Report 2006: Equity and Development*, New York, Oxford University Press.

Further reading

Beck, U. (2009) *World at Risk*, Cambridge, Polity Press.

McGregor, D., Dodman, D. and Barker, D. (eds) (2009) *Global Change and Caribbean Vulnerability: Environment, Economy and Society at Risk*, Kingston, Jamaica, University of the West Indies Press.

Payne, A. (2005) *The Global Politics of Unequal Development*, Basingstoke, Hampshire, Palgrave Macmillan.

Wilkinson, I. (2010) *Risk, Vulnerability and Everyday Life*, Oxford, Routledge.

You should also find it useful to search a journal database such as Academic Search Complete using key words such as 'vulnerability' and 'insecurity'.

Perspectives on development, technology and the environment

6

Peter T. Robbins

Introduction

The overarching aim of this chapter is to consider a number of different development perspectives, and in particular how they interface with thinking on technology and the environment. A related task is to examine some specifically environmental ideas and to consider their impact on technology and development. Key themes throughout the consideration of these perspectives are the extent to which development is seen as intrinsically positive or negative, and whether the development context is shaped by internal or external factors.

In summary, the aims of this chapter are to:

- explore some of the different perspectives on development, especially in terms of how they relate to thinking on technology and the environment

- investigate some perspectives on the environment and look at their relationship to technology and development.

Development is concerned with understanding the ways in which people in poorer countries try to improve the quality of their lives. As such, it is an important and evolving area of investigation. Since the leaders of most poorer or 'developing' countries try to raise standards of living by industrializing, development perspectives tend to look at the social, political and environmental effects of this economic and technological process.

The development field has gone through a number of theoretical and substantive changes since 1949, the date of US President Harry S. Truman's speech to the UN calling for it to develop the 'underdeveloped regions of the world', which is commonly seen as the start of the 'age of development' (Sachs, 1992; cf. Gilman, 2003). At the start of this 'age', from the 1950s to the 1970s, the beliefs of neoevolutionists that societies evolve was the dominant thinking, informed by an earlier generation of classical 19th century thinkers whose ideas originated in the work of Charles Darwin. They argued that to adapt and survive, societies require the ability to acquire the cultural attributes and structures of modern societies, such as a wide outlook on the world, rewards based on achievement, cities, a class system, bureaucracy, democracy and modern science and technology.

The modernization perspective of development emerged in the 1960s. Section 6.1 examines this perspective, which is still pervasive today. Subsequent sections deal with two perspectives that have offered major critiques of modernization: Section 6.2 looks at dependency and Marxism, while Section 6.3 examines post-development.

6.1 Modernization

Modernization theory was influenced by the liberal economic school that believed in the importance of free markets to address the social welfare needs of people more effectively than the state. Within much modernization thinking was a technological determinist view; so called because technology was seen to determine the shape of society. White (cited in Peace, 2004) produced an analysis of human history measuring social advancement in terms of the rates and methods of energy consumption of any given group. He also proposed a law of development, which linked energy consumption, energy efficiency and cultural development.

$$P = ET$$

Here E represents energy consumed per capita per year, T is the efficiency in utilizing the energy harnessed and P equals the degree of development defined in terms of products that are produced.

For him, there were five sequential stages of development, ranging from:

1   the least developed where people use their own bodies' physical power to produce useful energy

2   to the next stage where they use animals

3   then a stage focused on biomass that occurs alongside advances in agricultural production technology

4   followed by a stage defined by extraction, development and use of natural resources-based fuels, such as oil, gas and coal

5   a final stage in which power is derived from nuclear technology (White, cited in Peace, 2004).

Along with technology, modernization thinkers were particularly focused on the transmission of modern attitudes and values for the success of development. Lerner (1968) saw modern techniques in communicating ideas through the mass media as important, and Inkeles and Smith (1974) outlined a distinct set of attitudes, such as a readiness for new experience and openness to innovation, that would 'make men modern'.

Rostow (1971, see Figure 6.1) in *The Stages of Economic Growth* presented a work that was both a kind of social history of how economic growth took place in the North and a treatise on how development should unfold in the South. Rostow postulated that growth occurred in five stages:

- Traditional society
- Preconditions for take-off
- Take-off
- Drive to maturity
- High mass consumption.

Figure 6.1 Walt Rostow, US economist

According to Rostow, traditional society has limited production capability and its science and technology capabilities are not modernized.

Preconditions for take-off, which in Rostow's view is analogous with 'development', is the next stage and occurred in Europe roughly in the 17th and 18th centuries when 'modern science began to be translated into production functions in agriculture and industry' (Rostow, 1971). In other words, new production technologies emerged from scientific advancement. This happened alongside expansion of trade and development of the economic system.

Rostow argues that the stimulus for take-off in Britain and the USA (roughly the 18th and 19th centuries) was largely, but not wholly, technological; certainly new industries developed and agriculture intensified. But it was three factors working together – the build-up of capital, the surge of technological advancement, and a politically powerful group that saw this modernization as important – that was crucial.

In the fourth stage, the 'drive to maturity', the growing economy 'drives to extend its technology over the whole front of its economic activity' (Rostow, 1971). Historically, Germany, the USA, Britain and France went through the drive to maturity stage towards the end of the 19th century. The composition of the economy changes as new techniques come on stream and old industries die away. Goods that used to be imported are now produced locally, and new modern ideas and values emerge and replace traditional views. Technology became more refined and more complex and specialization occurred. At that point the economy moves beyond the industries that initially powered take-off, and applies the 'fruits of the most advanced modern technologies' (Rostow, 1971) to its growth.

The final stage, the age of high mass consumption, was achieved by the USA in the 20th century, and after World War II by most of Western Europe. In this stage, industrial sectors began to produce consumer durables like cars and refrigerators. Agricultural employment declined while industrial and services sectors grew. In the early 20th century the large-scale standardized production system developed by Henry Ford producing the Model T automobile allowed mass production of cars and other commodities, making them affordable to many people. At this point, continuing to develop technological capabilities was still important, but alongside this were growing concerns about social welfare, and the development of the welfare state.

The modernization perspective saw technology as a basis for social change. In other words, modernization thinkers saw responses to new technologies generating social change. For example, sometimes technologies are developed, but not widely used, then they are picked up by groups of people, at which point they become transformative. Innovation and technology are closely connected for modernization thinkers in the sense that scientists and engineers come up with ways to make life better for people and this interrelates with social change. To give a contemporary example, mobile telephones have had an important impact in the global South, where there is limited telecommunications infrastructure. They have connected diverse communities, giving people access to information, allowing for education and business transactions, and therefore development, to take place.

For Rostow, while countries go through the five stages in a linear fashion, the length each stage takes may vary from country to country. The model emphasizes development success rather than failure, which is the basis for the critique advanced by the dependency perspective that followed it.

The clearest and most persuasive conceptual critique of the modernization perspective was that advanced by Gusfield (1967), whose analysis focused on the problematic way tradition and modernity were often seen as opposed in modernization thinking. He argued that tradition, modernity and innovation actually often evolve together in the South. He also suggested that there was an implicit assumption in many modernization writings that Western political and economic forms were somehow the inevitable outcome of development and seen as superior to those in the South. In so doing, he questioned the linearity of much modernization writing, and the Darwinian notion that a society evolves more or less in a straight line from a traditional to a North American or European modern society. He wrote that modern ideas do not always replace traditional ones, as those of us who live in Europe or North America witness when our friends make their way to the homoeopathist or use Chinese herbal medicine. Another key point he made was that modernization does not necessarily weaken tradition, as evidenced by the traditional Muslim pilgrimage to Mecca in Saudi Arabia becoming possible for many Muslims worldwide through the mass availability of long-haul air travel.

Activity 6.1

Pause here and reflect on the relationship between modernization and tradition. In the country where you live, did modern ideas of economy and society replace traditional ones?

Spend no more than 10 minutes on this activity.

Discussion

I grew up in the USA, which is where many variants of the modernization perspective were developed. While I think that in the 1950s, when the modernization idea was formulated, modern economic and social forms were replacing traditional ones, in later decades we saw both the persistence of tradition, in terms of religious views and church attendance for example, and the resurgence of tradition. For example, farmers' markets had been disappearing in the early to mid-20th century and they are now flourishing in many towns and cities as people choose to buy local, organic produce directly from small-scale farmers rather than go to a supermarket and purchase food produced by large-scale chemicals-based agri-business.

While modernization was subjected to substantial criticism in the 1970s, due also to the failure of most countries in the South to develop in the ways predicted by its advocates, it was revived in the 1990s mainly to understand the developmental successes of countries like South Korea or city states like Singapore, Taiwan and Hong Kong (Crenshaw et al., 2000; Ingelhart and Baker, 2000; Kim, 1994). Modernization scholars also developed a specific environmental variant of the perspective around that time, ecological modernization (Spaargaren and Mol, 1992; Mol, 1995; Hajer, 1995), which argued that protecting the environment was not incompatible with meeting people's wants and needs through development. Ecological modernization had its roots in the thinking of Joseph Huber (2004) who believed that industrial society develops through three stages:

1 the industrial breakthrough

2 the construction of industrial society

3 the ecological shift of the industrial system.

This shift occurs through a process he calls 'super-industrialization', which involves the development of new technologies. Furthermore, like other modernization thinkers, he sees ecological modernization as a historical phase of modern society (Mol, 1995). Ecological modernization also draws upon what is called the 'reflexive modernization' school (Beck et al., 1994), specifically Beck's risk society (Beck, 1992, see Chapter 5). Beck emphasized the unperceivability of many 'high consequence' risks, such as climate change, or nuclear radiation, which we cannot smell, hear, see or feel.

Reflexive modernization has at its core the idea of reflecting back – so, for example, a pessimistic variant of this perspective might argue that it is modern institutions and modern life that have produced environmental problems, which those same institutions must now try to correct, and they may not manage it. A more optimistic variant of this idea, however, is that institutions do reflect back and in so doing they can adapt to incorporate environmental challenges through practices like developing environmental technologies, reusing materials and producing goods and services more efficiently.

Thus, these optimistic ecological modernization writers believe that 'the only possible way *out* of the ecological crisis is by going further *into* the process of modernization' (Mol, 1995, p. 42; italics in original). For them, ecological problems can be dealt with in a rational way by incorporating economists, natural scientists, corporate executives, engineers, sociologists, policy makers and others to deliver integrated **sustainable development** solutions (see Box 6.1). Indeed, for many, sustainable development – which, at its most basic, is that which meets current needs without compromising the ability of those in the future to meet theirs – is paradigmatic of ecological modernization (Hajer, 1995). This was criticized by some as treating sustainable development as a technological–managerial project. Such a project consists of the promotion of an agenda that argues that sustainability can be managed simply through a switch to greener technology, and otherwise pursuing 'business as usual'. This agenda does not allow for the interrogation of whether resource use needs to be more fundamentally restricted in order for sustainable development to be achieved (Robbins, 2001).

Box 6.1   Sustainable development

Although there have been many definitions of sustainable development, the one many people use was formulated by the Brundtland Commission in 1987, which defined sustainable development as development that 'meets the needs of the present without compromising the ability of future generations to meet their needs' (WCED, 1987). Since then, many writers have pointed out that sustainable development does not just have an environmental component, but also has economic and social features. In environmental terms, this means that natural resources should not be overused. In social terms, people should work together to address common goals for human health and wellbeing. In economic terms, social and environmental sustainability goals are economically feasible. These are referred to as the three 'interdependent and mutually reinforcing pillars' of sustainability, which evolve in an interlinked and interdependent way (United Nations General Assembly, 2005).

6.2   Marxism and dependency

Opposition to modernization's view of development, particularly in the 1970s and 1980s, centred on Marxist perspectives (see Kiely, 2013), and theories of 'dependency'. This model tried to explain why the global South was not developing as the North had in the past (see Figure 6.2).

DEPENDENCY THEORY

Figure 6.2 Developed countries represented as a baby dependent on developing countries (Source: Art of Lijen)

Writing in the 19th century, Marx himself was not particularly focused upon what came to be known as the South since his main interest was in the development of capitalism, which was an undeveloped or nonexistent model of economic organization in other parts of the world. Marx, like modernization theorists, used an analysis of history to propose that society evolved through various stages including primitive, slave-based, feudalist, capitalist, socialist and finally communist society. Whereas Marx saw change being driven by conflict between social classes of 'haves' and 'have-nots', Schumpeter, and other Marxist theorists of technological innovation, saw economic change being driven by innovation, concentrating economic power in the hands of the innovators and causing increased conflict between those innovators and their competitors (Schumpeter, 1976 [1942]).

Marx also had a technological determinist viewpoint in seeing technology driving societies. In *Poverty of Philosophy* (Marx, 1955 [1847]), he wrote that 'the windmill gives you the society with the feudal lord, [and] the steam mill the society with the industrial capitalist.' If space allowed, a larger discussion could be had here about Marx's concept of the forces of production that include technology, broadly defined, and how it relates to the base and superstructure model of society. Similarly, his views on the environment were defined in class terms, and he generally saw the development of capitalism and destruction of the environment going hand in hand. For example, he saw capitalist agriculture as progress in 'the art, not only of robbing the labourer, but of robbing the soil; all progress in increasing the fertility of the soil for a given time, is a progress towards ruining the lasting sources of that fertility' (Marx, 2007 [1867], p. 555). This line of thinking was continued with later Marxists, such as Gorz (1980, 1994) and Bahro (1986), who saw economic and environmental problems advancing alongside capitalist development. As Gorz said, 'we are dealing … with a crisis of capitalist accumulation, intensified by an ecological crisis …' (Gorz, 1980, p. 21; cf. Pepper, 1993).

The main advancement and critique of modernization during the 1970s and 1980s was the neo-Marxist dependency perspective, which emphasized imperialism (Mohan, 2013; Brewer, 1990), that is, the idea of how powerful capitalist groups or countries take over and exploit the less powerful for their own ends. It anticipates the withering of nation states and the predominance of the capitalist global economy, and saw a polarization between richer and poorer areas as the inevitable outcome of the development of capitalism.

Frank (1971, 1978) progressed the notion of Baran (1973) that it is actually in the interests of capitalists to keep the South as an 'indispensable hinterland', through a system of metropolitan and satellite areas where surplus is extracted. World metropolitan areas, for example the USA, underdevelop (or exploit and weaken) satellite areas, such as Mexico. Mexico City in turn takes advantage of smaller cities in Mexico, which then exploit rural areas.

Underdeveloped areas are forced through this process of underdevelopment to use sub-standard or obsolete technology. Wallerstein advanced dependency ideas further in *The Modern World-System* (Wallerstein, 1974; 1980; 1989), where he conceptualized a world capitalist system based on core (consisting of the richest countries), periphery (the poorest countries) and semi-periphery (the countries that were experiencing some development successes), in which wealthier areas underdeveloped poorer ones.

None of these theories really addressed the issue of social class, however, and when they did, they saw dominant classes in the South as simply 'comprador', from the Portuguese 'to buy', giving the impression of local elite groups that are bought by global interests. Thus, the focus of dependency perspective writers on exogenous factors impacting on development (i.e. factors from the 'outside', in this case the dominance of the metropolitan or core areas) made them vulnerable to critiques from orthodox Marxists such as Laclau (1971), who argued that the concept of relations of production, between capitalists and workers, was being ignored. Similarly, Brenner (1977) and Sender and Smith (1986) suggested that dependency writers' emphasis on underdevelopment neglected class struggle inside countries. Most audacious of all was the view of Warren (1980) that indigenous capitalist classes are emerging all over the world, and what the South needed was not less capitalism but more.

By the early 1990s, there was wide agreement that much development thinking was in a theoretical impasse. Neo-Marxist and orthodox Marxist critiques had largely cancelled each other out, and the collapse of communism in the Soviet Union signalled the end of many direct links to Marx in the literature (Ghosh, 2001). In the latter half of the decade, a wide range of post- and alternative development approaches, critical of the very (Western) idea of development began to emerge.

6.3   Post-development and ecocentrism

Writers from the post-development perspective direct their criticism at development itself, including both its capitalist and socialist varieties (Escobar, 1995; Rahnema and Bawtree, 1997; Nanda, 1999; Ziai, 2007). They base their analysis on the effects of President Truman's 1949 speech, which called for a 'brave new program for making the benefits of our scientific advances and industrial progress available for the involvement and growth of underdeveloped areas' (Sachs, 1992, p. 6). From that moment onwards, they argue, people in the South were defined as underdeveloped and in need of assistance. Development, and its associated technological innovations, became an obstacle to improving conditions of the poor and underprivileged, rather than a means to transform them. Post-development is a restatement of the critique of the modernization perspective, noted above, but it is also a powerful interrogation of the notion that industrialization is necessary for countries in the global south.

In this sense post-development represents also a critique of the dependency perspective, which has no quarrel with modernization as an abstract concept, but attacks the idea that it can occur for less powerful countries through allowing competition and free markets to reign supreme. Modernization as an abstract concept informs, therefore, the neoliberal, structuralist and interventionist approaches that are frequently encountered in development debates (Hanlin and Brown, 2013) even though these approaches have distinctively different takes on how to bring it about. Post-development, on the other hand, has greater synergy with the people-centred approaches to development (ibid).

However, while many find the critique conceptually satisfying, they are left wondering where to go next. The post-development perspective provides no obvious plan, other than to focus on building autonomous grassroots development.

The themes in post-development map well onto the **appropriate technology** movement and ecocentric environmental perspectives (Eckersley, 1992). The movement grew out of social and environmental concerns about problems with capital-intensive industrialization, that became especially pronounced during the energy crisis of the 1970s (see Box 6.2). Appropriate technology, on the other hand, is that which is small scale, environmentally sound and locally relevant (see Figure 6.3).

Box 6.2   The Sussex Manifesto

In 1970, a group at the University of Sussex produced the 'Sussex Manifesto' (Singer et al., 1970) for the UN, highlighting the importance of science and technology for development. While the UN deemed it too radical at the time, consigning it to the annex of a report, the manifesto nonetheless anticipated a number of approaches to innovation that are commonly accepted today. One example is the importance of adopting a systems approach, which means seeing science and technology innovation emerging from a system comprised of key agents (universities, the government and business) that provide an enabling environment for innovations to occur.

The Appropriate Technology
Collaborative: Guatemalan
Women Wind Weavers Project

Figure 6.3 Appropriate technology: Guatemalan Women Wind Weavers Project (Source: Flickr.com)

Ecocentric environmental perspectives recognize the moral standing of non-human, as well as human, life and seek to respect its right to unfold within the context of the Earth's sustainable development. They encompass a wide range of views that share the desire of eco-anarchists to disassemble or bypass the modern state in order to establish decentralized, autonomous and small-scale communities (Bookchin, 1971, 1982; Merchant, 1992). Such perspectives see our technology-reliant way of life as that which has brought the global environmental crisis to a head, seeing modern culture as incompatible with environmental sustainability. They also observe an inextricable link between the market economy and environmental decline. Thus, radical environmental groups, such as Earth First, which seek to sabotage technologies that destroy nature, place the Earth, rather than people, at the centre of their environmental politics, because they see human culture and its associated values and technologies as that which create environmental problems in the first place (Manes, 1990). Such ideas suggest that global industrialization, even that which promises environmentally sound technology transfer, brings local communities into the ecologically destructive global economy and are therefore ultimately unsustainable. In summary, such groups reject powerful groups' domination of the human as well as the non-human world, and embrace grassroots political action.

Activity 6.2

To what extent do you agree with the argument that the post-development perspective is more environmentally sound and technologically appropriate than the modernization and dependency perspectives?

Spend no more 10 minutes on this activity.

Discussion

The post-development perspective was formulated as a critique of the idea that poor countries need aspects of modernity – modern ideas, institutions and artefacts – possessed by richer countries in order to generate better livelihoods for their citizens. Its adherents believed improved livelihoods could come from local technological, environmental and socio-economic alternatives. So in that sense post-development is more technically and environmentally inclusive than the modernization and dependency perspectives, which mainly focused on the diffusion (or lack thereof) of modern technology and did not really address environmental concerns. That said, modern tools, techniques and institutions have greatly improved many aspects of social and economic life as well as the environment in developing countries. It can also be problematic to overly romanticize small-scale development. How you answer this question is really down to your own views of development, but it may be that all three perspectives have something to tell us about environmentally sound and technologically appropriate development.

Summary and looking forward

In many ways, development perspectives in the early 21st century are revisiting storylines that have been present from the beginning; classical 19th century sociologists from Tönnies (2001 [1887]) to Weber (2002 [1905]) showed an admiration for traditional society, untainted by modernity, while Marx (2007 [1867]) believed in the progression of history towards a more egalitarian form of social organization. Reflexively, development thinkers in their focus on post-development return to long-standing themes critical of both modernity and tradition.

Most development thinking has a strong streak of **technological determinism**; that is, most argue that technologies shape societies, which would be critiqued by scholars of science and technology who have argued since the mid-1980s that in reality this process is more complex (Hackett et al., 2007). The point was made that society also shapes technology, notably in a book by Mackenzie and Wacjman entitled *The Social Shaping of Technology* (1999), which maintained that technologies like weapons systems are very much a product of their powerful, often male, politician, business, scientist and engineer policy maker, funder and designer imaginations. This was part of a larger argument that technology is socially constructed (Bijker et al., 1989). Since then, many science and technology studies scholars see a mutual shaping of technology and society (Callon, 1986; Latour, 2005).

This chapter has looked at three perspectives on this intertwining of technology and society in particular: modernization, dependency and post-development, examining how they interrelate with views on technology and the environment. Modernization perspectives are often linear and based on an understanding that development occurs in well-defined stages; they also tend to focus on development success and on internal factors within countries that produce development outcomes. Developing modern science, technology and innovation is part and parcel of growth for modernization thinkers, especially that which is modelled on what has occurred in the North. This was the basis of many critiques of modernization by dependency and post-development theorists. They argued that Northern-style development is not occurring in the South for a whole variety of reasons. Some focused on the domination of the South by powerful groups in the North. Others emphasized the point that development is not as simple as exchanging traditional ideas and social formations for modern ones.

The post-development perspective spearheads the critique of big development, whether based on modernization or Marx-inspired communism, and dovetails nicely with calls for appropriate technology and ecocentric environmentalism. It advocates the belief that development as an idea has done more harm than good for the South, where people should be free to chart their own futures using locally relevant and sustainable technologies that allow them and their descendents to live in harmony with the Earth. However, these ideas have had difficulty being translated into practical development policies that can be scaled up to address national, and even global development issues.

In the next chapters, the issues of environment and sustainable development will be discussed in detail.

References

Bahro, R. (1986) *Building the Green Movement*, London, Heretic Books.

Baran, P. (1973) *The Political Economy of Growth*, Harmondsworth, Penguin.

Beck, U., Giddens, A. and Lash, S. (1994) *Reflexive Modernization: Politics, Tradition and Aesthetics in the Modern Social Order*, Cambridge, Polity Press.

Beck, U. (1992) *Risk Society: Towards a New Modernity*, London, Sage Publications.

Bijker, W., Hughes, T. and Pinch, T. (eds) (1989) *The Social Construction of Technological Systems*, London, MIT Press.

Bookchin, M. (1971) *Post-Scarcity Anarchism*, Berkeley, Ramparts (Published under the pseudonym 'Lewis Herber').

Bookchin, M. (1982) *Ecology of Freedom*, Palo Alto, Cheshire Books.

Brenner, R. (1977) 'The origins of capitalist development: a critique of neo-Smithian Marxism', *New Left Review*, vol. 104 (July/August), pp. 27–92.

Brewer, A. (1990) *Marxist Theories of Imperialism*, London, Routledge.

Callon, M. (1986) 'Some elements of a sociology of translation: domestication of the scallops and fishermen of St Brieuc Bay' in Law, J. (ed.) *Power, Action and Belief: a New Sociology of Knowledge*, London, Routledge & Kegan Paul.

Crenshaw, E.M., Christenson, M. and Oakey, D.R. (2000) 'Demographic transition in ecological focus', *American Sociological Review*, vol. 65, issue 3, pp. 371–91.

Eckersley, R. (1992) *Environmentalism and Political Theory: Towards an Ecocentric Approach*, London, University College Press.

Escobar, A. (1995) 'Imaging a post development era' in Crush, J. (ed.) *Power of Development*, London, Routledge.

Frank, A.G. (1971) *Capitalism and Underdevelopment in Latin America*, Harmondsworth, Penguin.

Frank, A.G. (1978) *Dependent Accumulation and Underdevelopment*, London, Macmillan.

Ghosh, B. (2001) *Dependency Theory Revisited*, Farnham, Surrey, Ashgate.

Gilman, N. (2003) *Mandarins of the Future: Modernization Theory in Cold War America*, Baltimore, Johns Hopkins University Press.

Gorz, A. (1980) *Ecology as Politics* (trans. P. Vigderman and J. Cloud), London, Pluto.

Gorz, A. (1994) *Capitalism, Socialism, Ecology* (trans. C. Turner), London, Verso.

Gusfield, J. (1967) 'Tradition and modernity: misplaced polarities', *American Journal of Sociology*, vol. 72, pp. 351–62.

Hackett, E., Amsterdamska, O., Lynch, M. and Wajcman, J. (eds) (2007) *The Handbook of Science and Technology Studies* (3rd edn), London, MIT Press.

Hajer, M. (1995) *The Politics of Environmental Discourse: Ecological Modernization and the Policy Process*, Oxford University Press.

Hanlin, R. and Brown, W. (2013) 'Contesting development in theory and practice' in Papaioannou, T. and Butcher, M. (eds) *International Development in a Changing World,* London, Bloomsbury Academic/Milton Keynes, The Open University.

Huber, J. (2004) *New Technologies and Environmental Innovation*, Cheltenham, Edward Elgar.

Ingelhart, R. and Baker, W. (2000) 'Modernization, cultural change and the persistence of traditional values', *American Sociological Review*, vol. 65 (February), pp. 19–51.

Inkeles, A. and Smith, D. (1974) *Becoming Modern: Individual Change in Six Countries*, Cambridge, MA, Harvard University Press.

Kim, K.-D. (1994) 'Confucianism and capitalist development in East Asia' in Sklair, L. (ed.) *Capitalism and Development*, London, Routledge.

Laclau, E. (1971) 'Feudalism and Capitalism in Latin America', *New Left Review*, vol. 67, pp. 19–38.

Latour, B. (2005) *Reassembling the Social: an Introduction to Actor Network Theory*, Oxford University Press.

Lerner, D. (1968) *The Passing of Traditional Society*, New York, Free Press.

Mackenzie, D. and Wacjman, J. (eds) (1999) *The Social Shaping of Technology* (2nd edn), Buckingham, Open University Press.

Manes, C. (1990) *Green Rage: Radical Environmentalism and the Unmaking of Civilization*, London, Little, Brown and Company.

Marx, K. (1955 [1847]) *Poverty of Philosophy*, Moscow, Progress Publishers.

Marx, K. (2007 [1867]) *Capital*, Volume 1, New York, Cosimo.

Merchant, C. (1992) *Radical Ecology: the Search for a Liveable World*, London, Routledge.

Mohan (2013).

Mol, A. (1995) *The Refinement of Production: Ecological Modernization Theory and the Chemical Industry*, Utrecht, Van Arkel.

Naess, A. (1989) *Ecology, Community and Lifestyle* (trans. D. Rothburg), Cambridge University Press.

Nanda, M. (1999) 'Who needs post-development? Discourses of difference, green revolution and agrarian populism in India', *Journal of Developing Societies*, vol. 15, issue 1, pp. 5–31.

Papaioannou, T. and Butcher, M. (eds) *International Development in a Changing World,* London, Bloomsbury Academic/Milton Keynes, The Open University.

Peace, W. (2004) *Leslie A. White: Evolution and Revolution in Anthropology,* University of Nebraska Press.

Pepper, D. (1993) *Eco-Socialism: From Deep Ecology to Social Justice*, London, Routledge.

Rahnema, M. and Bawtree, V. (eds) (1997) *The Post Development Reader*, London, Zed Publications.

Robbins, P.T. (2001) *Greening the Corporation*, London, Earthscan.

Rostow, W. (1971) *The Stages of Economic Growth*, Cambridge University Press.

Sachs, W. (1992) 'Environment' in Sachs, W. (ed.) *The Development Dictionary: a Guide to Knowledge as Power*, London, Zed Publications.

Schumpeter, J.R. (1976 [1942]) *Capitalism, Socialism and Democracy*, New York, George Allen & Unwin.

Sender, J. and Smith, S. (1986) *The Development of Capitalism in Latin America*, London, Methuen.

Singer, H., Cooper, C., Desai, R.C., Freeman, C., Gish, O., Hill, S. and Oldham, G. (1970) 'Draft introductory statement for the world plan of action for the application of science and technology to development', prepared by the 'Sussex Group', Annex II in *Science and Technology for Development: Proposals for the Second Development Decade*, New York, United Nations.

Spaargaren, G. and Mol, A. (1992) 'Sociology, environment, and modernity: ecological modernisation as a theory of social change', *Society and Natural Resources*, vol. 5, pp. 323–44.

Tönnies, F. (2001 [1887]) *Community and Society*, trans. J. Harris and M. Hollis, Cambridge University Press.

United Nations General Assembly (2005) *Follow Up to the Millennium Summit*, New York, United Nations.

Wallerstein, I. (1974) *The Modern World-System*, Volume 1, London, Academic Press.

Wallerstein, I. (1980) *The Modern World-System*, Volume 2, London, Academic Press.

Wallerstein, I. (1989) *The Modern World-System*, Volume 3, London, Academic Press.

Warren, B. (1980) *Imperialism: Pioneer of Capitalism*, London, Verso.

World Commission on Environment and Development (WCED) () (1987) *Our Common Future*, Oxford University Press.

Weber, M. (2002 [1905]) *The Protestant Ethic and the Spirit of Capitalism*, London, Penguin Books.

Ziai, A. (2007) *Exploring Post-Development: Theory and Practice, Problems and Perspectives*, Abingdon, Routledge.

Further reading

Hackett, E., Amsterdamska, O., Lynch, M. and Wajcman, J. (eds) (2007) *The Handbook of Science and Technology Studies* (3rd edn), London, MIT Press.

Milton, K. (1998) *Environmentalism and Cultural Theory*, London, Routledge.

Pieterse, J.N. (2010) *Development Theory* (2nd edn), London, Sage Publications.

Preston, P. (1996) *Development Theory: an Introduction*, Oxford, Blackwell.

Rist, G. (2008) *The History of Development: From Western Origins to Global Faith* (3rd edn), London, Zed Publications.

The challenge for environment, development and sustainability in China

Kelly Gallagher

Introduction

China provides a unique laboratory to examine the intersection of environment, development and sustainability. It is large in almost every dimension (Figure 7.1); it has the world's biggest population, the second-largest economy by one measure, a big land area, and it is the world's largest consumer of coal. This chapter will show how energy is at the heart of the 'environment' problem, and environment is at the heart of the 'energy' problem in China. The chapter reviews the development and environment challenges facing the country, and then examines the particular challenge of China's heavy reliance on coal for its energy needs. The chapter concludes with a discussion of what a more sustainable development path might look like in the Chinese context.

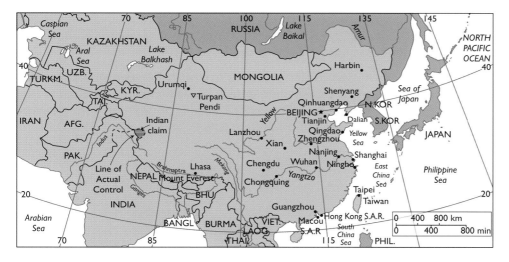

Figure 7.1   Map of the People's Republic of China

7.1   Development challenges in China

China's economic development during the past 40 years has been remarkable by nearly all metrics. During the 1970s, the Chinese economy was stagnant, and hundreds of millions of people languished in **poverty**. Since then, China has consistently been the most rapidly growing economy on earth, with average annual economic growth rates of 10 per cent since 1978 (Naughton, 2007). Adjusted for differences in cost of living in different countries, known as **purchasing power parity** (PPP), China is now the second-largest economy in the world (UNDP, 2007/2008) as measured by gross domestic product (GDP). Unadjusted per capita GDP (i.e. GDP per person) has grown from 1595 yuan (US$230) to 17 100 yuan (US$2500) during the past 30 years (Pan and Gallagher, 2009), while on a PPP basis China's per capita income in 2005 was US$6750 (HDI, 2008). As a result of this steady and rapid economic growth, an estimated 400 million people have been pulled out of absolute poverty since 1979 according to the World Bank (2003).

Despite these achievements, the Chinese government continues to face difficult development challenges. First, inequality is widening dramatically, which could cause instability and political unrest. Inequality is most stark between urban and rural areas, and especially between western and eastern coastal provinces. As of 2002, the incomes of urban residents were three times larger than rural incomes, and 99 per cent of the people living in absolute poverty were living in rural areas, especially in the western provinces. Infant mortality was three times higher in rural areas than in urban ones (World Bank, 2003). The '**Gini coefficient**' measure of inequality (where perfect equality = 0 and total inequality = 1, Hanlon, 2013) for China increased from 0.20 in the early 1980s to 0.47 in 2010 (*China Daily*, 2010), the latest for which year data are available. China now ranks seventieth in the world in terms of economic inequality, below Brazil, but not below Russia (UNDP, 2011). This inequality makes the Chinese government nervous about social stability, because as Shirk (2007, p. 54) notes: 'The Communist Party considers rapid economic growth a political imperative because it is the only way to prevent massive unemployment and labor unrest.'

The centrepiece of the government's twelfth five-year plan is restructuring the Chinese economy through encouraging domestic consumption, developing the service sector, shifting to higher value-added manufacturing, promoting energy efficiency and advancing scientific development.

The current goal is to transform its economic development pattern, addressing the energy and environmental challenges that have emerged from the rapid economic growth China experienced during the 1980s and 1990s.

7.2   Environmental challenges in China

China's population is the largest in the world, at 1.35 billion in 2012. One in every five people on earth lives in China. Although the vast majority of these still live in rural areas, it is estimated that about 18 million Chinese migrate to cities each year (UNFPA, 2007).

A major environmental problem in China is the lack of availability of fresh water. Two-thirds of China's cities lack sufficient water resources, and 110 cities suffer severe water shortages. An estimated 600 million people drink contaminated water daily (Hays, 2008). The inefficient agricultural sector is mainly to blame for over-use, though industries are not blameless either. The Chinese government estimates that 75 per cent of the river water that flows through urban areas is unfit for human consumption (Economy, 2007). One-third of China's cities do not have waste water treatment plants (CCICED, 2007) and, according to a recent survey by the State Environmental

Protection Administration, half of the waste water treatment plants do not work properly (China Economic Review, 2008).

China houses some of the largest hydropower installations in the world, most infamously the Three Gorges Dam. These hydropower stations have more localized but no less severe environmental impacts, including forced human relocation, inundation of agricultural lands and impacts on biodiversity. On the other hand, hydropower projects can help with flood control, irrigation and the provision of low carbon-emission electric power. High carbon-emission coal-fired power plants are also the fourth-largest source of waste water in the country (Sinton et al., 2000).

In China's biggest cities most of the urban air pollution comes from motor vehicles. The car population in China has grown dramatically, from fewer than 100 000 in 1990 to approximately 78 million in 2011 (*The Infrastructurist*, 2011). While the growth in new cars has been astounding, the total number is still small compared with the situation in the USA, which has a private vehicle population of 240 million (*The Infrastructurist*, 2011).

Chemical wastes in China are not well controlled, and numerous instances of accidental or deliberate releases of toxic wastes have been documented. Notably, the Songhua river in the north-east has suffered repeatedly from xylidine and nitrobenzene releases from factories, both of which are highly dangerous to human health. As with other environmental problems in China, lack of enforcement of existing environmental laws related to managing chemical and other toxic wastes (including electronic equipment wastes) is a major challenge to sustainability.

Activity 7.1

What would you identify as the two main environmental challenges in China? Given the myriad of problems facing the country, what factors did you prioritize in making your choice?

Spend no more than 5 minutes on this activity.

Discussion

As the summary above highlights, political, economic and social systems are all interconnected in contributing to China's environmental challenges, making it difficult to tease out single problems. However, as the next section elaborates, energy provision and use is a key factor.

7.3   Energy use and air pollution

China's energy-related challenges are many, including the need for energy to sustain economic growth, its increasing foreign dependency for oil and gas, the need to provide modern forms of energy to China's poor, its increasingly severe urban air pollution, its already massive acid deposition (commonly known as acid rain), the growing concerns domestically and internationally about global climate change, and access to affordable, advanced energy technologies to address all of the above challenges. Put simply, energy is at the heart of the environmental problem, and environment is at the heart of the energy problem (Holdren, 2008).

Total energy consumption in China 'increased by 2.3 percent/year between 1990 and 2002. Ever since 2002 it has increased at a rate of over 10 percent/ year. Final consumption followed the same trend as total energy consumption, although it increased at a slower rate per year. This very rapid growth was mainly driven by energy consumption in the industrial sector.' (*China Energy Efficiency Report*, 2011). Because of China's population, even if everyone consumed a very small amount of energy, China's total energy consumption would still be large.

Economically, China's growing energy consumption presents both challenge and opportunity. Energy sustains economic growth by providing fuel for factory boilers, electricity for lighting and machinery, and fuel for transportation services. Of course, energy provides heating and cooling services as well. During periods of energy shortages in China, factories are shut down entirely, or moved into a rotation where each factory must cease production periodically – once a week, or every other night. During the summer of 2004, for example, factories on the outskirts of Shanghai were forced to close two days a week due to the high demand for electricity to power air conditioners and insufficient supply (Fallon, 2004). Heavy snowstorms in central China in January 2008 contributed to severe electricity shortages in 31 provinces, caused primarily by an acute shortage of coal. This shortage was exacerbated by several factors, namely strong and persistent demand for coal, the closing down of small, unsafe coal mines, rising coal prices and price controls on electricity. Because the central government sets electricity prices, as coal prices rise but electricity prices stay the same, profit margins shrink until power producers are forced to shut down. As a result of the coal shortages, the Chinese government suspended coal exports for two months, causing coal prices to shoot up to all-time highs in the USA, Europe and Asia. China's largest copper producer, Jiangxi Copper Co., shut down some plants due to the high coal prices and lack of availability, as did some steel, zinc and aluminium producers (Oster and Davis, 2008).

The economic costs of China's air pollution are high. According to a report from the Chinese government and the World Bank, conservative estimates of morbidity and premature mortality associated with ambient air pollution in China was equivalent to 3.8 per cent of GDP in 2003 if premature death was valued at 1 million yuan per person. Acid rain, caused mainly from sulphur dioxide (SO_2) emissions from coal combustion, is estimated to cost 30 billion yuan in crop damage (mostly for vegetables) and 7 billion yuan in material damage annually. This damage is equivalent to 1.8 per cent of the value of the crop output.

Providing better energy services to the poor in order to improve the quality of life for those still reliant on traditional forms of energy such as charcoal, crop wastes and dung is a preoccupation of the Chinese government as part of its socio-economic development strategy. Nationally, 96 per cent of rural households have access to electricity, although in some provinces the figure is much lower, such as in Guizhou where 80 per cent of households lack access (LBNL, 2001).

One rising concern is that as China imports greater amounts of energy, prices of these commodities will rise until supply catches up, and price spikes are especially likely during supply disruption events. After China became a net oil importer in 1994, its demand for global oil supplies grew rapidly as it became the second-largest consumer of oil in 2004, and it is now the third-largest oil importer in the world (BP, 2008). China's escalating demand contributed strongly to the rise in world oil prices during the first part of this century as suppliers scrambled to catch up. It appears that China is beginning to affect world coal prices as well. In the first six months of 2007, China imported more coal than it exported for the first time in history. Overall, China's coal demand grew nearly 9 per cent in 2007, indicating that Chinese coal demand could double by 2015.

The other big challenge is to supply enough energy, especially electricity, to meet the very high demand created by Chinese industry. Industry consumes the majority of electricity supplied, accounting for 74 per cent of total demand (NBS, 2006, Chapter 7). On the opportunity side, the Chinese energy sector represents an exciting market opportunity for Chinese and foreign energy services companies alike. In 2006, China installed 101 gigawatts (GW) of new power plants, 90 GW of which was coal-fired power. In 2007, China installed an additional 91 GW for a total of 713 GW (China Electricity Council, 2008). To put these numbers in perspective, Germany's entire electricity system in 2005 was 124 GW (Eurostat, 2008). China's total generation capacity was estimated to be around 1050 GW at the end of 2011 (China.org.cn, 2011).

Just in the last decade, China has emerged as a major consumer of oil, and there is strong potential for China to become a major natural gas consumer as well, especially if it tries to reduce its greenhouse gas emissions (natural gas is much less carbon-intensive than coal). About half of China's oil imports come from the Middle East, but Angola became the largest single supplier in 2006, and, indeed, China has invested heavily in energy resources in Africa. Although there have been several new oil discoveries in China, Chinese reserves are on the decline. China has relatively few natural gas reserves domestically, and therefore uses virtually no natural gas in its power sector. To offset this, it is trying to increase production of coal-bed methane, a form of natural gas extracted from coal deposits. If China decides to increase its reliance on natural gas, it will have to import. If it begins to import large quantities from either the Persian Gulf or Russia, the geopolitical implications would be significant. China's long-term energy security is not only dependent on having sufficient supplies of energy to sustain its economic growth, but it will be equally dependent on its ability to manage the growth in energy demand without causing intolerable environmental damage.

7.4   The particular challenge of coal

China's main energy resource endowment is coal (Figure 7.2). Coal accounts for 93 per cent of China's remaining fossil fuel resources. In China, the majority of the electricity is derived from coal, with only 26.53 per cent derived from carbon-free energy sources (hydropower accounts for 213.4 GW, wind power is 31.07 GW and nuclear power is 10.82 GW (Good Environment, 2011)). Although nuclear and wind power have been growing rapidly in recent years, coal is so dominant that it is unlikely that the current mix of electricity supply can be significantly altered any time soon. Natural gas is not commonly used for power generation due to the high price and lack of availability of the fuel (see above). China is aggressively pursuing renewable energy, and ranks number one in the world in some respects, such as in its installation of solar hot water and small hydropower. It ranks fifth in the world in terms of installed wind capacity, and fourth in terms of ethanol production (Martinot, 2007). Still, China's non-hydro renewable capacity is a tiny fraction of primary energy supply, which is completely dominated by coal.

Figure 7.2   China's coal-dependent economy

Coal is at the heart of China's environmental woes, with major implications for human health. Particulate matter from coal is a major air pollutant. Average concentrations of PM10 (particles the size of 10 microns or less that are capable of penetrating deep into the lung) in China's cities are extremely high, ranging from (in parts per million) 255 in Panzhihua, 150 in Beijing, 140 in Chongqing to 100 in Shanghai. These numbers compare with 45 in Los Angeles and 25 in New York. PM10 can increase the number and severity of asthma attacks, cause or aggravate bronchitis and other lung diseases, and reduce the body's ability to fight infections. Certain types of people are especially vulnerable to PM10's adverse health effects, including children, the elderly, exercising adults and those suffering from asthma or bronchitis (CARB, 2003). In addition, each year more than 4000 miners die in China's coal mines, mostly due to accidents (Biallo, 2008).

Sulphur dioxide emissions from coal combustion, a major source of acid deposition, rose 27 per cent between 2001 and 2005. Acid rain predominantly affects south-eastern China, and Hebei Province is most severely affected, with acid rain accounting for more than 20 per cent of crop losses (World

Bank and SEPA, 2007). In terms of global climate change, coal emits the most greenhouse gas emissions of any fossil fuel and accounts for approximately 80 per cent of China's carbon dioxide (CO_2) emissions. The possible adverse impacts of climate change on China are likely to concern:

- Water supply and agriculture due to changing rainfall patterns and disappearing glaciers. For example, precipitation decreased by 50–120 mm per year along the northern Yellow River between 1956 and 2000, an already arid region. Conversely, precipitation increased by 60–130 mm per year along the southern Yangtze River from 1956 to 2000, an area that has been plagued by heavy flooding. The mountain glaciers on the Tibetan plateau are receding rapidly, with major implications for fresh water supply in already water-stressed northern China.

- Sea levels, where a rise of 30 cm would cause massive coastal inundation, which Chinese scientists estimate would cost 115–120 billion yuan in economic losses to the major delta areas of the Pearl, Yangtze and Yellow Rivers, including the Gulf of Bohai.

7.5   Achieving sustainable development in China

It is challenging to imagine China (and most other countries) achieving true environmental sustainability, if one defines a sustainable process or condition as 'one that can be maintained indefinitely without progressive diminution of valued qualities inside or outside the system where the process operates or the condition prevails' (Holdren et al., 1995, p. 3). But it is not, in fact, difficult to imagine environmental conditions being vastly improved, nor is it hard to imagine China formulating a new mode of industrialization that is far cleaner and more efficient than the US model, for example. There are already signs of this with over a quarter of China's electricity derived from carbon-free energy sources (Good Environment, 2011) and China's commitment to its twelfth five-year plan. Indeed, one could even envision a future where the Chinese government decided to embark on a completely new growth strategy that championed sustainable development precisely because the environmental woes currently afflicting China are so severe and costly to its society.

To achieve dramatic environmental improvements in China, a comprehensive and far-reaching incentive system would have to be created. Experience to date suggests that even though much more energy-efficient and cleaner technologies have been developed, sometimes within China, they are not widely adopted in the country. The proposition that late-industrializing countries like China would leapfrog to the most sustainable technologies available has not been borne out, and in fact many limits to leapfrogging have been identified. Most importantly, it is clear that the processes of leapfrogging, **technology transfer** and cooperation, and accelerated deployment of environmental technologies are not automatic (Ohshita and Ortolano, 2002; Gallagher, 2006; Lewis and Wiser, 2007).

Many barriers to **technological leapfrogging** exist in different contexts, including the higher costs of some cleaner technologies, lack of knowledge about or access to those technologies, and insufficient incentives to adopt them. Indeed, without clear and consistent incentives for firms to produce and consumers to purchase cleaner products and services, they often fail to do so. Especially because environmental quality is a public good, government has a special role to play to design and enforce environmental laws and regulations, which in turn create the appropriate incentives for producers and consumers alike.

Activity 7.2

How does this need for a government role in environmental regulation sit with the idea of neoliberal development?

Spend no more 10 minutes in this activity.

Discussion

Neoliberal models of development would suggest that it is up to the market to find solutions to environmental problems. For example, when the cost of coal is too expensive, other sources of energy will be sought. With technological innovation and entrepreneurship, the cost of alternative energy sources will decline and replace fuels such as coal. However, unfettered development as industrialization could be blamed for creating much of the environmental damage we see today (as discussed in the previous chapter). Therefore, if we regard environmental quality as a public good we are suggesting a role for the state and civil society in managing it.

The Chinese government recognizes and is tackling many of China's environmental problems. The government, for example, has issued strong targets for energy efficiency and renewable energy. The target for renewable energy is 15 per cent of primary energy by 2020 (Martinot, 2007). As a step towards achieving this, one of the targets in the twelfth five-year plan is for non-fossil fuels to reach 11.4 per cent of total energy consumption by 2015. In addition, it has issued six main environmental laws and nine natural resources laws, while the State Council has released 28 environmental administrative regulations and the Ministry of Environmental Protection has published 27 environmental standards. Reportedly, more than 900 local environmental rules have been promulgated as well (Liu, 2007). Many of these laws and regulations are somewhat weaker than their counterparts in the USA and Europe, but some are actually stricter or more far reaching. China's passenger car fuel-efficiency standards, for example, are considerably more stringent than those approved by the US Congress in 2007.

On the other hand, enforcement of China's environmental policies is highly uneven. Some cities like Beijing in its run-up to the 2008 Olympics went to tremendous lengths to clean up their local factories and reduce air and water pollution. Generally, local environmental enforcement is lax and undermines the relatively good policies that have been issued by the central government. For its part, the central government has thus far failed to provide adequate resources to strengthen the Ministry of Environmental Protection. There is no adequate system of environmental data collection, distribution and analysis, which further complicates the enforcement effort because without irrefutable data about pollutant emissions and effluent releases, the government lacks a fundamental tool that would enable it to judge and act upon non-compliance with the law. All of these deficiencies demonstrate the need for more effective government institutions to promulgate and enforce regulations.

In Europe and the USA, the environmental movement was and continues to be critically important to the passage and enforcement of landmark environmental laws. The formation of public interest groups or NGOs like the World Wildlife Fund, Greenpeace, Natural Resource Defense Council and Sierra Club as well as 'green' parties created new and powerful political forces. These parties and NGOs advocated for environmental protection by educating citizens, pushing for new laws, monitoring enforcement and suing firms or government agencies for non-compliance. In Japan, a culture of conservation sprang from the realization during World War II that it is a country with large resource needs but few endowments of natural resources.

In China, environmental groups are allowed to form, but usually only for the purposes of public education. A somewhat bizarre form of NGO called 'government-owned non-governmental organizations' (GONGOs) initially emerged. More 'pure' environmental NGOs now exist, but they are still mostly confined to public education activities. The government has apparently given the media permission to report on environmental abuses, and it has established 'hotlines' for citizens to call to report environmental infractions. Still, it is clear that criticism of government policies, and especially the Communist Party itself, is not acceptable. Average citizens and NGOs are not potent political forces with respect to the formation of environmental policies today in China. There is, however, a growing reliance on academia to inform environmental policy making, where university and research institute experts are encouraged to make suggestions, recommendations and even relatively modest constructive criticisms to the government. It is difficult to imagine that China would be able to forge a sustainable path without the help of NGOs and institutions, given the large size of its economy and population.

The final crucial component of a transition to an environmentally sustainable future in China is money. Large financial resources will be needed because even though China is already a successful industrializing country, there are competing demands for available financial resources. If the rest of the world wants China to move more quickly to reduce its environmental impact on the planet, then other countries will almost certainly need to provide greater financial resources to help. Money will also be needed for investment in technological innovation. Investments in the research, development, demonstration and deployment of more environmentally sustainable technologies will reduce the costs of these technologies in the near term and provide a better menu of options for the future.

Summary and looking forward

The challenge for environment, development and sustainability in China is enormous because of its large population, heavy reliance on coal and energy intensive economy. Coal is at the heart of China's environmental woes, with major implications for human health. In terms of the causes of global climate change, coal emits the most greenhouse gas emissions of any fossil fuel. It accounts for approximately 80 per cent of China's CO_2 emissions. To achieve dramatic environmental improvements in China, a comprehensive and far-reaching incentive system would have to be created. Government has a special role to play to design and enforce environmental laws and regulations, which in turn create the appropriate incentives for producers and consumers alike. But while the Chinese government recognizes many of the country's environmental problems, there is a need for more effective government institutions to promulgate and enforce regulations in China. The next chapter extends these discussions on environment and sustainability from a national to the global scale.

References

Biallo, D. (2008) 'Can coal and clean air co-exist in China?', *Scientific American*, 4 August 2008, [online] http://www.sciam.com/article.cfm?id=can-coal-and-clean-air-coexist-china (Accessed 1 February 2012).

British Petroleum (BP) (2008) *Statistical Review of World Energy*, BP, [online] http://www.bp.com/statistical review, June.

California Air Resources Board (CARB) (2003) *Air Pollution – Particulate Matter Brochure*, Sacramento, CA, California Air Resources Board.

China Council for International Cooperation on Environment and Development (CCICED) (2007) 'Global experiences and China's solution: environmentally sound chemicals management in China', CCICED Issues Paper, [online] http://www.vancouver.sfu.ca/dlam/ (Accessed 09 January 2009).

China Daily (2010) 'Country's wealth divide past warning level', *China Daily*, [online] http://www.chinadaily.com.cn/china/2010-05/12/content_9837073.htm (Accessed 13 March 2012).

China Economic Review (2008) *China's Environment 2008*, Hong Kong, China Economic Review Publishing.

China Electricity Council (2008) *Nation-Wide Power Sector Statistics Newsletter for 2007*. (in Chinese), [online] http://www.cec.org.cn.

China Energy Efficiency Report (2011) [online] http://www05.abb.com/global/scot/scot316.nsf/veritydisplay/63246e62080610aec12578640050f217/$file/china.pdf (Accessed 8 February 2012).

China.org.cn (2011) 'China power shortfall may hit up to 40GW', Beijing, State Council Information Office and China International Publishing Group, [online] http://www.china.org.cn/business/2011-10/28/content_23748327.htm (Accessed 8 February).

Davis, S.C. and Diegel, S.W. (2007) *Transportation Energy Data Book: Report ORNL-6978*, Oak Ridge National Laboratory, Oak Ridge, US Department of Energy.

Economy, E. (2007) 'The great leap backwards?, *Foreign Policy,* vol. 86, issue 5, pp. 38–59.

Eurostat (2008) Infrastructure – electricity – annual data, Luxembourg, Eurostat. Downloaded from http://epp.eurostat.ec.europa.eu (Accessed ??).

Fallon, B. (2004) 'Energy shortage hits Chinese firms', *BBC News*, http://news.bbc.co.uk/2/hi/business/3602678.stm (Accessed 8 February 2008).

Gallagher, K.S. (2006) 'Limits to leapfrogging? Evidence from China's automobile industry', *Energy Policy*, vol. 34, pp. 383–94.

Good Environment (2011) 'China gets over a quarter of its electricity from clean energy sources', [online] http://www.good.is/post/china-gets-over-a-quarter-of-its-electricity-from-clean-energy-sources/ (Accessed 8 February 2012).

Hanlon, J. (2013) 'Inequality – does it matter?' in Papaioannou, T. and Butcher, M. (eds) *International Development in a Changing World*, London, Bloomsbury Academic/Milton Keynes, The Open University.

Hays, J. (2008) 'Water shortages in China', [online] http://factsanddetails.com/china.php?itemid=390&catid=10&subcatid=66 (Accessed 8 February 2012).

HDI (2008) *Human Development Index, Fact Sheet for China*, [online] http://hdrstats.undp.org/countries/country_fact_sheets/cty_fs_CHN.html.

Holdren. J.P. (2008) 'Science and technology for sustainable well-being', *Science*, vol. 319, pp. 424–34.

Holdren, J.P., Daily, G. and Ehrlich, P. (1995) 'The meaning of sustainability: biogeophysical aspects', in Munasinghe, M. and Shearer, W. (eds) *Defining and Measuring Sustainability: The Biogeophysical Foundations*, Washington, DC, World Bank.

The Infrastructurist (2011) 'There are now 1 billion cars on the road', posted by Eric Jaffe [online] http://www.infrastructurist.com/2011/08/24/new-report-global-car-population-tops-1-billion/ (Accessed 8 February 2012).

Lawrence Berkeley National Laboratory (LBNL) (2001) *China Energy Data Book*, Version 5.0, Berkeley, Lawrence Berkeley National Laboratory..

Lewis, J.I. and Wiser, R.H. (2007) 'Fostering a renewable energy technology industry: an international comparison of wind industry policy support mechanisms', *Energy Policy*, vol. 35, pp. 1844–57.

Liu, X. (2007) 'Building an environmentally-friendly society through innovation: challenges and choices', Background Paper, China Council for International Cooperation on Environment and Development.

Martinot, E. (2007) *Renewables 2007 Global Status Report, REN21*, Paris, Renewable Energy Policy Network.

Naughton, B. (2007) *The Chinese Economy: Transitions and Growth*. Cambridge, MA, MIT Press.

National Bureau of Statistics (NBS) (2006) *Statistical Yearbook of 2006*, Washington, DC, China National Bureau of Statistics.

Ohshita, S.B. and Ortolano, L. (2002) 'The promise and pitfalls of Japanese cleaner coal technology transfer to China', *International Journal of Technology Transfer and Commercialisation*, vol. 1, nos. 1 and 2, pp. 56–81.

Oster, S. and Davis, A. (2008) 'China spurs coal-price surge', *The Wall Street Journal*, 12 February 2008, A1.

Pan, J. and Gallagher, K.S. (2009) 'Global warming: the road to restraint' in Allison, G., Guoliang, G., Rosecrance, R., Tung, C.H. and Wang, J. (eds) *Power and Restraint: a Shared Vision of the US China Relationship*, New York, Public Affairs.

Shirk, S. (2007) *China: Fragile Superpower*, Oxford University Press, New York.

Sinton, J.E., Fridley, D.G., Logan, J., Yuan, G., Bangcheng, W. and Xu, Q. (2000) *Valuation of the Environmental Impacts of Energy Use in China*, Washington, DC, World Resources Institute.

United Nations Development Programme (UNDP) (2007/2008).

United Nations Development Programme (UNDP) (2011) *Human Development Report: Sustainability and Equity: a Better Future for All*, New York, United Nations,

[online]
http://hdr.undp.org/en/reports/global/hdr2011/download/en/ (Accessed 8 February 2012).

United Nations Population Fund (UNFPA) (2007) *State of the World's Population*, New York, United Nations.

World Bank (2003) 'China: promoting growth with equity', *Country Economic Memorandum, Report No. 24169-CHA*, 15 October 2003, Washington, DC, World Bank.

World Bank and State Environmental Protection Administration (SEPA) (2007) *Cost of Pollution in China: Economic Estimates of Physical Damages*, Washington, DC, World Bank and China State Environmental Protection Administration.

Further reading

Chinese Government (2008) 'China's policies and actions for addressing climate change. White Paper issued by the Chinese Government, 29 October 2008, [online] http:/www.english.gov.cn/2008-10/29/content_1134544.htm (Accessed ??).

Economy, E. (2007) 'The great leap backwards?', *Foreign Affairs*, vol. 86, issue, 5. pp. 38–59.

Gallagher, K.S. (2006) *China Shifts Gears: Automakers, Oil, Pollution, and Development*, Cambridge, MA, MIT Press.

World Bank and China State Environmental Protection Administration (SEPA) (2007) *Cost of Pollution in China: Economic Estimates of Physical Damages*, Washington, DC, World Bank and China State Environmental Protection Administration.

Environment, inequality and the internal contradictions of globalization

8

Raphael Kaplinsky

Introduction

We are currently in the midst of a period of triumphalism about the unstoppable nature of deepening **globalization**, the belief that the forces of globalization are irresistible, that there will be no end to the ever-deepening and ever-widening removal of the cross-border barriers to the flows of products, **production factors** (people and **capital**), ideas and technology. The view that globalization is unstoppable echoes that of an earlier era, the period ending with World War I. The last decades of the 19th century represented a similar phase of rapidly deepening global integration. Yet this process came to an end in an abrupt and brutal form, with the loss of millions of lives in the World Wars. It was half a century later that we entered a new phase of global integration.

The primary reason for the descent of the global economy into war in the early years of the 20th century was the failure of the old imperial powers to allow a new entrant – Germany – to play a key role in the forming of **global architecture**. A similar challenge faces the global regime now that dynamic new entrants from Asia and South America are rising in the economic league and will soon be seeking to have this reflected in the role they play in the fashioning of the global political and institutional architecture.

This chapter addresses the sustainability of the global system, and will do so by focusing on three themes (Kaplinsky, 2005). The first is to understand how the very nature of capitalist development leads to the degradation of the **global commons**, to global warming and to climate chaos. Second, it is also in the nature of current processes of globalization that inequality deepens and poverty endures, often reinforcing pressures on the environment. Third, this combination of environmental impacts and inequality sets up internal contradictions that are likely to undermine the sustainability of the globalization process itself. All of this leads us to question globalization–triumphalism and requires us to think about new and innovative ways in which humankind can continue to survive and prosper, living with, rather than in command of, nature.

The innovation imperative, the environment and global warming

There are many reasons why the **command economies** of the Soviet system collapsed, but perhaps the most important is that they failed to deliver the goods. That is, they neither grew as rapidly as nor delivered the quality and variety of goods of their capitalist counter-parts. Joseph Schumpeter, an Austrian economist of the mid-20th century, provided the explanation for this systemic deficiency (Schumpeter, 1942). Schumpeter showed how the very breathing of the capitalist economy requires **innovation** where entrepreneurs, who are defined by their capacity to turn ideas into profit, respond to competition by introducing new products and processes. Innovation and expansion are at the core of the capitalist system; they are its internal motor.

Writing some centuries before Schumpeter, Adam Smith provided the key to understand how this accumulating motor of capitalism fuels a globalizing economy. Using an example of a pin factory, Smith showed how the division of labour led to an increase in productivity. Moreover, he argued, 'the division of labour depends on the extent of the market' (Smith, 1976 [1776]), that is, the bigger the market, the greater the division of labour, the greater the gains in productivity, and the higher the profit to the innovating capitalist.

Thus in summary, the argument for the inevitability of globalization runs as follows:

- Innovation and growth are at the core of the capitalist system.
- Capitalism triumphs because of its ability to innovate and grow faster.
- Increasingly, this growth takes a global form, as new large-scale technologies develop and new forms of firm and factory organization (of which the division of labour is an early example) result in increasingly global **value chains** (Chang et al., 2013) producing for global markets.

This ever-expanding global system makes enormous demands on the environment because, amongst other things, global value chains and global markets require transport, and transport uses energy. There is no need here to go into the extent of these resource demands, nor the impact this is having on the global climate. Forget for the moment the localized pollution that results from the ever-deepening exploitation of the earth's biosphere – the pesticides in cotton production, the cancer (mesothelioma) arising from asbestos production, the pollution of Alaskan waters through oil spillages. As we are increasingly aware, these localized environmental impacts pale into insignificance when we see the rapidly growing impact on the global climate. We are not just in an era of global warming and climate change, but one of growing unpredictability and climate chaos (Sachs, 2004). The global capitalist **accumulation** system is making greater demands on the biosphere than it can sustain. For humankind to survive, to live in peace and in security, the accumulation motor needs either to be switched off or perhaps even to be put in reverse. At the very least, the energy intensity of this innovation system needs to be reversed (Stern, 2006).

Activity 8.1

What did Adam Smith and Joseph Schumpeter contribute to our understanding of global capitalism?

Spend no more than 10 minutes in this activity.

Discussion

Adam Smith and Joseph Schumpeter are two of the most influential economists even today. Smith's model of the division of labour is reflected in the Fordist model of production where labour is divided according to task and employees become specialized. This takes on a global scale when we see the connections between different sites of production in global value chains, where, for example, labour may be divided into farmers who grow crops, transport networks that move them around the globe, factory workers that process the products, marketing professionals that devise means to increase sales, and retail employees who sell it (see Chang et al., 2013, for a discussion on global value chains. Schumpeter treated innovation as the most important driving force of capitalism. His theory of economic development distingushed between inventions and innovations. An invention is just an idea for an improved product or process. By contrast, an innovation is about the commercialization of a new product or process. This distinction between invention and innovation is reflected in globalized models of capitalist development. Competition for new technological innovations is key to accumulation of capital and social reproduction.

8.1 The innovation imperative, and global poverty and inequality

The theory of comparative advantage that underlies modern theories about trade can be traced back to the writings of Adam Smith and David Ricardo in the late 18th and early 19th centuries (Smith, 1976 [1776]; Ricardo, 1973 [1817]). By comparative advantage, Ricardo meant that countries should specialize in those activities in which they performed relatively well. The theory provides a particular perspective on global poverty, one that sees it as a residual phenomenon. That is, global poverty can be seen as a temporary condition, a condition that can be alleviated if all producers specialize in their areas of comparative advantage and enter the global system – the poor remain poor because they fail to join in. In the words of the World Bank: '[i]n sum, global economic integration has supported poverty reduction and should not be reversed' (World Bank, 2002, p. xi).

There is, however, a key assumption in the intellectual architecture of this win–win approach to globalization of which Ricardo was fully aware. Specialization in areas of comparative advantage only leads to a win–win outcome in a world of full employment, that is, if all producers have a role to play, a product to produce that someone else both wants and can afford to buy. What happens if this world of full employment does not exist?

Here we need to be informed by both Thomas Malthus and Karl Marx. Malthus, a British political economist writing in the same era as Smith, argued that the growth of population would exceed the capacity of humankind to produce the necessities required to feed it. He was wrong, of course, in the sense that our present innovating and highly productive production system is clearly able to feed the world's current population (in principle, if not in practice). However, can it continue to do so on a sustainable basis, or will our demands for present consumption undermine our capacity to deliver adequate consumption in the future (Sachs, 2004)?

Writing about 50 years later, Marx, too, had something to say of relevance to the win–win outcome to globalization. He argued that the technical progress that is key to the capitalist innovation system was inherently labour saving, and that this led to a systemic tendency towards a '**reserve army of labour**' (Marx, 1970 [1876]). In an environment of surplus labour, where productive capacities exceed consumption (in other words, where supply exceeds effective demand) there is a 'race to the bottom' for all those who do not have unique capabilities to offer. They are subject to the intensity of global competition and wages decline. In this race to the bottom, global poverty is not so much residual but relational, that is, a direct consequence of the workings of the global system (Bernstein, 1990). It is not just that real wages and absolute standards of living may decline, but that the other side of the income spectrum has seen relative gainers, able to insulate themselves from competition through special attributes that they are able to exploit to a global audience – high-end professionals, celebrities, sports people, innovators, and so on. Their incomes rise disproportionately in a global arena, leading to rising inequality, another form of poverty (see Hanlon, 2013).

What do the facts show? (For a detailed analysis see Kaplinsky, 2005.) Let us begin with poverty understood as an absolute condition, focusing on the US$1 per day target which is the key Millennium Development Goal. The number of people globally living below the US$1 per day level has remained stable since 1990 but rose between 1993 and 2006 in sub-Saharan Africa, Latin America and South Asia (World Bank, 2007).

Viewing poverty as a relative issue in relation to income distribution, the outcome has been unambiguous. In virtually every respect, as globalization has deepened, so the distribution of income within and between countries, regions, classes and genders has become more unequal (Cornia and Court, 2001; Kaplinsky, 2005). China has also played an important role in the worsening distribution of income. With 20 per cent of the world's population, growing inequality in China has meant that, notwithstanding its rapid growth rate, the population-weighted global distribution of income has widened even further (Milanovic, 2005).

Those people subject to global competitive pressures – unskilled workers and increasingly also semi-skilled and information technology (IT) workers – have experienced growing levels of unemployment and seen their relative incomes decline (Hira, 2004). This has not just been a phenomenon experienced in low-income developing countries, but in the rich countries as well, where income distribution has tended to worsen significantly over the past decade or two (Cornia and Court, 2001). In the USA (1966–2001), the top 1000th of the population gained more total growth than the bottom 20 per cent, and the top 1 per cent more than the bottom 50 per cent (Dew-Becker and Gordon, 2005, p. 36). In the UK, the minimum wage is lower in real terms than it was two decades ago (Toynbee, 2003).

Will things improve? Will these global labour markets tighten? Almost certainly not. The total industrial labour force in the 14 largest Organisation for Economic Cooperation and Development (OECD) economies in 2002 was 79 million. In the same year, China's manufacturing sector employed 83 million (Kaplinsky, 2005). More to the point, it is estimated that China's reserve army of labour – those waiting to enter paid employment and currently working in very low-productivity activities – was in excess of 100 million. To make matters worse, an increasing number of this labour force is educated and skilled, and if that was not bad enough, by 2020, India's labour force will exceed that of China. There are no signs of the global reserve army of labour drying up.

Activity 8.2

Are technological innovation and productivity growth solutions to problems of global inequality and absolute poverty?

Spend no more than 10 minutes in this activity.

Discussion

As was noted in the previous chapter, technological innovation has an ambiguous role in solving problems of inequality and poverty. Schumpeter spoke of both 'bandwagon effects' of new technological products and 'creative destruction'. While new technology can create new jobs in novel industries, for example new energy sectors such as wind farms, subsequent declines in other sectors could lead to increasing unemployment. Increasing productivity, or efficiency, may create wealth but if this is not distributed evenly then some groups in society may not be able to develop the resilience to the risks of economic downturn.

8.2   What does this portend for the sustainability of globalization?

What do these observations about the environment, climate and income distribution have to tell us about the sustainability of globalization? They suggest that globalization suffers from an internal contradiction, that is, developments that arise from its success are at the same time a threat to its future.

This contradiction can be seen in two example. First, the current trajectory of continued global growth is quite clearly unsustainable in environmental terms (Stern, 2006). The energy required to transport products in extended global value chains is placing impossible demands on the planetary biosphere. If humankind gets round to taking action to stop global warming and climate chaos, this will necessarily have to be at the expense of the current trajectory of energy-intensive production systems, probably through much higher prices for energy. The logic of shipping low-value vegetables, fruit and components around the world will be lost and profitable production systems will necessarily place a greater emphasis on proximity. Food miles, for example, are ascending in consumer consciousness as they ponder the rapidly evolving change in global climate patterns.

Second, globalization forces alterations in economic specialization. The result is frequent and significant change in employment patterns, work organization and institutional design. Perhaps more importantly, it has also led to significant changes in the pattern of income distribution (see above).

The consequence is that life appears to have become more insecure for many, including for articulate professionals in the high-income economies. To a significant extent this growing anxiety and unease is a direct consequence of the imperative for continual reinvention forced by global competition. For example, during the late 1990s, the managers of General Electric (GE) subsidiaries (one of the largest US conglomerates) were expected to evaluate and weed out the poorest-performing group of employees on an annual basis however competent they were in performing their allocated tasks. In the early years of the millennium, GE promoted a '70:70:70 policy' – 70 per cent of activities to be outsourced; 70 per cent of this outsourcing to be off-shored (that is, sent abroad); and 70 per cent of this 'off-shoring' to go to low-wage economies. It is an agenda of uncertainty, distrust and fear. This is echoed in the worldview of the former head of Intel, Andy Groves, who wrote a best-seller entitled *Only the Paranoid Survive* (Groves, 1996). In each case the prognosis was change – 'reinvention', 'reorganization', 'business process engineering' – an ongoing agenda not just in the private sector but even in state-owned bureaucracies such as the UK's National Health Service and educational systems. This world of insecurity, fear and anxiety engenders opposition to globalization, the more so as the professional classes in the high-income economies are now being threatened by the off-shoring of their own jobs to India and other lower-wage economies. This opposition can also be seen in the worldwide 'Occupy Movement' that began in 2011.

The lessons of the 19th century provide an important backdrop in understanding these possible developments in the early 21st century (Williamson, 1998). After five to six decades of growing global integration, the world economy turned inwards after 1914 with the outbreak of World War I, and the outward momentum was only regained in the decades after 1950. In between saw a period of inward focus and a reduction in economic integration. This reversal of global processes followed directly from the success of late-19th century integration. Cheap grain imports into continental Europe led to a decline in agricultural profits. This resulted in the imposition of tariffs against agricultural imports in much of Europe. Second, there was a mass emigration of unskilled Europeans as 60 million people, often literally walking across Europe, made their way to the USA between 1820 and 1914. This forced down wages in North America, and led to growing controls against migration. At the same time, the competitiveness of US manufacturers threatened the survival of European manufacturing. This resulted in the imposition of tariffs against imported manufactures, and set in train a series of 'beggar my neighbour' policies in which countries reacted against each other by ratcheting up protection against imports. Finally, the demand for growing markets and resources led to the expansion of colonialism, which spurred the imperialist rivalries that helped to fuel World War I. In each case, the seeds of change are to be found in the workings of the 19th-century global economy, and arose as a direct consequence of its success.

We can also see an interaction between the environmental, social and political internal contradictions of the contemporary capitalist production system.

Pushed to the margin of subsistence by the unequalizing and impoverishing nature of globalization, populations encroach further on fragile physical environments, exacerbating pressures on local ecologies. This leads to or deepens political conflict, as in the case of Darfur, the civil-war-torn region of Sudan, contributing to the breakdown of ordered rule (i.e. good governance) and thus providing seedbeds for forces opposing the onward march of global integration. At another level, China's energy requirements are growing to fuel its investments in infrastructure (more than 300 million people are expected to migrate to the urban areas in the coming two decades), its manufacturing sector and its commitment to private forms of transport. This is leading to growing competition for access to oil and gas in Africa and other resource-rich regions, with as yet unknown consequences for the global political architecture (see also Mohan, 2013). Will it herald a new phase of imperialist rivalry for resources, eerily similar to that of the late 19th century?

8.3 What is to be done?

We are accustomed to think positively, to find a solution for every problem (Figure 8.1). This is just as well, since the threats confronting humankind in general, and the historically advantaged West in particular, are very substantial. There is no simple answer to the growing problems besetting the globalizing economy, but there are three environment-related issues that need to be addressed.

Figure 8.1 Sorting out globalization? G8 world leaders in Tokyo, Japan, 2008 (Source: Getty Images)

First and foremost is the environmental challenge in general and climate change in particular. The aggregate numbers are overwhelming – the biosphere simply cannot withstand the pressures that sustained global growth will place on it. This has multiple consequences. We need to find a more efficient path for the generation, distribution, and consumption of energy, developing a range of energy-saving technologies and organizational structures. More rational – that is higher – energy pricing is one part of the solution, but it is only one. If it is the only solution, then higher energy prices will exacerbate the gap between the global haves and have-nots, both within and between countries. We also need to reduce material consumption patterns in the rich countries, placing greater emphasis on leisure and services, particularly if consumption in the developing world is going to grow as living standards are raised. China adds a new coal-fired power station every four days (see Chapter 7), and however efficient new forms of carbon capture might be, the expansion of energy consumption in the emerging economies is only environmentally sustainable if consumption in high-income countries is reduced.

Second, for many people and many countries, globalization is less a route to higher living standards and more a force for immiseration (economic impoverishment) (Kaplinsky, 2005). The injunction to deepening globalization involves a fallacy of composition – that is, it works for individual countries, acting in isolation, but not when all countries follow the same route (Mayer, 2002). Unfettered access to global competition, in the context of global excess capacity, means impoverishment for those without unique skills. This is the case for much of Africa and Latin America, and for a growing number of people in Western Europe and North America (whose reserve armies of labour are not just China and India, but also Eastern Europe and Central America).

In principle, incomes can be provided for these marginalized communities through the redistribution of the fruits of increased growth and productivity, but realpolitik stands in the way – the rich will not pay the taxes required to fund this redistribution, and they are increasingly able to avoid taxes in a world of liberalized financial flows. It is, perhaps, necessary to revisit the virtues of protection, but in a world of regional preferences that will at the same time allow for enhanced scale and productivity growth with a less extended and energy-intensive transport infrastructure. This means a greater emphasis on intraregional integration reflected in trade, governance systems, financial flows, migration and other elements that have become so important in the globalizing world of the past few decades.

Third, the entry of China, and soon India, as growing sources of global economic demand and supply needs to be reflected in the global political architecture. For decades this has been the playground of the rich Western countries. For example, the head of the World Bank has always been a US nominee, whilst that of the International Monetary Fund is a European appointee. How durable this division of spoils turns out to be will be an indicator of the degree to which currently hegemonic powers are willing to accommodate new entrants to the global political table.

These three factors interact. The politics of growing inequality, economic imbalances between newly emergent Asian economies and the USA and the EU, and unemployment are leading to growing opposition to globalization in many countries who have previously enthusiastically embraced it. To an increasing extent, opponents of globalization are focusing on its environmental excesses as a key point of opposition, particularly as energy prices rise. In hindsight, seen from a perspective of the earth's biosphere, the unequalizing tendencies inherent in current structures of globalized production systems may prove to have been a godsend.

Summary and looking forward

There is a widespread 'triumphalist' belief that globalization as we know it is unstoppable, but three issues challenge this belief:

- The nature of capitalist development leads to the degradation of the global commons, to global warming and to climate chaos. This is because the search for profitability leads to over-consumption by many, and because of the extended and energy-intensive transport arteries of global production systems.

- Current processes of globalization deepen inequality. This leads to growing political hostility to globalization from the marginalized, and deepens poverty, often reinforcing pressures on the environment.

- The combination of environmental impacts and inequality sets up internal contradictions that are likely to undermine the sustainability of the globalization process itself.

All of the above requires us to think about new and innovative ways in which humankind can continue to survive and prosper, living with, rather than in command of, nature. The environmental impact of globalization is integral to all three challenges and the next chapter will look at specific causes and the consequences of climate change for our future.

References

Bernstein, J. (ed.) (1990) *The Food Question: Profit vs People*, London, Earthscan.

Chang et al. (2013).

Cornia, A.C. and Court, J. (2001) *Inequality, Growth and Poverty in the Era of Liberalization and Globalization,* Policy Brief No. 4. Helsinki, Wider.

Dew-Becker, I. and Gordon, R.J. (2005) 'Where did the productivity growth go? Inflation dynamics and the distribution of income', Working Paper, 11842, Cambridge, National Bureau of Economic Research, [online] http://www.nber.org/papers/w11842 (Accessed 16 January 2012).

Groves, A.S. (1996) *Only the Paranoid Survive*, New York, Doubleday.

Hanlon (2013).

Hira, R. (2004) *Implications of Offshore Sourcing*, Mimeo, Rochester Institute of Techonlogy.

Kaplinsky, R. (2005) *Globalization, Poverty and Inequality: Between a Rock and a Hard Place*, Cambridge, Polity Press.

Marx, K. (1970 [1876]) *Capital: a Critique of Political Economy*, volume 1, London, Lawrence and Wishart.

Mayer, A.J. (2002) 'The fallacy of composition: A review of the literature', *The World Economy*, vol. 25, issue 6, pp. 875–94.

Milanovic, B. (2005) *World Apart: Measuring International and Global Inequality*, Princeton NJ, Princeton University Press.

Mohan (2013).

Ricardo, D. (1973 [1817]) *The Principles of Political Economy and Taxation*, London, Dent.

Sachs, W. (2004) 'Climate change and human rights', *Development*, vol. 47, issue 1, pp. 42–9.

Schumpeter, J. (1942) *Capitalism, Socialism and Democracy*, London, Unwin University Books.

Smith, A. (1976 [1776]) *An Enquiry into the Nature and Cause of the Wealth of Nations* (4th edn), Oxford, Oxford University Press.

Stern, N. (2006) *The Economics of Climate Change: The Stern Review*, Cambridge, Cambridge University Press.

Toynbee, P. (2003) *Hard Work. Life in Low Pay Britain*, London, Bloomsbury Academic.

Wikipedia (n.d.) Welcome to Wikipedia, [online] http://en.wikipedia.org/wiki/Main_Page (Accessed 11 January 2009).

Williamson, J.G. (1998) 'Globalization, labor markets and policy backlash in the past', *Journal of Economic Perspectives*, vol. 12, issue 4, pp. 51–72.

World Bank (2002) *Globalization, Growth, and Poverty: Building an Inclusive World Economy*, Washington, DC, World Bank and Oxford, Oxford University Press.

World Bank (2007) Key Indicators: Regional Data from the WDI Database, [online] http://siteresources.worldbank.org/DATASTATISTICS/Resources/reg_wdi.pdf (Accessed 17 September 2007).

Further reading

Dicken, P. (2007) *Mapping the Changing Contours of the Global Economy*, London, Sage Publications.

Kaplinsky, R. (2005) *Globalization, Poverty and Inequality: Between a Rock and a Hard Place*, Cambridge, Polity Press.

Milanovic, B. (2005) *World Apart: Measuring International and Global Inequality*, Princeton, NJ, Princeton University Press.

Stern, N. (2007) *The Economics of Climate Change: The Stern Review*, Cambridge, Cambridge University Press.

Climate change: causes and consequences for development

Roger Blackmore

Introduction

> There is no bigger problem than climate change. The threat is quite simple, it's a threat to our civilization.
>
> *Professor Sir David King, UK Government Chief Scientific Adviser, 2000–2007*
> *(King, 2004)*

This chapter sets out to answer two questions about climate change:

- Why is the Earth getting warmer?
- How significant are the changes going to be?

Much of the data and evidence supporting the answers have been provided by the Intergovernmental Panel on Climate Change (IPCC), set up in 1988 by the United Nations Environment Programme and the World Meteorological Organization to improve understanding about global warming. The IPCC is an extraordinary example of international and interdisciplinary collaboration between scientists and other academics across the world. Their efforts have advanced significantly our understanding of how the Earth's physical and biological systems, its atmosphere, oceans, land, ice, and the living world including ourselves, interact and influence each other. At the same time the information and evidence underpinning this understanding has been debated openly and vigorously in the media.

9.1   Why is the Earth getting warmer?

We now know that the Earth is getting warmer. Eleven of the 12 years between 1995 and 2006 were the warmest observed since instrumental records began in 1850, and every year brings new evidence of changes to climate and weather, and their environmental impacts. According to the latest report from the IPCC:

> Warming of the climate system is unequivocal, as is now evident from observations of increases in global average air and ocean temperatures, widespread melting of snow and ice, and rising global mean sea level.
>
> *(IPCC, 2007, p. 4)*

The report makes clear that this 'unequivocal warming' is outside the normal range of climate variability observed in recent centuries. In other words, the climate change now being observed is not just part of a natural cycle; there must be a new factor affecting the Earth's climate.

To understand what this might be, consider what determines the temperature of the Earth. Almost all the energy reaching the Earth's surface comes from the Sun (a much smaller flow comes from the Earth's hot interior). The Earth's temperature is controlled by the balance between the energy arriving from the Sun and that radiated out to space from the Earth as heat. This balance is influenced by four important factors: the temperature of the Sun; periodic changes in the Earth's orbit that affect the distance from the Sun to the Earth; the nature of the Earth's atmosphere; and the amount of sunlight reflected away from the Earth's surface (and thus not available to warm it). The last factor varies considerably with the weather and the seasons – snow and clouds reflect strongly, oceans and vegetation weakly.

Over timescales of thousands to millions of years the temperature of the Sun and the Earth's orbital patterns have varied. However, over the timescale of current global warming, approximately the past hundred years, these factors have not changed enough to explain the measured increase in temperature. What has changed significantly has been the composition of the atmosphere, in particular the concentration of certain gases critical to the temperature balance, known as greenhouse gases.

The greater part of the Earth's atmosphere, when dry, is made up almost entirely of three gases: nitrogen, 78 per cent by volume; oxygen, 21 per cent; and an inert gas, argon, 0.9 per cent. These three gases do not interact significantly with heat radiation from the Sun or the Earth. If these were the only gases in our atmosphere the Earth would be in a deep freeze, its mean temperature would be approximately –18 °C. The two main naturally occurring greenhouse gases are carbon dioxide (CO_2) and water vapour; others include methane and nitrous oxide. They are normally only present in small amounts, but their impact is significant. They act by absorbing the heat radiated from the Earth, and distributing it within the atmosphere. Most of the heat escapes to space, but, as Figure 9.1 illustrates, some is sent back to the Earth's surface and to the lower layers of the atmosphere where it is effectively trapped, warming both. The overall effect, known as the natural greenhouse effect, is to warm the Earth by about 30 °C to its current mean value close to 15 °C. Life depends on the warmth of the Sun being trapped in this way much as a greenhouse keeps warm on a sunny day; without it the Earth would not be habitable. (Note that the figures in this paragraph do not take account of reflected sunlight which, as noted above, is variable.)

The main reason for recent global warming can be described simply. (Sometimes a distinction is made between global warming, i.e. temperature rise alone, and global climate change, i.e. its wider impacts, but in this chapter the two are used interchangeably.) For several centuries, ever since the Industrial Revolution, Western societies have been extracting and burning fossil fuels such as coal, oil and gas to provide energy for industry, domestic use and transport, and as a result have been releasing CO_2 into the atmosphere. Today, most countries are heavily reliant on these sources for their energy. In addition, deforestation releases CO_2, and the practices of modern agriculture release methane and nitrous oxide. This has set in motion a chain of events: the release of greenhouse gases into the atmosphere leads to higher concentrations in the atmosphere that, in turn, cause additional

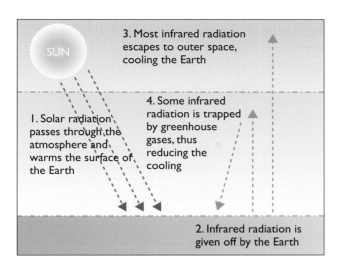

Figure 9.1   The greenhouse effect

warming of the Earth. This new factor affecting the Earth's climate is called the anthropogenic or enhanced greenhouse effect, and it is caused by human economic activity.

Global emissions of greenhouse gases arising from economic activity have grown rapidly since pre-industrial times, due to a combination of growth in global population and growth in energy use per person. Between 1850 and 2000, global population rose from just over one billion to six billion and energy use per person rose sevenfold (Open University, 2005). More people enjoyed a higher standard of living through increased consumption of goods and use of services, in spite of continuing poverty for many. In recent decades, the pace of greenhouse gas emissions has accelerated, increasing by 70 per cent between 1970 and 2004. After a short time lag the Earth's climate has responded by warming rapidly.

Figure 9.2(a) shows the contribution of the key greenhouse gases to total emissions in 2004, expressed as CO_2 equivalents, that is, the amount of CO_2 that would have the equivalent effect. The most important greenhouse gas is clearly CO_2. The main cause of CO_2 release is the burning of fossil fuel, which accounts for about three-quarters of CO_2 emissions. Land use changes, particularly deforestation, account for most of the rest with a small contribution from cement production. Methane (CH_4) is the next biggest contributor with 14 per cent, followed by nitrous oxide (N_2O) with 8 per cent. Agricultural practices are the main source of both of these gases.

Figure 9.2(b) shows the contribution of economic sectors to global greenhouse gas emissions in 2004. This is the nub of the problem: almost all economic activities today contribute to emissions. Reducing these emissions presents many and diverse challenges. The carbon stored in fossil fuels, which took millions of years to form, is being released back to the atmosphere in the space of a few hundred years. This rate of release far exceeds the capacity of the Earth's natural processes to remove it from the atmosphere by returning it to the oceans, soils and plants. This is why atmospheric concentrations of all greenhouse gases have increased dramatically since the original UK Industrial Revolution in the 18th century.

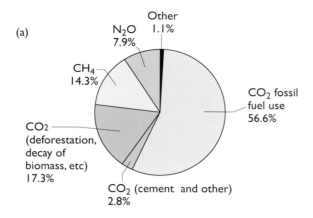

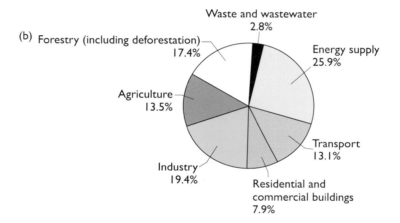

Figure 9.2 (a) The contribution of the key greenhouse gases to total emissions in 2004; (b) the contribution of economic sectors to global greenhouse gas emissions in 2004

Figure 9.3, which shows concentrations of CO_2 and other greenhouse gases in the atmosphere over the past 2000 years, illustrates this point. Until approximately 1750, concentrations of the three greenhouse gases remained roughly constant. Since then they have risen rapidly: CO_2 has risen by a third, methane has more than doubled, and nitrous oxide has increased by nearly 20 per cent.

9.2   How significant are the changes going to be?

[S]cientists are virtually screaming from the rooftops now. The debate is over! There is no longer any debate in the scientific community about this. But the political systems around the world have held this at arm's length because it's an inconvenient truth, because they don't want to accept that it's a moral imperative.

Gore (2006)

There are two reasons why scientists have been 'screaming from the rooftops' recently. The first is to do with timescales. Figure 9.3 clearly shows how much CO_2 and other greenhouse gases have increased in the past few hundred years, but how unusual is this on a longer timescale? Ice cores taken from sites on the Antarctic ice cap contain air trapped in bubbles that provide a record of the state of the atmosphere for the past 800 000 years. Analysis of this air (Lüthi et al., 2008) has shown that the Earth's climate over this period has swung eight times between long, cold glacial periods and warmer interglacial periods more like our present climate. Throughout this period, temperatures have varied from 6–8 °C colder than now to a few degrees warmer, while CO_2 concentrations in the atmosphere have fluctuated within a fairly narrow range of 180 ppm (parts per million) to 300 ppm. But the current level of CO_2, 386 ppm (2008), is now much higher than this range and rising rapidly. The implication is clear. If current levels persist, let alone continue to rise, the Earth is likely to become much warmer than it has been for nearly a million years. While the Earth has experienced higher levels of greenhouse gases and warmer climates in its long geological history, we humans, who have only existed on the Earth for about 250 000 years, have not.

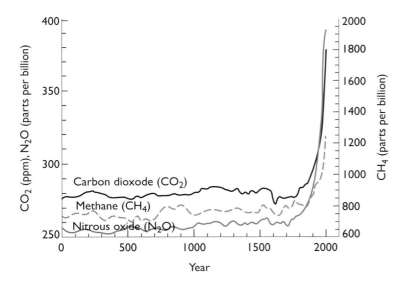

Figure 9.3 Concentrations of CO_2 and other greenhouse gases over the past 2000 years

In stark contrast to these long timescales, the time horizons of many governments are short. Their primary focus is likely to be the next election or next crisis, not the next generation. It is hard for most governments and organizations to plan far ahead into the future even though energy supplies and infrastructure take decades to change, not years. Yet many of the greenhouse gases already added to the atmosphere will persist for the next 100 years, committing future generations to a warmer world and unknown climate shocks. So far, governments have found it hard to rise to Gore's moral challenge.

The second reason for growing concern comes from the computer models that climate scientists use to explore the interactions between the atmosphere and other parts of the Earth.

Increased computer power has allowed their models to include more interactions between the oceans, land, ice, the living world and the atmosphere, leading to realistic outputs. Global circulation models are now able to model past and current climates accurately enough to demonstrate both that global warming is now occurring and that it cannot be caused by natural variability alone – it can only be explained by human activity. They are also warning that future global warming may be more damaging and more rapid than earlier models have suggested. Modelling outputs are starting to produce some scary results.

Two examples, one from modelling and the other from the real world illustrate this point. Currently, over half of the additional CO_2 added to the atmosphere is absorbed by vegetation and dissolves in the oceans. However, as the climate warms, warmer oceans hold less CO_2, bacteria in warmer soils break down organic matter faster and release more greenhouse gases, and some tropical forests could die back as drought becomes more common. Results from models (Cox et al., 2000; Cox and Jones, 2008) suggest that, as warming progresses, forests and oceans will lose some of their ability to take up CO_2 and in some cases may start to release it. In either case, the result would be to amplify and accelerate the effects of global warming.

The second example is the effect on the climate of disappearing glaciers, snow and ice in a warmer world. Snow and ice reflect most of the sun's energy back to space, keeping snow-covered areas cooler. When there is less snow, this cooling no longer happens, so in regions where snow and ice are in retreat, for example around the Arctic, warming is expected to be enhanced. Models show this by predicting a much greater rate of warming in and around the Arctic than elsewhere on the globe. What they have not predicted is the speed of the retreat of Arctic ice in the summer, or of glaciers on Greenland (Pfeffer et al., 2008). In the summers of both 2007 and 2008 the sudden decline of Arctic ice surprised and alarmed the people monitoring events (NSIDC, 2008).

For scientists, as Gore pointed out, the debate about the reality of climate change is now over. The focus has moved on to a better understanding of its impacts, and providing more useful forecasts for governments and communities. A major focus is to communicate to leaders at all levels the significance of future changes and the need for prompt action. One approach is to predict more specific impacts expected at different levels of warming. For example, the UK Government Stern Review (HM Treasury, 2006a) predicted that a 1 °C rise will mean the disappearance of small mountain glaciers and severe damage to coral reefs. A 2–3 °C increase will see significant changes in water availability and falling crop yields in many developing regions. With an increase of 4 °C, sea level rise will threaten major world cities including London, Shanghai, New York, Tokyo and Hong Kong. These examples illustrate what might happen if adaptive measures are not taken, but it is not possible to predict with precision that a particular event will occur at a particular temperature. The effects of future climate change are still difficult to predict accurately because they are unlikely to act in isolation and will add to existing pressures on vulnerable human and natural systems.

In spite of these caveats, the general trends should be clear. If global temperatures rise to 2 °C or more above pre-industrial levels – and the Earth is already half a degree warmer now – a series of major, damaging impacts are predicted to occur.

A rising number of people are threatened by hunger and from regional water shortages, and are at risk from a rising intensity of storms, droughts, floods and heat waves. In addition, irreversible processes may begin to destroy the Amazonian rainforest and melt the Greenland ice sheet (which would add 7 metres to sea levels), and a significant proportion of all species may become extinct.

Activity 9.1

With so much evidence pointing to the human contribution to climate change that is likely to have a dramatic impact on livelihoods and lifestyles globally, why do you think governments find it hard to accept the need to reduce greenhouse gas emissions?

Spend no more than 10 minutes in this activity.

Discussion

Previous chapters have noted several possible reasons. In Chapter 6, it was noted that modernization is embedded in an ideology of progress and success. For proponents of modernization, it could be difficult to grasp that modernization could actually be detrimental and regressive. International relations could also be a reason. Leaders of countries who are currently economically powerful, such as the USA and the UK, may be unwilling to make the first move to address climate change for fear of losing out to another country, or for fear of declining living standards in the short term in their own country that could lead to political instability. Other factors could include the influence of interest groups such as industry lobbies and religious organizations.

9.3   Paths to action

The goal of climate change policy makers has always been to prevent this situation occurring. This is stated in Article 2 of the UN Framework Convention on Climate Change:

> The ultimate objective … is to achieve … stabilisation of greenhouse gas concentrations in the atmosphere at a level that would prevent dangerous anthropogenic interference with the climate system. Such a level should be

achieved within a time frame sufficient to allow ecosystems to adapt naturally to climate change, to ensure that food production is not threatened and to enable economic development to proceed in a sustainable manner.

(UNEP/WMO, 1992 p. 4)

Many would consider that 'dangerous interference' is already occurring and that the examples just described demonstrate that the rise in global temperature needs to keep below 2 °C to avoid the worst consequences of climate change. To achieve this goal, models now indicate that concentrations of all greenhouse gases in the atmosphere need to be held back to the equivalent of 450 ppm CO_2. This would require global emissions to fall eventually by 80 per cent or even 90 per cent of current levels – a much tougher target than had been thought only a few years ago, and one that requires action be taken as soon as possible to have any prospect of success. In the words of the head of climate change for the UK government: 'If action is delayed or is slow, then there is a significant risk of much larger increases in temperature' (Pope, 2008).

A further issue concerns the unequal distribution of the impacts of climate change. As has been noted in previous chapters, the wealthy can afford the measures needed to adapt more than the poor. The subsistence farmers and fishermen of the Ganges or Nile deltas (and many others) are far more vulnerable to climate hazards than Londoners protected by the Thames Barrier, and have fewer financial and other resources to help them recover from rising sea levels, floods or storms. In general, developing countries are much more vulnerable than developed, and the weakest economies are the most vulnerable. Some regions are particularly susceptible due to their geography, for example small islands and the large delta regions of Africa and Asia, while in others, such as Arctic nations and dry areas in low latitudes, the early effects of climate change are likely to be particularly acute.

The unequal distribution of impacts is of importance for another reason. It contrasts the fortunes of developed countries that have been responsible for most greenhouse gas emissions until recently, with developing countries that have not but are suffering disproportionately. Inequity has dogged global negotiations to reduce greenhouse gas emissions. Developing countries want to see developed countries acting first, whereas developed countries are fearful that if countries such as China follow their path of development, then greenhouse gas emissions will soar. To find some way round this stand-off blame is not a likely foundation of a constructive agreement. Professor Stephen Pacala (a US climate scientist) turned his attention to the behaviour of individuals rather than nations. He did this by estimating the CO_2 emissions of everyone in the world ranked by their income, a task he described as 'not particularly easy'. What he found was a stark contrast between the CO_2 emissions of the poor and the rich. The contribution from the poorest half of humanity is less than 7 per cent of the total.

The 3 billion poorest people … emit essentially nothing. The take-home message here is that you could increase the emissions of all those people by putting diesel generators or anything you wanted into their lives and it would not materially affect anything I'm going to say [about stabilising carbon dioxide to 450 ppm]. In other words, the development of the desperately poor is not in conflict with solving the climate problem, which is a problem of the very rich. … In contrast, the rich are really spectacular emitters.

(Pacala, 2007)

The rich he described as the top 500 million who earn somewhat more than the average US citizen, and are found in all countries, rich and poor. This 7 per cent of humanity emit half of all emissions, and reducing these levels is necessary to have any chance of reaching the targets. Pacala's approach changes the focus from countries and actions by 'them', to individuals and our own responsibilities. It is likely, for example, that some of the authors of this book, while not the richest individuals, are creating very high carbon footprints as they fly from conference to conference. Change has to begin at home.

Activity 9.2

Reflect on climate change and vulnerability. Why, according to Pacala, is tackling climate change a problem for the wealthy? Do you agree that individual actions to reduce carbon emissions can be an effective way to manage climate change?'

Spend no more than 10 minutes in this activity.

Discussion

Pacala's argument is that it is wealthy countries that have benefited from industrialization at the expense of others. Therefore, those countries, and those of us who live in them, have a responsibility to address the impact of climate change. Our individual actions, for example over-consumption, have contributed to climate change, therefore we need to adapt our lifestyle to ensure that it does not detrimentally affect others. As with campaigns that aim to make development personal (see Chapter 10), the campaign against climate change is also focusing on what individuals can do. You may think about not flying so often or cycling instead of driving your car.

However, it is also argued that these actions are not enough in themselves. Institutions, in particular the state, need to establish economic and social frameworks that ensure climate change is managed equitably, to protect those who are most vulnerable.

Summary and looking forward

This chapter has examined how the Earth's climate has warmed in recent decades due to changes in its atmosphere, specifically increases in CO_2 and other greenhouse gases. This increase has been the result primarily of the use of fossil fuels in processes of industrialization. The level of greenhouse gases now far exceeds that of the past 800 000 years and is increasing rapidly. Greenhouse gases persist in the atmosphere for centuries rather than years, already 'committing' the Earth to significant further warming. Climate models are signalling a growing risk that climate change may be more rapid and damaging than earlier thought. Yet government's short time horizons for planning are not addressing the issue adequately. Societies move even more slowly, taking decades to change intrastructure. Climate impacts become more damaging with rising temperatures, affecting all societies and ecosystems, but are spread unequally. The most vulnerable people are the poor, who are not the cause of the problem.

When discussing climate change, it is all too easy to be overwhelmed by the scale of the problems it poses and the inadequacy of most political responses or the effect of individual action. To avoid the dangers and damaging impacts of climate change, there is clearly a need both to reduce emissions of greenhouse gases dramatically and to prepare for and adapt to the changes already in the pipeline. It is time, however, to move away from the narrative of doom and gloom to one of opportunities and solutions. Continents in the tropics and subtropics, for example Africa, South America and southern Asia, are going to be hardest hit by climate change, yet they hold most of the planet's renewable resources in the form of energy from sunlight, rainfall and fresh water, stores of biodiversity and young people. Their populations mostly lack capital to develop these resources in sustainable ways, but they have the potential and the natural resources to be a major part of the solution to the global challenges of climate change and sustainable development.

Simple mechanisms such as the transfer of new, clean technology coupled with fair trade could transform the outlook. As Stern points out in his review of the economics of climate change (HM Treasury, 2006b), acting now and committing spending now is going to be much less costly in the medium term than doing nothing, and there is still time to avoid the worst impacts of climate change.

Avoiding the effects of climate change are starting to be taken seriously in new development strategies, in particular focusing on holistic approaches that take the environment into account in assessing wellbeing.

References

Cox, P.M., Betts, R.A., Jones, C.D., Spall, S.A. and Totterdell, I.J. (2000) 'Acceleration of global warming due to carbon cycle feedbacks in a coupled climate model', *Nature*, vol. 408, pp. 184–7.

Cox, P.M. and Jones, C. (2008) 'Climate change: illuminating the modern dance of climate and CO_2', *Science*, vol. 321, pp. 1642–4.

Gore, A. (2006) *An Inconvenient Truth*, Paramount Classics, Paramount Pictures, USA.

HM Treasury (2006a) *Stern Review: the Economics of Climate Change, Part 1: Climate Change – Our Approach*, London, HM Treasury London, [online] http://www.hm-treasury.gov.uk/sternreview_index.htm (Accessed 17 June 2009).

HM Treasury (2006b) *Stern Review: the Economics of Climate Change, Executive Summary*, London, HM Treasury, [online] http://www.hm-treasury.gov.uk/sternreview_index.htm (Accessed 17 June 2009).

Intergovernmental Panel on Climate Change (IPCC) (2007) 'Summary for policymakers' in Contribution of Working Group I to the Fourth Assessment Report of the Intergovernmental Panel on Climate Change, *Climate Change 2007: the Physical Science Basis*, Cambridge: Cambridge University Press.

King, D. (2004) Quoted in an interview with The Climate Group, The Office of Science and Technology, London, [online] http://www.theclimategroup.org/news_and_events/professor_sir_david_king/ (Accessed 20 October 2008).

Lüthi, D., Le Floch, M., Bereiter, B., Blunier, T., Barnola, J.-M., Siegenthaler, U., Raynard, D., Jouzel, J., Fischer, H., Kawamure, K. and Stocker, T.F. (2008) 'High-resolution carbon dioxide concentration record 650,000–800,000 years before present', *Nature*, vol. 453, pp. 379–82.

National Snow and Ice Data Centre (NSIDC) (2008) 'Arctic sea ice down to second lowest extent; likely record low volume', Press Release, National Snow and Ice Data Centre, University of Colorado, USA, [online] http://nsidc.org/arctic/news/ (Accessed 20 October 2008).

The Open University (2005) *Population and Energy Use*, [online] http://www.open.ac.uk/T206/longtour.htm, accesssed November 2005.

Pacala, S. (2007) 'Equitable solutions to greenhouse warming: on the distribution of wealth, emissions and responsibility within and between nations', Address to the 35th Conference of the International Institute for Applied Systems Analysis, 13–16 November 2007, Vienna, [online] http://www.iiasa.ac.at/Admin/INF/conf35/docs/programme.html?sb=3 (Accessed 20 October 2008).

Pfeffer, W.T., Harper, J.T. and O'Neel, S. (2008) 'Kinematic constraints on glacier contributions to 21st-century sea-level rise', *Science*, vol. 321, pp. 1340–3.

Pope, V. (2008) 'The Met Office's bleak forecast on climate change', *The Guardian*, 1 October 2008.

United Nations Environmental Programme (UNEP)/World Meteorological Organisation (WMO) (1992) *United Nations Framework Convention on Climate Change*, Geneva, United Nations Environment Programme and World Meteorological Organisation, Information Unit on Climate Change.

Further reading

Henson, R. (2008) *The Rough Guide to Climate Change* (2nd edn), London, Rough Guides.

Lynas, M. (2007) *Six Degrees: Our Future on a Hotter Planet*, London, Fourth Estate.

Maslin, M. (2008) *Global Warming: a Very Short Introduction* (2nd edn), Oxford, Oxford University Press.

Making international development personal

10

Sarah C. White

Introduction

Each autumn, hundreds of thousands of people across the UK and the USA get involved with Christmas shoebox campaigns, filling a shoebox with items – small toys, stationery, sweets, toiletries, accessories – as gifts for children in difficult circumstances in far away countries (see Figure 10.1). The largest of these – Operation Christmas Child – celebrated 20 years of its programme in 2010, which it claimed had 'brought joy into the lives of over 80 million children worldwide' (Figure 10.2, Samaritan's Purse, 2011). The appeal of such campaigns is beyond question. While other charities report reduced giving and 'donor fatigue', the shoebox campaigns have successfully mobilized people through schools and churches to send well over one million shoeboxes from the UK and Ireland every year from 2001 to 2010.

Figure 10.1   Caitlyn Hawley and Ellie Cowley of Sheffield with the shoeboxes they collected on their joint birthday party. The girls asked their friends to come with shoeboxes instead of presents (Source: Samaritan's Purse)

Figure 10.2 Haitian girl receiving a shoebox at a distribution centre (Source: Samaritan's Purse)

What is it about such campaigns that people find so appealing? In large part, it is probably their immediacy. Like child sponsorship, they offer a direct link to an individual, an opportunity to 'put a smile on a child's face'. For some there is an explicitly religious motivation, a way of 'showing God's love'. But for most it is the sense of human connection or a moral duty that is at the heart of the appeal. Filling the boxes mimics an old-fashioned pleasure of Christmas giving, when small tokens were appreciated with no expectations of price tags measured in hundreds of pounds. Packing the boxes brings people together in a warm glow of shared goodwill. The gifts are small and personal: you can imagine the happiness they will bring. Fundraising material reinforces this as it shows small children opening boxes with pleasure and excitement on their faces. And immediacy is also promised through the delivery of the boxes. The very box that you have packed will be taken by the organization, loaded on a lorry and delivered directly into the hands of a child in need.

Making development personal is, therefore, a very powerful activity. Personal images and stories tug at the heartstrings and motivate us to take action. What is true for Christmas gift boxes also holds for longer term work in relief and development. Personal stories help us feel we understand distant contexts and bring them down to a scale that makes us feel we can get involved. Even large organizations like the World Bank, which rely mainly on generalized models and statistics, reserve a space in their publications and communications for the more immediate, intimate stories, to show the human impact of the programmes they are pursuing.

Such stories and pictures do not just portray the recipients of development, of course. The key characteristic of the personal is that it establishes relationship. Therefore, Christmas shoebox publicity shows not only smiling children receiving the boxes, but also smiling volunteers filling and sending them. As the relationship is only imagined, however, it is also safe. To fill a shoebox is a limited, tangible thing. The gift is to an (idealized) image of a child, a child whose situation of need means they will simply be happy with what they are given, not a real child who might appreciate some things and not others, or come back with further, inconvenient demands. World Bank publicity has exactly the same function, if at a different level. It too shows the organization as powerful and humane – able to intervene effectively in ways that change people's lives for the better, and caring about the least well off. It too is apparently able to enter and leave a situation at will. In making development personal, we are not then simply promoting a particular view of others. We are also, very importantly, telling a story about ourselves.

This chapter aims to identify and interrogate the processes through which development is made personal. This brings together two related but distinct strands of argument. In the first place, the chapter will consider how the growing concern with 'wellbeing' in international development policy and practice takes forward the agenda of 'making development personal'. In the second place, making development personal is also a call for **reflexivity** in how we evaluate development; it is a call to pay attention to the way that who we are makes a difference to what we see, how we act and how people respond to what we say and do. As we become more conscious of our own identities and values, however, this also prompts us to ask more questions about the ways that other people's identities are being represented and the kinds of relationships that are assumed or established in development work. This critical reflection gives a new perspective on one of the major claims within the international development industry over the past 40 years; that it is increasingly focusing on the social and the personal, rather than simply measuring economic indicators, showing greater sensitivity to those at the margins, and increasingly concerned with the 'voices of the poor' (Narayan, 2000). This chapter weaves together these two strands as a way to consider the benefits and disadvantages of different models of development, and where we might go from here.

Activity 10.1

Thinking critically about the Christmas shoebox campaign, would you regard this as a form of development or 'charity', and is there a relationship between the two? How does it make development personal?

You might also spend a few minutes thinking about how your own beliefs about development impact on how you evaluate this campaign?

Do not spend more than 10 minutes on this activity.

Discussion

It is clear that the campaign establishes in this relationship of giving a connection between the direct action of the donor and the recipient. The imagery associated with giving is of kindness and generosity. Images of misery and poverty are transformed to that of happiness and excitement as a result of having received the shoebox. This type of imagery in NGO fundraising campaigns has received much criticism from development specialists and social scientists who argue that it perpetuates a sense of dependency between donors and aid recipients; the shoebox campaign does not challenge any of the core structural reasons as to why poverty exists, but instead perpetuates a paternalistic relationship between the giver and receiver.

However, an opposing view of the campaign would emphasize that both givers and recipients are gaining some benefit from their interaction. It would focus on the generosity of those who make up the shoeboxes and perhaps critique the development specialists and social scientists as elitist, not leaving any space for ordinary people to get involved in trying to make a difference. Other NGOs have argued that in order to ensure that development and poverty reduction remain in the attention of people in countries like the UK it is necessary to construct campaigns that make development personal, using this type of imagery.

The following sections will take up these ideas by first examining the shift in development policy to focus increasingly on 'wellbeing', as an example of making development personal, and then review the impact of history, scale, power and agency on the role of the personal in development.

To trace the whole story of development's engagement with the personal would be a major task, well beyond the scope of a single chapter. Instead, we concentrate on its current phase: the growing momentum to make the achievement of wellbeing the goal of international development policy. At the macro level, this is part of a move to go beyond GDP as a measure of national progress. This has been advanced most notably by Joseph Stiglitz, Amartya Sen and Jean-Paul Fitoussi in a report for President Sarkozy (Stiglitz et al., 2009). At the micro level, wellbeing brings together established agendas for participation with growing recognition of the psycho-social, especially in post-conflict situations. More than any other development approach, it brings the personal to the centre of attention. If you want to know about someone's wellbeing, you cannot simply rely on external measures, you need to ask him or her how s/he is thinking and feeling. People's own subjective perceptions, rather than simply their objective circumstances, are therefore central to a wellbeing approach. As Copestake (2008) puts it, wellbeing marks out a 'discursive space' that allows new kinds of questions to be asked and new kinds of answers to be sought. In place of the predominant policy preoccupation with what is problematic and negative, a focus on wellbeing asks people what they would like, and what they aspire to, which has brought a new energy into discussions of public policy and administration.

Wellbeing can encourage a 'joined-up', more holistic approach to policy, which considers relationships between different areas of life (as in the 'work–life balance') and between economic achievement, environmental sustainability and human fulfilment. We can see here how programmes that focus on wellbeing could also be applied to development in industrialized countries. A focus on wellbeing leads to asking *how* programmes are implemented and the terms of interaction between staff and the people they serve. For example, beyond the achievement of targets, are people being treated in ways that respect their dignity and enhance self-confidence? This draws attention to the need to consider the quality, not just the quantity of what is provided, and the process of implementation, not just the end results.

Focusing on wellbeing is also a prompt for reflexivity. As wellbeing is something which concerns us all, questioning other people about their wellbeing almost inevitably leads us to think about our own. At an individual level this may challenge taken-for-granted assumptions about who is well off and who is needy, who is in a position to advise and who is in need of help. At a collective level also, wellbeing has the potential to break down the familiar binaries of global North and South, developed and developing, modern and 'traditional' that have marked default ways of thinking in international development (see Hanlin and Brown, 2013). In 2007, for example, UNICEF produced shock waves in the UK when it produced a 'score card' of child wellbeing in rich countries, and the UK came at the bottom of the list. (UNICEF ranked 20 countries in this order: the Netherlands, Sweden, Denmark, Finland, Spain, Switzerland, Norway, Italy, Ireland, Belgium, Germany, Canada, Greece, Poland, the Czech Republic, France, Portugal, Hungary, the USA, the UK (UNICEF, 2007).Whatever the merits of the particular measures UNICEF used, the potential to reverse conventional assumptions is an important advance, considering the way that value has been codified in racial and other terms through the recurrent contrast of 'the rest and the west' (Hall, 1992). However, the wellbeing approach is not without limitations, which will be examined as we go along using the core themes that we have been considering throughout this book: history, scale, power and agency.

The following section will consider history, recounting the narrative of a shift in development from economic model to a set of programmes increasingly sensitive to social and personal concerns, suggesting some alternative ways that the story might be interpreted. It will then look at scale and how making development personal at times can collapse, and at other times can accentuate local and global relationships. An important question is whether wellbeing can deliver on its promise to bring the personal into development policy making, right across the scale from national and international statistics to community self-help projects and individual empowerment.

Looking at power and agency, we consider the politics of how an emphasis on personal responsibility may be incorporated in policy, and how values regarding difference, be it gender, ethnicity or normative ideas of good and bad lives, are embedded in culture and, therefore, definitions of wellbeing. At the individual level, we look at how scope for agency and autonomy has been seen as a key dimension of people's wellbeing. Finally, we return to the questions of relationship and reflexivity, as we consider the processes through which development is made personal, not only for others, but also for ourselves.

10.1 A history of the personal in development

While it is tempting to emphasize what is new and distinctive about the concept of wellbeing in development, the story can also be told in other ways. One way, as suggested above, is to see the present advocacy of wellbeing as the latest stage in a cumulative drive to 'make development personal'. This section explores this perspective and uses it to reflect on the nature of the story of international development's history more broadly.

International development is commonly presented in terms of policies based on statistics and hard facts, its models developed by economists skilled in determining the distribution of resources in particular ways. However, development is also about the telling of tales, the spinning of stories, in which it presents itself and the world in ways calculated to convince, to elicit support, or even to beguile. One function of this is to make dominant models appear natural. This returns to Mohan's argument of the role of cultural hegemony in development policy (Mohan, 2013). There are many stories in development, some contradictory, some deeply intertwined. Despite a premium on novelty, few of the stories are new, rather they twist together old archetypes of heroes and villains, of fall and salvation, of folly and enlightenment, of achievement in the face of great obstacles, of tragic pride. The story that international development is increasingly 'making development personal' is one of these strands, and, as usually told, goes something like this.

The roots of development, as noted in Hanlin and Brown (2013), go back at least to 19th century colonialism, but the birth of the 'industry' is generally dated to the mid-1940s, and the formation of the Bretton Woods Institutions (the IMF and the World Bank). In the 1950s and 1960s there was a general confidence that economic growth along with social, political and technological modernization would enable poorer countries to 'catch up' with the modernity of the West (see Chapter 6). In the 1970s, however, came recognition that the benefits of economic growth were not 'trickling down' as planned, and that where there was growth there could also be increasing inequality. This led to the formulation of 'basic needs' approaches, with direct targeting of 'the poor'. It was also at this time that women and gender began to be taken more into account, and this led to the social aim of empowerment being introduced alongside economic concerns with income generation.

The 1980s saw a shift from state- to market-based economic paradigms with the IMF and World Bank advancing 'structural adjustment' and 'stabilization' measures that involved massive cuts to government programmes. Recognition that these resulted in considerable damage to some of the most vulnerable in societies led UNICEF to proclaim the need for 'adjustment with a human face' (Cornia et al., 1987). From the 1980s into the 1990s, there was a growing emphasis on the importance of participation in development, which sought to shift 'beneficiaries' from being passive targets of others' plans to having an active role in shaping and carrying out development themselves. This has taken many different forms. Minimally, it has attempted to ensure community buy-in and some local resource mobilization as counterpart to outside funding. More significantly, it has summoned support for previously excluded groups to contest local elections or for people to devise and evaluate their own community programmes. It has also led to a broader concern with the 'voice' of poorer or otherwise disadvantaged people. After women, children were the first population group to be marked for special recognition, signalled by the near universal ratification of the Convention on the Rights of the Child (CRC) in 1989/90. Through the 1990s and 2000s, other groups have followed – people with disabilities, youth, elderly people – and other social issues, such as race (to a limited degree), culture and religion.

From 1990, the *Human Development Report* of the United Nations Development Programme (UNDP) was launched, to offer a more human-centred alternative to the economic focus of the World Bank Development Reports. This was supported by a growing movement to provide a more social account of economics, in the form of Amartya Sen's entitlements and capabilities approach (Sen, 1981; Johnson and Farooki, 2013). This sought to emphasize what (poor) people can be and do in practice, rather than simply looking at the absence of formal constraints. It subsequently evolved into a strong identification of development with freedom (Sen, 1999). Livelihoods frameworks were also devised to overcome narrow income-based indicators of poverty. Instead of working from bureaucratic categories that divided people's lives up into different sectors (e.g. health, education, agriculture, transport, etc.) these frameworks sought to see people's lives more holistically. This again aimed to highlight that people were active, dynamic agents. It also opened space to recognize that people draw on many different kinds of 'capital' in constructing their livelihoods: social, political, and cultural, as well as the more familiar physical and economic forms. In the 2000s, there has been a rediscovery of the importance of basic provision by the state, with resurgent interest in social protection programmes. As already noted, it is at this point that wellbeing enters the stage, with its distinctive focus on the 'subjective' dimension of people's own values and perceptions as a central policy and programmatic concern.

Taken on its own terms, this telling of the story frames development as a linear progress towards greater enlightenment and increasing inclusiveness. This clearly chimes with the more general idea of historical change as social progress, of which international development plays a part. An alternative narrative frame might emphasize continuity rather than change, and cycles rather than linear progression. Popular participation, for example, has been an abiding concern. While development programmes might like to present themselves in technical or managerial terms, in fact they are political programmes that need popular support if they are to succeed. In one way or another, therefore, participation – and how to make people participate appropriately, in forms that support rather than undermine the planners' intentions – is a recurrent theme. One of the earliest sociological studies of a development intervention, the 'New Deal' Tennessee Valley Authority in the USA, was published in 1949. The focus of this study is popular participation, and the different ways in which elements within the Authority sought to capture and co-opt participation for their own interests. As the author states, one of the abiding aims of development agencies is to turn 'an unreliable citizenry into a structured, readily accessible public' (Selznick, 1966 [1949], p. 220).

Similarly, concerns with psychology and culture (including religion) are not new. These ideas were a strong part of the modernization agenda of the 1960s. There is also continuity in the politics that underlie such interests. 1960s US theorists of social and political modernization were concerned with managing social and political change in the context of Cold War fears of advancing communism. 'Winning hearts and minds' was seen as an important complement to military strategies, and for many the linkages were even more direct. Prominent academics such as Samuel Huntington (1965, 1968) and Walter Rostow (1960, see Chapter 6), for example, doubled as advisors to the Pentagon and the CIA on US strategy in Vietnam. The rediscovery of culture and religion in 21st century development thinking appears to be an indication of growth in cross-cultural sensitivity and awareness that has come with increasing globalization. But paradoxically, it is also linked directly to the threat some forms of radical Islam are perceived to pose to Western dominance, and the wish to 'wage war on terror' (for example, Huntington, 2003). These recurring concerns suggest that the story is only partial, and there is a darker side to relations. This is the military support to dictators, undercover involvement in the politics of supposedly sovereign nations, the worldwide industry in arms and munitions, direct military aggression and economic plunder by some transnational corporations (see Brown and Hanlin 2013). Here again the pattern is cyclical and repetitive, setting in trail further spirals of violence and dispossession played out within and between countries of the global South. Considered in this light, the comforting tale of development's increasing humanity begins to look rather one-sided. Coming back to the idea of reflexivity, therefore, it is important to look beyond the story and consider what interests might underlie the policies and outcomes of development throughout history. For example, encouraging women to participate in economic activity may be seen as liberating them from patriarchy, but it might also serve the interests of transnational capital in the expansion of labour and consumer markets.

Finally, the very linearity of the story suggests that there is just one (international, European–US led) story to be told. Economic development and industrialization was the great goal of the 20th century for many nations, and national planning the signatory move of all governments newly free from colonization (Robertson, 1984). But there was never one conception of what development might be. The USSR model of socialist development was very different from Mao Zedong's vision for China. Gandhi's vision of self-reliance in India contrasted sharply with Nehru's commitment to industrialization. Nyerere's vision of African socialism in Tanzania was very different from Nkrumah's vision of scientific socialism in Ghana. While development might serve as a common rallying cry, therefore, what development means has always been essentially contested.

Therefore, there are many different ways that the story of development has been told. All of them include some perspectives and exclude others, highlight some features and cast others into shadow. The point is not to claim that one story is true and another false, but to draw attention to the processes that underpin the dominance of some stories and the marginalization of others. A large part of the difference in narratives derives from *who* is doing the telling. As a common saying puts it: 'where you stand depends on where you sit.' Put more academically, this links to Edward Said's (1978) study of Orientalism, in which he rejects the distinction between 'pure' and 'political' knowledge. For Said, the European art, literature and historical studies that produced Western knowledge about the Arab and Islamic world, for example, throughout the European imperial period was not simply academic or cultural, but infused with 'a Western style for dominating, restructuring, and having authority over the Orient' (Said, 1978, p. 3). In international development we have an explicit concern with policy, the 'what should be done' question, which brings the power of particular development discourse even nearer to the surface.

Therefore, rather than taking dominant narratives at face value, we need to consider the way they are framed: what and who they exclude and include, what is represented as 'good' and 'bad' development. As we asked with reference to the shoeboxes, what images of others do different models of development present, what do they imply about the 'self' or the institution that is doing the describing, and what do they imagine is the relationship between these two, the 'self' and the 'other'? It is also necessary to ask about the political implications of the changes they describe or enact. To what extent do they promote liberation or greater social control? To what extent do they enable people to speak out with a genuinely different voice, or might they neutralize any alternative by re-casting it in the terms of an established and authorized version? As the incorporation of wellbeing into international development policies increasingly gathers momentum, it is important to remember that this approach, like others, requires critical assessment.

Activity 10.2

The events and policies mentioned above may be familiar to you, but are retold and represented here to illustrate that development has always been contested.

If you were to tell your own story about processes of change in your life or your neighbourhood what events, policies, agencies and actors would you include and why? How have the changes, or what others might call development, been contested and by whom? In your view, has there been improvement in your own or others' way of life or standard of living as a result of these changes? Have there been any downsides to this change? Can you link these changes to deliberate policies of development that may originate locally or even globally? Once you have your answers to these questions you might like to show them to another member of your family or someone you know from the same area to see if they have the same perspective on change as you.

Spend no more than 40 minutes on this activity.

Discussion

This activity is another example of making development personal by placing yourself at the centre of change, as an object of development if you like. While your answer will be very context specific, you might want to think first about the history of your area. Has it been influenced by particular industries or particular people? The north of England, for example, was once the heart of industrialization but in the later half of the 20th century this sector began to decline, which impacted on the living standards of people in the region. Some have argued that government policies in the 1980s in particular hastened this decline, which was met with resistance from trade unions who contested these changes. If you were to ask a local resident, a unionist and a member of the government for their assessment of change during that period you are likely to get very different answers! We could also draw international links to this example, seeing at the same time an increase in connections between British industry and global markets where products could be manufactured offshore and imported back to Britain. Analyzing change in this way not only personalizes development, but also shows the interconnections between local and global scales, which we will examine more closely in the next section.

10.2 Scaling up the personal

The Christmas shoeboxes demonstrated how the promise of personal connection can seem to cut through geographical distance and the complexity of international relations. This collapsing of scale and distance is perhaps the most vital technique in the portfolio of those who seek to mobilize or motivate people to action. It is the foundation of some of the most successful movements for change. The slogan 'think global, act local', for example, has been a cornerstone of popular environmental mobilization. Another is the boycott of South African goods sponsored by the Anti-Apartheid movement, which made people's everyday supermarket choices a political issue. In both cases, an imaginative identification with an apparently distant person or situation is linked to the possibility of personal action in an immediate practical context. The action both derives from the sense of personal connection and in turn affirms it, as it establishes or thickens a tangible association. And of course, the hallmark of globalization is the increasing density of such links across national borders, whether or not they are consciously recognized (e.g. see Mohan and Butcher, 2013).

The paradox of globalization is that it not only increases the density of links across borders, at times making the world feel smaller, it can also increase distances and dissolve any sense of personal responsibility. For example, the transnationalization of industry has reduced connections between producers and consumers. Food is grown at unprecedented distances from where it is consumed; clothing is produced thousands of miles away from where it is sold. Choices of what to eat or wear, therefore, seem to take place in a vacuum, an entirely personal matter with no wider consequences. The trading agreements that determine their price, the environmental impact that their production involved and the consequences of these for those who grew or made them, seem almost literally to belong to another world.

One way of making these connections more visible is to 'humanize' international statistical indicators of development. The most influential example of this has been the Human Development Index (HDI), adopted by the UNDP in 1990. The HDI is a composite index that brings together national indicators of life expectancy, years in schooling and GNP per capita (Johnson and Farooki, 2013). A still fuller picture may be gained through the Multidimensional Poverty Index, which combines ten indicators across the three dimensions of health, education and living standards (UNDP, 2011). These go some way towards a more comprehensive measure of wellbeing, but they still rely only on external measures. For statisticians, the additional attraction of wellbeing is its use of subjective indicators to measure the outcomes of national or even international policy at the individual level. This promises a direct link from the corridors of power to people's living rooms; from the necessarily blunt and generalized instruments of policy to the rather intimate specificity of how people are feeling about their lives.

There is much debate about how credible it is to use subjective wellbeing in measuring national progress (see Box 10.1). Some people dismiss it out of hand, preferring to stay with apparently objective indicators. Others accept the validity of subjective measures at a local level, but are doubtful about how you can understand a subjective view without some sense of the context from which it emerges. Many would agree with James (2008, p. 76) that 'it is very awkward to try and apply [wellbeing] to interests outside the immediate life of individual persons and their close circle.' Still others, however, maintain that aggregate measures of mood or satisfaction in different areas of life do give us meaningful results. The Warwick Edinburgh Mental Wellbeing Scale (WEMWBS), for example, asks people to respond to 14 statements about how they have been feeling and functioning mentally over the previous two weeks. Lower scores in Iceland three months after the banking crash in 2008 than shortly before it are claimed by researchers to show that such very personal indicators are able to pick up changes in sentiment at a national scale (Guðmundsdóttir, 2009).

Box 10.1 Subjective wellbeing

The field of subjective wellbeing is led by psychologists, though with a considerable following amongst economists. It is primarily quantitative and predominantly concerned with measurement. Intellectually, the main dispute is whether more emphasis should be placed on satisfaction and pleasure or on meaning and fulfilment as the foundation of being happy with your life.

The leading school of thought tends towards the first view, defining subjective wellbeing as a combination of cognitive (thinking) satisfaction measures and affective (feeling) measures of happiness or other emotions. Sometimes the satisfaction measures concern 'life as a whole' and sometimes they are broken down according to specific domains or areas (see Diener et al., 1985, for a very commonly used approach). The emotions are usually grouped into two types, positive and negative, with separate questions about each, as most theorists believe that having a negative feeling is not the same as simply the absence of a positive feeling (see Watson et al., 1988).

Examples of the second approach see wellbeing as deriving from satisfaction of 'basic psychological needs' (for example, Ryan and Deci, 2000) or 'positive psychological functioning,' (for example, Ryff, 1989). Both of these include the ability to exercise autonomy along with competence and positive relationship with others in their understanding of personal wellbeing.

Subjective measures have also been used to argue the negative long-term effects of unemployment on mental wellbeing (Seaford, 2010). There remain, however, good reasons to be cautious. It is not clear what such generalized measures can tell us that we do not already know from other sources. There is also a dangerous level of political indeterminacy and space for cooption for what could be considered non-progressive agendas. Correlations do not prove causation (see Hanlon, 2013). For example, the finding that unemployment correlates with lower levels of subjective wellbeing could be read as showing that unhappy people are more likely to lose their jobs and find it more difficult to get another, rather than that losing their jobs undermines people's sense of wellbeing (see Stiglitz et al., 2009). The political and policy outcomes of these two readings would be diametrically opposed.

The Icelandic example raises another interesting question: can collectivities, at the scale of the community or the nation, have a sense of wellbeing? You may have come across the term 'depressed neighbourhoods' and we know that local renewal and regeneration schemes can increase a local sense of pride and raise people's aspirations. Scheper-Hughes (1992) describes how people in the *favela* (slum) that she studied in Brazil saw themselves as having 'bad blood' and weaker bodies than the rich people who lived in town. In these cases, the notion of collective wellbeing seems to indicate more than just the aggregate of how people within them are feeling about their lives as individuals. Or perhaps more accurately, the relationship seems to run in the reverse direction, that is, the individual sense of wellbeing is derived from the collective, rather than the other way around. This would represent a considerable challenge to the dominant assumption amongst some wellbeing theorists, that the locus of wellbeing lies within the individual.

While governments and development agencies may wish to emphasize the personal as a means to rally people to their cause, much of development policy and practice tends to obscure the particularity implied by personal connection. Kothari (2005) points out that colonial administration, the predecessor to international development, often valued highly in-depth, personal, country-specific knowledge including the understanding of language or culture. By contrast, contemporary bilateral and multilateral development agencies have often emphasized translocal technical 'expertise' over place-specific knowledge and been captivated by the potential for context-free models with their scope for 'scaling up'. This model can be institutionalized in the structure of international donor communities if staff spend much of their lives in meetings, administration, workshops and reporting, locked in the capital city with a small group of people very much like themselves. Some organizations, including ActionAid International and the World Bank, have taken to providing staff with 'immersion' programmes to counteract this, giving staff an opportunity for a brief while to 'live the lives of the poor and understand poverty in all its dimensions' (World Bank, 2003 cited in Eyben, 2006, p. 64). This follows a practice that has long been part of participatory development: building in time for outsiders to take part in some activity with people as a way to build rapport and come to understand something more of their lives. There is, of course, a high potential for such initiatives to be tokenistic, patronizing and a significant waste of poor people's time. The fact that they are taking place, however, does indicate recognition of the power of personal encounter to generate a reflexive process, and some auto-critique within development agencies of their comfort zones within institutional and work practices.

While personal contact can help to overcome differences in culture and experience, it can also have the opposite effect. Here again we hear echoes of the colonial past. Colonial knowledge was clearly grounded in (often unexplored) assumptions of the national and racial superiority of the colonizing power (Kothari, 2005; Memmi, 1974 [1957]; Said, 1978; Mudimbe, 1988). Development geographies of global North and South, imageries of scale and categories of developed/developing and universal/specific are susceptible to a similar charge (Mohanty, 1988; Matlanyane-Sexwale, 1994; White, 2002; Kothari, 2006). Such consciousness receives relatively little reference in the 'on-stage' professional productions of development's drama: the official reports, meetings and exercises in 'policy dialogue'. However, in 'off-stage' informal, personal interaction they are often a powerful presence, ghosts of the ancestors that thicken the air in international discussions in which the terms of development policy and practice are hammered out (Crewe and Fernando, 2006). Personal interaction can, as the 'immersion' idea assumes, be the means through which people are challenged to new kinds of insight, and to seeing things for a moment from a very different point of view. But it is also in personal encounters and unconscious behaviours that we enact our gendered/classed/racial/ethnic selves, and often reproduce through our interactions the power relations in which they are inscribed.

Analyzing international development policy and practice at different scales highlights that it is a deeply political process (Chatterjee, 1993). One aspect of this is that different ideological perspectives will result in very different policy prescriptions. But another aspect is that personal dynamics, commitments, values and who has the ear of whom are the stuff by which policy is also influenced. Eyben (2006), reflecting on the interface between bilateral donors and recipient governments, talks of how in-depth personal relationships are critical if the donors are to be effective in influencing policy in the countries where they give aid. The resonance of such an approach with colonial perspectives on administration perhaps offers further support for the cyclical view of development's history advanced above. The next section, however, will explore further the role of power in making development personal.

Activity 10.3

Look again at the definition of 'subjective wellbeing' in Box 10.1. Summarize what you think are its advantages and disadvantages. Do you see the possibility to scale up such an approach to address national or international development challenges such as inequality or environmental degradation? Think of an example from your own locality.

Do not spend more than 20 minutes on this activity.

Discussion

While there are advantages to wellbeing as a measure of development as noted in earlier sections, an area of criticism is that it is based on individual emotional and cognitive states. Some might also argue that, like other development agendas before it, wellbeing has stemmed from Western preoccupations, in this case with happiness. Given that many in the global North are materially better off it is perhaps not surprising that development has taken this turn towards more non-material, even spiritual, matters. However, for many in the global South, basic survival is still the priority; the need for food, clean water and shelter. Given this greater focus on the individual it could be argued that it is difficult to see how wellbeing could be applied at larger scales, the national or the international level, for example. National leaders such as David Cameron (the UK) and Nicolas Sarkozy (France), at the time of writing, have made open attempts to, such as happiness, to inform their policy approaches to national development, but a set of appropriate indicators is yet to be established.

10.3 The personalization of power and agency

As we saw in the previous sections, narratives about 'the personal' are implicitly, and at times explicitly, about power. It is about development becoming more democratic, about ordinary people having a greater say in what is happening to them. The centrality of subjectivity within wellbeing approaches aims to build on and advance this, to produce a 'person-centred' approach that begins with people's lives in the round and seeks to enable them to meet their own aspirations.

While this seems something to be welcomed, there are also reasons for caution. The holistic character of wellbeing can be used to mask power relations and inequalities. How wellbeing is defined, whose wellbeing matters and where responsibility lies for bringing it about are all influenced by power relations. Sometimes these are overt, with one person asserting his or her claims against those of others. But they can also be implicitly, deeply embedded in the shared meanings that make up the culture within which people live their lives. For example, during a research project in rural India carried out by the author and colleagues, a woman made the following comment: 'According to our Hindu faith a woman's happiness lies in her family being happy' (White et al., 2011, p. 22).

There are a number of things we can draw from this. Most obvious is the gender dimension. While most people who took part in this project identified helping others as important, women seemed to have a particularly central role in maintaining the wellbeing of others, often at the expense of their own (see Figure 10.3). Interviews referenced strong mothers who manage to support their families in the face of their husbands' incompetence or absence (often through death). The centrality of women in the household is not reflected, however, in positive gender indicators. In 2001, in the region where this study took place, the state of Punjab, only 874 females were born for every 1000 males, against the Indian national average of 933. This reflects widespread son preference expressed through sex selective abortion and infanticide or neglect of female babies. The incidence of domestic violence is also unusually high. This suggests that the statement above may itself be a product of particular power relations: that it is not only that women find fulfilment in making their family happy, but that the wellbeing of women in their own right may be culturally defined as secondary to that of others. This is not, of course, a pattern that is limited to India or to the global South.

Figure 10.3   Low income Indian women in Amritsar carry home branches and twigs to use as firewood when cooking. However, collecting firewood, a task undertaken by women, places strain on their bodies (Source: Getty Images)

The other issue that this statement draws to our attention is that happiness, as part of wellbeing, is not something that just occurs naturally, but is culturally and, in this case, religiously defined. In fact, in this research in India and Bangladesh, the authors found that discourses about wellbeing and about religion were very difficult to disentangle. People talked about material needs: to have enough money, a house, a job and so forth. However, even these were commonly circumscribed in moral terms, by stressing, for example, that 'money isn't everything', that it is important to 'live within one's means' and to 'be satisfied with what one is given'. The following statement was more explicit than most in the study about the importance of religion, but it is not untypical:

> My view is that life is a blessing, a gift that we receive from God. If we have come upon this earth then it is also essential that we do our duty and side-by-side always remember to take his name. It is only if we perform meritorious actions in this life that we can be prepared for what comes afterwards. Apart from that, it is important that one looks after one's family; that one works hard; that we walk on a righteous path and tell the truth and perform good acts. Without all of this, life is meaningless. The rest is in God's hands.

> *(White et al., 2011, pp. 20–21)*

Such discourses might not strike us immediately as being about power, but of course they are. They tell people how they should behave. They mark some actions as impermissible and exclude people who do not conform. They are the basis on which judgements are made, judgements of oneself and of others. As Foucault (1981) has argued in his *History of Sexuality*, power is by no means always negative or always about domination and control. It is also implicated in the constitution of desire, of what gives life meaning, of what people understand as making for happiness. There is nothing inherently sinister in this, but it is important to recognize it. Narratives of wellbeing that are packaged in academic or scientific terms are no less culturally based, no less bearers of ideology, no less from a particular point of view, than those narratives that stem from religious tradition.

Following Foucault a little further, there are two implications to consider. The first is that wellbeing may become a political tool. Rose (1989) applies Foucault's analysis to the question of how modern states secure the governance of their citizens. While legal and policy sanctions on misbehaviour clearly exist, critically, Rose argues:

> a citizen subject is not to be dominated in the interests of power, but to be educated and solicited into a kind of alliance between personal objectives and ambitions and institutionally or socially prized goals or activities.

(Rose, 1989, p.10)

The appeal of wellbeing is, of course, precisely that it is a positive charge that the majority of people are attracted to. We need to pay attention, therefore, to the particular ways in which wellbeing is defined politically, and the distributive outcomes that these might have. Indicators that people are 'poor but happy' could be used, for example, to argue for cutting development aid. Identifying wellbeing as something that inheres within the individual and is his or her own responsibility could be used to justify the reduction of state services or to argue against affirmative action policies (Sointu, 2005).

The second implication derives from Foucault's upending of the conventional narrative that the 20th century was an age of sexual freedom, liberated from the constraints of 19th century moralism. To the contrary, he maintained that the explosion of talk about our intimate lives has opened us up to ever greater intrusion, and ever greater surveillance. This is also a concern for wellbeing perspectives, and for the interest in 'making development personal'. Asking about people's families, their feelings, their hopes and their sense of self is clearly more intrusive than the conventional preoccupations with income and asset-holding. While this may offer a means to challenge stereotypes and re-orient power relations, it will not necessarily do so.

Within development, the complicated relations between power and the personal have been most fully explored by feminists, particularly in the area of women or gender and development. A key aspect of the feminist movement had been consciousness-raising groups, in which women came together to reflect on the ways in which they had learned the habits of subordination, learned to see themselves as less able, less valuable, than men. By no means all of those who joined development agencies in the 1970s and

1980s to work with women on gender issues were feminists. But for those who were, reflection on their own experience and the power-play that existed in personal relationships was an important part of the empowerment process. This provided an important forerunner for subsequent thinking on personal wellbeing.

Jo Rowlands' (1997) book, *Questioning Empowerment*, provides a good example of this. Reporting on her observations amongst women in NGOs in Honduras, she identified three aspects of empowerment: the contextual or material, that is, what belonged to the wider environment; the 'structural', that is, what belonged to the character of the organization; and '"inner" psychological or psycho-social processes' (Rowlands, 1997, p. 110) (see Figure 10.4).

Figure 10.4   Women help in the distribution of electoral kits in Tegucigalpa, Honduras, on 24 November 2008 in preparation for the general elections – an example of women empowering themselves and others (© AFP/Getty Images)

She states that it was the last category that provided 'the most significant area of change' that people perceived, such that she identified it as 'the "core" of the empowerment process' (ibid, p. 111). She goes on:

> Central to these [psychological and psycho-social processes] are the development of self-confidence and self-esteem, and a sense of agency, of being an individual who can interact with her surroundings and cause things to happen. I would also include 'dignity' in the core aspects. This is a word that many of my interviewees used, to mean self-respect, self-esteem, and a sense of being not only worthy of respect from others, but of having a right to that respect. I have also included 'a sense of self within a wider context'. Although not as explicitly identified in interviews, it seems to be an essential part of the 'core' if the individual is to be able to move out of the gender-assigned roles that her context and culture have given her.
>
> *(Rowlands, 1977, pp. 111–12)*

While the 'core' concerned how women felt about themselves, it was also profoundly social. As Rowlands (1997, p. 95) states: 'Part of the empowerment process is learning to stop criticizing others and oneself.' The effect of this is that one can then be empowering to others in turn. One of the women described it like this:

> Before, with my children, I would hit them and get hysterical with them and all that. Now I don't do that. I treat my children with love. I don't go around hitting them, I care for them. Who else is going to care for them for me? Before I used to hit them with a belt like a madwoman, when I just lived shut in the house. If my mother says to me 'the kids did such and such, you should hit them for it, you haven't hit them,' I say 'no, if I don't care for my children, who will?'

(Rowlands, 1997, p. 54)

The focus here on the substantive content of people's experience is clearly very different from the very thin and abstracted character of the dominant approach to subjective wellbeing introduced above.

The final way in which a focus on personal wellbeing can make a real difference in development practice is in drawing attention to the terms on which the staff of organizations engage with clients – and indeed relate to one another. Here again there is a debt to feminism and its insistence that 'the personal is political'; that how you behave in personal interaction is a bearer of social power. But the debt is more direct than this. Mitchell (1995) points out that international development discourse and practice frame 'the object of development' as something external, 'out there', rarely seeing organizations themselves as part of the picture. This is part of the conventional construction of development agency noted above. An important part of the women in development/gender and development agenda, however, was to blow apart this tendency to locate all problems in 'the field'. Instead, a major part of the argument was that gender was also an issue 'back here' in the sexist assumptions and behaviour within the agencies themselves.

Relating this back to wellbeing, the significance of personal relationships in enhancing or undermining wellbeing is frequently noted. In the 1990s, social relationships captured the imagination of development organizations such as the World Bank under the terminology of 'social capital'. This followed the work of Robert Putnam and others, who argued that the extent of development depends on the quality of associational life, social networks and trust in the community (for example, Putnam, 1995). Following the default tendency in international development to look outward at 'the field', however, social capital tends to be considered only in relation to the 'target group' and their links with family, friends or neighbours. What this misses is that a significant degree of 'social capital' can inhere – for good or ill – within the relationships associated with intervention itself. Devine (2002), for example, describes how it was having strong patronage relations with the local NGO in Bangladesh that determined who amongst the poor gained access to land in a land redistribution programme.

Fraser (1997, p. 25) points out that in the USA: 'Public assistance programmes "target" the poor, not only for aid, but for hostility.' It is not unusual to find that hostility made material in the physical barriers erected between staff and clients, the character of the building claimants are made to attend, the way that their waiting is managed. Some would argue, of course, that claiming benefits should not be made too attractive, and that all means should be used to encourage clients to seek alternatives. However, for those taking a wellbeing perspective, the institutional denial of claimants' dignity cannot be defended. Similarly, organizations that use participatory rhetoric can in reality be hierarchical internally. Across the global North and South, fault lines of gender, class, caste or ethnicity can be found that separate staff and clients, complete with the misinformation and prejudice that accompanies such inequalities. A discourse of 'deserving' and 'undeserving' poor is part of these divisions. Instead of challenging this state, however, hierarchical relationships established within development projects can actually reinforce it, and become themselves the means through which class-, caste- or ethnicity-based antagonism is reproduced. This is expressed in numerous ways, through disparaging terms used to refer to clients, as 'ignorant', 'primitive' or 'backward'; institutionalized deference such as making people wait; lecturing clients; material extraction, either in bribes or patterns of gifting in which staff receive village produce yet never give anything in return (see also Pigg, 1992). While these practices may be commonplace, it is rare to find an organization in which this becomes an explicit focus for staff reflection.

Such patterns, of course, are unlikely to enhance wellbeing, although it should be noted that these things are not always clear-cut. As in the case described by Devine mentioned above, in some cultural contexts patron–client relations may offer the main means that people can use to help them achieve goals, and provide security and protection. In such circumstances, clients may assume an attitude of inferiority as they actively seek a patron whom they then draw into a web of obligation, mobilizing their weakness as part of a claim. This suggests a question to reflect on at the close of this section. How far do ideas of agency or empowerment carry cultural baggage? For 'us' to recognize 'their' agency, do they have to express it in 'our' way?

Activity 10.4

Given the different power relationships involved in development, from local to international relations, as well as culturally relative understandings of what wellbeing means, how would you design a project to enhance wellbeing in your local community?

Do not spend more than 20 minutes on this activity.

Discussion

First of all, who did you define as needing 'wellbeing' and why? Did you include yourself or did you target a particular group. If so, what do you think is the power relationship between yourself and that group? These are very personal questions designed to help you think, if you haven't already done so, about how power at different scales impacts on how you have constructed your view of the world.

Now, take it a step further and think about how your view of the world has been constructed. You might think of books you've read (feminist ideas, for example, or economists), ideas from your family and friends, or from religion, government statements or the media. All of these sources can reinforce your own subjective understanding. Which sources of information have a more powerful influence over constructing your point of view about development and the meaning of wellbeing? Where have these sources of information developed their perspective? Undertaking a process of critical self-reflection may feel a bit uncomfortable at times as we challenge our own entrenched beliefs, but as we hope you've seen from this chapter, it is an invaluable process to begin to develop an understanding of where your own perspective comes from, how it influences your thinking about the world, and why development programmes, even with the best intentions, can fail or succeed.

Summary and looking forward

This chapter has considered the issue of making development personal through the prism of wellbeing, and has linked this to the core themes of history, scale, power and agency that have been considered throughout this book. Overall the orientation has been towards reflexivity, to think again over what we already 'know' and to consider how this constructs the people who give and the people who receive; the people who write and the people who are written about; the people who are photographed and the people who view the pictures.

The chapter began by considering how development is made up of many narratives, and how each of these is grounded in a particular set of power relationships, and a particular point of view. It then considered scale and the challenges of shifting wellbeing from an individual approach to an indicator for national development.

Finally, power and agency were considered. Here we looked at how wellbeing and the personal can be coopted, either to reconfirm social and cultural inequalities, or in the pursuit of a non-progressive political agenda. The importance of agency to people's sense of wellbeing was considered, particularly in the context of empowerment programmes and the significance of the terms on which development agencies interact with those they seek to serve. The ambivalent scope of personal interaction to improve development outcomes on the one hand and reinforce tensions on the other was also noted.

To finish, consider the argument that in our increasingly interdependent world, international development does not need to be *made* personal, it *is* personal. We contribute to the form it takes in everyday choices about what to wear, what to eat or how to travel. Whether we choose to think about it or not, each of these choices may have an effect on the livelihood or living conditions of someone on the other side of the globe. Learning tools focused on in this chapter, such as self-reflection and critical evaluation, help us to question the role of government, media, development agencies and even ourselves. This enables us to challenge 'taken for granted' assumptions, and above all make it clear that how we act, what we consume, and how we talk to and about others, matters in our interdependent world. Of course, it is important not only to critique development but also to look for practical solutions, and taking wellbeing as a focus can sharpen these choices considerably. What would the world look like if human fulfilment and environmental sustainability were really at the centre of policy? What would it mean locally, in your school, your workplace, your neighbourhood, your city centre if they were organized so as to promote their inhabitants' wellbeing? What would it mean to international relations, if the wellbeing of individual countries were seen to derive from relationships within the global community? When you begin to think about it you realize what a fundamental reorientation of political, economic and social life it would mean. How might it challenge, or perhaps fulfil, the kind of 'personal', charitable link promised by the shoebox campaigns?

While wellbeing may be a newcomer to international development, it is a concept with a very long history. It reflects perhaps *the* core human question, asked by religious and philosophical thinkers throughout the ages: what does it mean to live well? (See, for example, Haidt (2006) who tracks how thinkers have approached the allied notion of happiness throughout human history.) Thought about like this, we might see international development as one set of answers to this question, answers born out of the characteristic 20th century preoccupations of economic growth, national sovereignty, social modernization and technological innovation. For some in international development, wellbeing may still mean no more than this: a way of rebranding an old set of ideas, practices and relationships without any substantial change. For others, however, to talk about wellbeing in development signals something more distinctive. In being unavoidably moral and political, it explodes any idea that development is simply technical or that a particular kind of development is inevitable. In being unashamedly personal, it emphasizes that how we relate to one another in our personal, work, consumer and political lives makes a difference. For people who think like this, the entrance of wellbeing on the development landscape signifies that development by itself is no longer able to contain people's aspirations. There is a need for a bigger vision.

References

Brown, W. and Hanlin, R. (2013) 'Introducing international development', in Papaioannou, T. and Butcher, M. (eds) *International Development in a Changing World*, London, Bloomsbury Academic/Milton Keynes, The Open University.

Chatterjee, P. (1993) *The Nation and Its Fragments: Colonial and Post-colonial Histories*, Princeton, NJ, Princeton University Press.

Copestake, J. (2008) 'Wellbeing and international development: what's new?', *Journal of International Development*, vol. 29, issue 4, pp. 00–00).

Cornia, A.C., Jolly, R. and Stewart, F. (1987) *Adjustment with a Human Face: Protecting the Vulnerable and Promoting Growth*, Oxford, Clarendon Press.

Crewe, E. and Fernando, P. (2006) 'The elephant in the room: racism in representations, relationships and rituals', *Progress in Development Studies*, vol. 6, pp. 40–54.

Devine, J. (2002) 'Ethnography of a policy process: a case study of land redistribution in Bangladesh', *Public Administration and Development*, vol. 22, pp. 403–14.

Diener, E., Emmons, R.A., Larsen, R.J. and Griffin, S. (1985) 'The satisfaction with life scale', *Journal of Personality Assessment*, vol. 49, pp. 71–5.

Eyben, R. (ed). (2006) *Relationships for Aid*, London, Earthscan.

Foucault, M. (1981) *The History of Sexuality, Volume 1: An Introduction*, Harmondsworth, Penguin.

Fraser, N. (1997) *Justice Interruptus: Critical Reflections on the 'Post-Socialist' Condition*, London, Routledge.

Guðmundsdóttir, D.G. (2009) 'The impact of economic crisis on mental well-being and happiness', presented at the 1st World Congress on Positive Psychology, Philadelphia, USA, 18–21 June 2009.

Haidt, J. (2006) *The Happiness Hypothesis: Putting Ancient Wisdom to the Test of Modern Science*, London, William Heinemann.

Hall, S. (1992) 'The West and the rest: discourse and power', in Hall, S. and Gieben, B. (eds) *Formations of Modernity*, Oxford, The Open University.

Hanlin, R. and Brown, W. (2013) 'Contesting development in theory and practice', in Papaioannou, T. and Butcher, M. (eds) *International Development in a Changing World*, London, Bloomsbury Academic/Milton Keynes, The Open University.

Hanlon, J. (2013) 'Inequality – does it matter?' in Papaioannou, T. and Butcher, M. (eds) *International Development in a Changing World*, London, Bloomsbury Academic/Milton Keynes, The Open University.

Huntington, S.P. (1965) 'Political development and political decay', *World Politics*, vol. 3, pp. 386–430.

Huntington, S.P. (1968) *The Political Order of Changing Societies*, New Haven, CT, Yale University Press.

Huntington, S.P. (1996) *The Clash of Civilizations and the Remaking of World Order*, New York, Simon and Schuster.

James, W. (2008) 'Well-being: in whose opinion, and who pays?' in Corsin, J. (ed.) *Culture and Well-Being: Anthropological Approaches to Freedom and Political Ethics,* London, Pluto Press.

Johnson, H. and Farooki, M. (2013) 'Thinking about poverty' in Papaioannou, T. and Butcher, M. (eds) *International Development in a Changing World*, London, Bloomsbury Academic/Milton Keynes, The Open University.

Kothari, U. (2005) 'From colonial administration to development studies: a post-colonial critique of the history of development studies' in Kothari, U. (ed) *A Radical History of Development Studies*, London, Zed Publications.

Kothari, U. (2006) 'An agenda for thinking about "race" in development', *Progress in Development Studies*, vol. 6, pp. 9–23.

Matlanyane-Sexwale, B. (1994) 'The politics of gender training', *Agenda*, vol. 23, pp. 57–63.

Memmi, A. (1974 [1957]) *The Colonized and the Colonizer*, London, Souvenir Press.

Mitchell. T. (1995) 'The object of development: America's Egypt' in Crush, J. (ed.) *Power of Development*, London, Routledge.

Mohan, G. (2013) 'Rising powers' in Papaioannou, T. and Butcher, M. (eds.) *International Development in a Changing World*, London, Bloomsbury Academic/ Milton Keynes, The Open University.

Mohan, G. and Butcher, M. (2013) 'Spaces of development: cities, mobilities and ecologies' in Papaioannou, T. and Butcher, M. (eds) *International Development in a Changing World*, London, Bloomsbury Academic/Milton Keynes, The Open University.

Mohanty, C.T. (1988) 'Under Western eyes: feminist scholarship and colonial discourses', *Feminist Review*, vol. 30, pp. 61–88.

Mudimbe, V.Y. (1988) *The Invention of Africa: Gnosis, Philosophy and the Order of Knowledge*, Bloomington and Indianapolis, IN, Indiana University Press.

Narayan, D. (ed.) (2000) *Voices of the Poor: Can Anyone Hear Us?* Washington, DC, World Bank.

Office for National Statistics (ONS) (2011) 'Measuring national well-being', [online] http://www.nmhdu.org.uk/news/measuring-national-wellbeing/ (Accessed 5 February 2012).

Pigg, S.L. (1992) 'Inventing social categories through place: social representations and development in Nepal', *Comparative Studies in Society and History*, vol. 34, issue 3, pp. 491–513.

Putnam, R.D. (1995) 'Bowling alone: America's declining social capital', *Journal of Democracy* , vol. 6, issue 1, pp. 65–78.

Robertson, A.F. (1984) *People and the State: An Anthropology of Planned Development*, Cambridge, Cambridge University Press.

Rose, N. (1989) *Governing the Soul: The Shaping of the Private Self*, London, Routledge.

Rostow, W.W. (1960) *The Stages of Economic Growth: A Non-Communist Manifesto*, Cambridge, Cambridge University Press.

Rowlands, J. (1997) *Questioning Empowerment: Working with Women in Honduras*, Oxford, Oxfam.

Ryan, R., and Deci, E. (2000) 'Self-determination theory and the facilitation of intrinsic motivation, social development, and well-being', *American Psychologist,* vol. 55, pp. 68–78.

Ryff, C.D. (1989) 'Happiness is everything, or is it? Explorations on the meaning of psychological well-being', *Journal of Personality and Social Psychology*, vol. 57, pp. 1069–81.

Said, E.W. (1978) *Orientalism*, New York, Routledge and Kegan Paul.

Samaritan's Purse (2011) 'About Operation Christmas Child', [online] www.operationchristmaschild.org.uk/about (Accessed 8 August 2011).

Scheper-Hughes, N. (1992) *Death without Weeping: The Violence of Everyday Life in Brazil*, Berkeley, University of California Press.

Seaford, C. (2010) 'Well-being: human well-being and priorities for economic policy-makers', nef working paper 2.

Selznick, P. (1966 [1949]) *TVA and the Grass Roots: A Study in the Sociology of Formal Organization*, New York, Harper and Row.

Sen, A. (1981) *Poverty and Famines: An Essay on Entitlement and Deprivations*, Oxford, Oxford University Press.

Sen, A. (1999) *Development as Freedom*, Oxford, Oxford University Press.

Sointu, E. (2005) 'The rise of an ideal: tracing changing discourses of wellbeing', *The Sociological Review*, vol. 53, issue 2, pp. 255–74.

Stiglitz, J., Sen, A., Fitoussi, J.-P. (2009) *Report of the Commission on the Measurement of Economic Performance and Social Progress*, [online] http://www.stiglitz-sen-fitoussi.fr/documents/rapport_anglais.pdf (Accessed 5 February 2011).

United Nations Development Programme (UNDP) (2011) 'Multidimensional Poverty Index (MPI)', *Human Development Reports*, [online] http://hdr.undp.org/en/statistics/mpi (Accessed 8 August 2011).

United Nations International Children's Fund (UNICEF) (2007) 'Child poverty in perspective: an overview of child well-being in rich countries', Innocenti Report Card

7, Florence, UNICEF Innocenti Research Centre, [online] http://www.unicef.org/media/files/ChildPovertyReport.pdf (Accessed 5 February 2012).

Watson, D., Clark, L.A. and Tellegen, A. (1988) 'Development and validation of brief measures of positive and negative affect: the PANAS scales', *Journal of Personality and Social Psychology*, vol. 54, issue 6, pp. 1063–70.

White, S.C. (2002) 'Thinking race, thinking development', *Third World Quarterly*, vol. 23, issue 3, pp. 407–19.

White, S.C., Devine, J. and Jha, S. (2011) 'Religion, development and wellbeing in India', RaD Working Paper 54, University of Birmingham.

World Bank (2003) p. 202.

Further reading

Rowlands, J. (editor) (1997) 'Analysing empowerment, a dynamic view' in *Questioning Empowerment Working with Women in Honduras*, Oxford, Oxfam.

Smith, M. and Yanacopulos, H. (2004) 'The public faces of development: an introduction', *Journal of International Development*, vol. 16, pp. 657–64.

White, S. (2010) 'Analysing wellbeing: a framework for development policy and practice', *Development in Practice*, vol. 20, issue 2, pp. 158–72.

Epilogue

Melissa Butcher and Theo Papaioannou

Throughout this book, and its companion volume, *International Development in a Changing World*, we have argued that to comprehend the complex and multifaceted nature of development, that is, to generate new perspectives on its economic, social, political and cultural processes, it is important to analyze it through a framework of power, agency, scale and history. This framework is both explanatory and normative, helping us explore questions of what 'is' international development, and also the contested question of what international development 'should' be.

Studies of power in international relations have been highlighted as essential for understanding new perspectives on development. The chapters in this book have ranged from discussions of military power and its impact on development (Brown), governmental power that can determine who is in need and if they should be rescued (Aradau), to institutional power that can both increase and decrease the vulnerability of different populations (Smith). Joseph Hanlon asked the question of whether the power of civil society, such as non-governmental organizations, can make a difference, or perhaps make matters worse. At the other end of the scale, Sarah White focused on the agency of individuals, to negotiate the terms and conditions of their own lives, although always aware of the power relations around them.

The intersection between power and agency is an ever-present feature of development that marks not only relations between states, institutions and people but also the production of knowledge itself. The prevalent use of statistics, for example to measure development, or the dominance of particular theories, and subsequent ideologies, such as of 'modernization' (Robbins), highlights how those with power have swayed the model of development at any given period of time. But power as such is not immutable. The different levels of agency that individuals and institutions possess can lead to shifts in borders and thinking, as relationships are negotiated. For example, we have seen a move away from analyzing development purely through economic indicators towards 'happiness' or wellbeing indices.

As suggested in many of the chapters in this book, power and agency can be exercised at different scales, impacting on models and practices of development at local, national, regional and international levels. This multi-scalar perspective makes visible the interconnections inherent in development processes in a globalized world. We've seen the example of trafficking discussed in Chapter 4, where questions of security for women are tied to local economic conditions and transnational linkages between countries that form the routes to both negative and positive freedom. But perhaps nowhere are the scalar interconnections of development more evident than in debates on the future of energy and the impact of climate change. For example, the growing of bio-fuels in Brazil, while perhaps solving some energy problems and creating wealth there, also created vulnerability in many other countries that are internationally linked to Brazil through its agrarian exports. This shift from food to fuel production in one locality increased vulnerability for thousands, including people living in Western countries, as food prices rose in the face of declining production.

However, as the various case studies in this book have highlighted, there is a differential impact of factors such as climate change on countries as a result of history. A historical perspective has often been forgotten in development policy and practice that emphasizes the 'modern' and the next big idea. Yet case studies can show how an understanding of history can also generate a better understanding of development in practice and why one country, such as Haiti, may have very different outcomes to its neighbours (Chapter 5). In this analysis we should also take into account the place of Haiti in international relations (power and scale) and geographical factors such as its vulnerability to cyclones.

Incorporating these perspectives, it has been part of the explicit aim of this book, and its companion volume, to emphasize a holistic approach to development, taking into account the past to be able to understand the present and why some development practices have been successful or failed. You may finish this book with a sneaking suspicion that history repeats itself when it comes to development: that there are always powerful forces within international relations that will attempt to sway development thinking and practice in a particular direction for self- or national interest as much as humanitarian motivations. But we finish with a reminder of new perspectives on agency. Whether in individual choices or within collectives, we are not only subject to a changing world, but have the potential to drive that change as well.

Glossary

accumulation

Generally the amassing of objects of wealth; the increase in wealth or the creation of wealth.

appropriate technology

The movement in favour of intermediate technologies for development that is small scale, labour intensive, energy efficient, environmentally sound and locally controlled.

benevolence

The disposition to do good, a charitable feeling that protection implies.

capital

Often used loosely to refer to a manufacturer's machinery and agricultural equipment, but more broadly any form of wealth capable of being employed in the production of more wealth.

civil society

Tends to refer to those institutions, organizations and actors that operate beyond the public sphere or organized politics and government. In this context, alongside citizens and small groups, both not-for-profit organizations such as non-governmental organizations, and for-profit institutions such as private corporations can be said to be part of civil society.

civil war

Collective killing and use of force for some collective purpose, mainly within one country and where the fighting is primarily between the people of that country. Often one side is able to use the coercive capacities of the state.

coercive peacekeeping

When not all parties to a violent conflict agree to a peace accord, and it is necessary to use force to keep the peace.

Cold War

The state of hostility between the USA and the Soviet Union from 1947 to 1991. It was called a 'cold war' because it did not involve a direct violent confrontation between the two sides, and thus was not a 'hot war'. It was assumed that direct confrontation would lead to Mutually Assured Destruction (MAD).

command economy

Economy in which production (generally under the control of state-owned enterprises) was planned in detail centrally by the state. They are associated with communist party governments, in contrast to the capitalist market system.

development in reverse

In this context, refers to processes of deindustrialization in developed countries such as the USA's 'Rustbelt' but can also be applied to developing countries who see their living standards fall and witness loss of services such as education and healthcare as a result of war, civil conflict, economic crisis and structural adjustment policies.

distributional role

In the context of the state, the state deciding who gets what when and how.

emergency

A natural disaster or war or violence that poses an immediate threat to life and health. If the local community or country cannot cope, outside help may be needed.

empowerment

The process through which people can be actively involved in acting in and shaping their world. This includes, but is not restricted to, incorporation in political processes of decision making.

fear

The feeling of anxiety or apprehension that something may be dangerous or harmful, or that the unknown consequences of change may be harmful.

food security

Exists where adequate food supplies are grown, processed, not withheld, transported and distributed to consumers at prices that consumers can afford to pay on a global scale.

Gini coefficient

A measure of inequality. The value can be between 0 and 1, where 0 is equality and 1 is inequality. Any value between 0 and 1 represents the level of inequality in a country and is one way of comparing inequality between countries.

global architecture

The structure of the global economic and political system of firms, nation states and their interactions which is governed by sanctions for those who either do or do not conform.

global commons

That which no one person or state may own or control and which is central to life. The two most obvious examples are the oceans and the air we breathe.

global risks

According to Beck, *three logics or types of global risk* that together interact to shape the world as we understand it – environmental crises, global financial risks and terrorist threats. Terrorism is seen as distinct as an intentional act resulting from planning and deliberation, whereas economic crises and environmental crises derive from multiple causes working together organized in poorly understood systems and thus are seen as more likely to be perceived as a matter of chance and misfortune.

globalization

At its most general, the increasing interconnectedness of the world, through various avenues including increased flows of economic, political and religious ideas across regions.

human development

According to the UN, the process of enlarging people's choices and building human capabilities.

humanitarian relief and aid

Emergency and/or other urgent relief in cash or in kind, including food aid and short-term reconstruction.

human trafficking

Defined by the UN as the recruitment, transportation, transfer, harbouring or receipt of persons, by means of the threat or use of force or other forms of coercion, of abduction, of fraud, of deception, of the abuse of power or of a position of vulnerability or of the giving or receiving of payments or benefits to achieve the consent of a person having control over another person, for the purpose of exploitation.

innovation

Already in glossary of TD223 Block 2 see *technological innovation*.

internal or civil wars

Wars fought primarily within a single state, often over control of that state, although outside forces can also play a role.

international relief

A relief effort to one country by other countries, which may or may not be the product of humanitarian intentions.

intervention

Any action taking place in another country, normally requested by that country, but there is a debate about the circumstances in which it might be permitted to intervene without a request.

legitimacy

Legitimate power is defined by Beetham as power that is exercised according to established rules, which are in turn justified in terms of the values of that society and where there are explicit demonstrations of consent by the population.

limited war

War that is used as an instrument of specific policy goals, utilizing limited means, and contained in terms of scope and duration.

masculinity

A series of elements that we take for granted in social action, but which emerge from particular characteristics of male identities.

negative freedom

'Freedom from' coercion and violence.

nuclear warfare

Used only twice (by the USA against Japan in 1945), nuclear weapons formed the basis of systems of deterrence involving the threat of mutually assured destruction between the opposing Cold War superpowers between 1945 and 1991.

oligarchic political class

An elite group in society who make decisions on behalf of the rest of a society. They are often cohesive (have a homogenous social composition due to family, educational and economic background), conscious (of their role in society and their status) and conspiratorial (reluctant to yield control to democratic forces). The term often used to describe the oligarchy in the USA is the military–industrial complex.

peacekeeping

Civilian, police and military intervention during or after a violent conflict to first stop and prevent violence, as well as building links between the sides in the violent conflict, and finally to help build security and political institutions to prevent future violence and coordinate relief efforts.

peacekeeping plus

Peacekeeping when not all parties agree to the peace and some groups wish to sabotage it, and thus involves a greater readiness to deploy military force against one or both sides.

political power

The ability to get your favoured outcomes in whatever area of politics is under consideration.

positive freedom

'Freedom to', the capacity of acting in the world.

poverty

Defined in this book in material terms where its measurement is based on the level of household expenditure. The World Bank has defined 'absolute' poverty as living on less than US$1 per day in purchasing power parity (PPP) terms. This definition is thought by others, however, to be too narrow. A broader approach defines poverty as having multiple dimensions, such as low income, poor literacy, poor health, poor access to clean water and sanitation, and so on. A third approach defines poverty in terms of social exclusion – the ability to play a full part in the society in which one lives.

principle of sovereignty

The absolute power of a people and its state and its government over its internal affairs within a given territory, which means other countries normally cannot intervene without permission from an organization or international alliance, such as the UN.

production factors

The resources employed to produce goods and services.

protection

Not only means shielding somebody from danger, but also implies subordination, benevolence and masculinity. It depends on a third party – most often the state – which takes on the role of protector.

proxy war

Occurs when two countries choose to fight their 'hot war' in a third country, instead of going to war directly against each other. Each country supports, promotes and sometimes even creates one side (typically an opposition guerrilla movement) as a proxy. The USA and Soviet Union fought proxy wars in Angola, Mozambique, Nicaragua and elsewhere. China and the USA engaged in this in the Korean War although the Chinese and US armies became directly involved.

purchasing power parity

(PPP) A value put on goods and services in different countries (and in this book, GDP) which has been adjusted to account for different costs of living in the countries. One reason for making a PPP adjustment is that non-traded goods tend to be cheaper in developing countries, and so a given currency will go further in some countries compared to others.

reflexivity

Assumes that a person's thoughts and ideas are inherently biased. Personal reflexivity in the context of carrying out research is about how a person's background, values, belief and understanding affect the outcome and the process of one's research. In Chapter 10, reflexivity has two meanings. It refers to how a person's background, values, belief and identity affect their actions and perception as well as how others respond to what they say and do. It also refers to the process of thinking through critically how identity is represented.

regulative role

In the context of the state, refers to creating the 'rules of the game' for politics.

reserve army of labour

Those who are unemployed, but, if given the chance, would seek to be employed; they are waiting to join the labour force.

responsibility to protect

Responsibility of states to protect their citizens from avoidable catastrophe, including hunger; the international community shares that responsibility. Sometimes this is also associated with plans to prevent similar problems emerging and rebuilding or reconstructing buildings, critical infrastructures and governance.

right to intervene

See *intervention*.

risk society

Approach developed by Beck that sees risks and hazards generated by technological knowledge in industrial society as open to anticipation, where causal attribution is feasible and technical solutions (technofixes) can be found because these risks were localized and calculable. Contemporary risks are often unexpected, creeping and insidious, and responsibility for the effects is often hard if not impossible to establish (see *global risks*)

scientific uncertainty

The problem of establishing clear causal relations between a cause and effect in a particular situation that corresponds to existing knowledge of likely causes.

security dilemma

The idea that one state's accumulation of greater military power, even if done with defensive intent, will be interpreted by others as creating a threat to their security, and they will respond in kind.

social contract

A contract made between state and citizens, according to which the former ensures security in exchange for the latter relinquishing some (or most) of their freedoms in the state of nature.

solidarity (global)

Mutual support, particularly when individuals or groups support similar people who are in difficulty – people who are on strike, suffering from a natural disaster, etc. Global solidarity is support from many countries for people struggling for freedom or harmed by an emergency.

subordination

A hierarchy of power in which one individual or group is perceived or acted upon as inferior to another.

survival

Defined in International Relations as the equivalent of security and can refer to physical survival or the survival of a political order, of values, communities, or even nature.

sustainable development

The pattern of development that, according to the UN, 'meets the needs of the present without compromising the ability of future generations to meet their own needs'.

technological determinism

The belief that socio-economic structures and cultural values are driven by a society's technology.

technological leapfrogging

The possibility of poorer countries adopting cleaner, greener technologies without first having to go through the stage of employing dirty technologies as the now-rich countries did during their development.

technology transfer

Partly concerns the transfer of products, machinery and processes from one (typically richer) country to another (typically poorer) country, sometimes through investment by a large foreign firm in the country and sometimes through development aid. Crucially, to be successful it also requires transfer of skills, and maintenance and management capabilities, so that the receiving country can develop its own technological capacity over time.

total war

War aimed at the destruction of the opposing state and involving the total mobilization of a country's economy and population to achieve this end.

vagaries

Unexpected or inexplicable changes in situations such as economic crises (hence the term the vagaries of the markets or climate). They can also be associated with sudden changes of behaviour and unusual forms of agency such as mass migration, mass protest and economic depressions.

value chain

Describes the full range of activities that are required to bring a product or service from conception, through the different phases of production (involving a combination of physical transformation and the input of various producer services), delivery to final consumers and final disposal after use.

vicissitudes

Hardships or difficulties associated with changing social and natural conditions. They are often associated with disasters or unexpected disruptions which radically affect everyday life, including income and shelter.

vulnerability

Susceptibility to injury and harm, which can take both physical and psychological forms as well as censure and public criticism. It is associated with risks and need for protection when exposed.

wellbeing

At a simplistic level, what makes people feel 'well' and 'being well'. However, this concept is context specific, highly contested and very personal (some would say very subjective). Many people link wellbeing to health and happiness. Others relate it to a reasonable standard of living, a good relationship with one's family/community or something more intangible, such as freedom.

Acknowledgements

Grateful acknowledgement is made to the following sources for permission to reproduce material in this book.

Chapters 7, 8 and 9 previously published in Wilson, G., Furniss, P. and Kimbowa, R. (2009) *Environment, Development and Sustainability*, Oxford, Oxford University Press/Milton Keynes, The Open University. (Open University copyright.)

Figures

Figure 1.1 Out of copyright; **Figure 1.2** Adapted from: http://blogs.ubc.ca/astu400e2010/2010/09/16/un-structure-simplified/; **Figure 1.3** Out of copyright; **Figure 1.5** © Taken from:www.latrobe.edu.au/screeningthepast/25/rose-of-rhodesia/appendix-f.html; **Figure 2.1a** © Time & Life Pictures/Getty Images; **Figure 2.1b** © Time & Life Pictures/Getty Images; **Figure 2.1c** © Michael Dunning/Getty Images; **Figure 2.4a** © Nick Gordon/Getty Images; **Figure 2.4b** © Anonymous/AP Press Association; **Figure 2.5b** Taken from: Google Images; **Figure 3.1** © Canadian Red Cross; **Figure 3.2** © Ariadne Van Zandbergen/Getty Images; **Figure 3.4** © United Nations; **Figure 3.5** Taken from: www.aljazeera.com/programmes/2011/12/201112249934367210.html; **Figure 3.6** © AFP/Getty Images; **Figure 4.4** © Taken from: Google Images; **Figure 4.5** UNODC 2006; **Figure 4.6** Courtesy of Legal Rights Institute; **Figure 5.1a** Taken from: www.wordpress.com; **Figure 5.1b** © AFP/Getty Images; **Figure 5.1d** PA Photos; **Figure 5.2** © Magnus Manske/Flickr.com. This file is licensed under the Creative Commons Attribution 2.0 Generic License; **Figure 5.3** © Her Majesty the Queen in Right of Canada, Environment Canada, 2003. Reproduced with the permission of the Minister of Public Works and Government Services Canada; **Figure 5.4** © Smith, M. and Pangsapa, P. (2008) *Environment and Citizenship* Zed Publications; **Figure 5.5a,b** © Taken from: www.travelinghaiti.com; **Figure 5.6b** Taken from: Google Images; **Figure 5.7** Ideal Stock/Alamy; **Figure 5.10** © Mark Smith; **Figure 5.11a** Trinidad & Tobago Guardian; **Figure 5.11b** NGOs, CBOs and Community members participate in the Break the Silence: end child sexual abuse walk, in Barrackpore, South Trinidad (Trinidad and Tobago), in April 2011. **Figure 6.1** © Yoichi R Okamoto/LBJ LIBRARY; **Figure 6.2** © www.lijenhuangart.com; **Figure 6.3** © J.S.Barrie/Flickr.com. This file is licensed under the Creative Commons BY-NC; **Figure 8.1** © Koichi Kamishoda/Getty Images; **Figure 10.1** www.samaritans-purse.orguk/operation-christmas-child; **Figure 10.2** www.samaritans-purse.orguk/operation-christmas-child; **Figure 10.3** © Narinder Nanu/Getty Images; **Figure 10.4** © AFP/Getty Images.

Text

Box 5.1 © Vidal, J. (2010) 'Global Food Crisis Forecast as Prices Reach Record Highs', Guardian News and Media Limited.

Index